The Debt Trap

Cheryl Payer

The Debt Trap

The IMF and the Third World

Monthly Review Press
New York and London

Copyright © 1974 by Cheryl Payer
All Rights Reserved

Library of Congress Cataloging in Publication Data

Payer, Cheryl, 1940-
   The debt trap.

   Includes bibliographical references and index.
   1. International Monetary Fund.   2. International finance.
3. Underdeveloped areas—Finance. I. Title
HG3881.P36   1975   332.1'52   74-24794
ISBN 0-85345-375-6
ISBN 0-85345-376-4 Pbk.

Monthly Review Press
62 West 14th Street, New York, N.Y. 10011
47 Red Lion Street, London WC1R 4PF

Manufactured in the United States of America
10   9   8   7   6   5   4   3

Contents

Preface

I have tried (for the most part unconsciously) to produce this book in a manner consistent with the philosophy which underlies its discussion of the relations among peoples and nations.

Therefore I have rejected the invidious division of labour, typical of the academic and publishing world, which assigns the more tedious tasks to persons who never enjoy the rewards of authorship. Both from necessity (for I received no financial assistance except the publisher's advance) and from conviction, I have no research assistants, secretaries, or typists to thank in this space; I did the work myself. Nor did I have a spouse who would take charge of the time-consuming mechanics of living while I carried on the higher intellectual labour.

I am, however, happy to acknowledge the advice and criticism of other scholars who have read chapters of the manuscript for which they have particular competence. Many are clearly my superiors in intellect, experience, and specialized knowledge; but the spirit has been invariably that of exchange between equals, even if the profit has sometimes been entirely on my side. Those whom I have to thank for this assistance include T. D. Allman, Carmel Budiardjo, Robert Cassen, Eprime Eshag, Jonathan Fast, Albert Fishlow, Armando Garcia, Alec Gordon, Alejandro Lichauco, Stefan Markowski, Ingrid Palmer, Christopher Roper, Herman Starobin, Bob Sutcliffe, Paul Sweezy, Rosemary Thorp, Carlos Waisman, and Thomas Weisskopf. I owe special thanks to Harry Magdoff, who inspired my first research on the subject and has encouraged and assisted me at every stage of the preparation and writing of this book. The responsibility is mine if I have persisted in error despite the good advice received from these colleagues.

Particular thanks are due to the staffs of the Library and Press Library of Chatham House, whose high professional standards have eliminated most of the frustrations familiar to researchers tracking down sources.

With the exception of one brief, informal interview, my only contact with the staff of the International Monetary Fund has been through their published writings.

*

Two chapters have been published previously:

Chapter Three (Philippines) Copyright © 1972 by *Journal of Contemporary Asia.*

Chapter Four (Indonesia) Copyright © 1974 by Random House Inc. From *Remaking Asia: Essays on the American Uses of Power*, edited by Mark Selden, published by Pantheon Books, a division of Random House, Inc. Reprinted by permission of Pantheon Books.

Introduction

In Indonesia, Brazil, Cambodia, and Argentina the military seize power from elected governments or popular rulers. Within a few weeks of the coup a mission from the International Monetary Fund arrives in each country to advise the new rulers on the reorganization of their economy.

In the Philippines, Colombia, and Ceylon, candidates for the post of President or Prime Minister campaign for election on a platform of opposition to the IMF. Months, or even weeks, after the election is won, the same leaders forget their campaign promises and come to terms with the IMF – having found it as impossible to live without it as to live with it.

In communist Yugoslavia, the IMF is unobtrusively in attendance whenever major economic reforms are introduced which make the country more open to Western trade and investment. In Laos and Cambodia, though, the IMF lends its prestige and expertise to prop up anti-communist governments and ensure continued Western control of Indochina.

What is this powerful but publicity-shy institution? How can it exercise such a profound influence on the politics and policies of so many countries?

The International Monetary Fund is the most powerful supranational government in the world today. The resources it controls and its power to interfere in the internal affairs of borrowing nations give it the authority of which United Nations advocates can only dream.

This tremendous power does not inhere in the corps of economists who staff the IMF, nor even in the Board of Governors appointed by its member nations. The IMF must be seen as the keystone of a total system. Its power is made possible not only by the enormous resources which it controls (about $29 billion in national quota subscriptions, plus its recently acquired power to create international money in the form of Special Drawing

Rights), but more significantly as a result of its function as an international credit agency. All of the major sources of credit in the developed capitalist world, whether private lenders, governments, or multilateral institutions such as the World Bank group, will refuse to lend to a country which persists in defying IMF 'advice'. The real importance of the IMF lies in the authority delegated to it by the governments and capital markets of the entire capitalist world.

Since its founding at the end of the Second World War, the IMF has been the chosen instrument for imposing imperialist financial discipline upon poor countries under a façade of multilateralism and technical competence. In this era, the status of a country's relationship with the IMF is the most accurate guide to the fate of its aspirations to autonomous development.

This book is about the efforts of poor nations to gain some control over their own economies, and the role of the IMF in frustrating those efforts. My intent is to extend the critical analysis of the IMF as an obstacle to autonomous national development which has been pioneered by Magdoff, Hayter, and Frank.[1]

This is not an institutional study of the International Monetary Fund. It pays little attention to differences within the Fund, or to the negotiations over particular decisions. The emphasis here is on the constitutional and structural factors which severely limit the scope for bureaucratic politics and discretionary decision-making, and ensure that the policies of the IMF are consistently in the interests of its capitalist masters. It is the study of a system, and not of the incidental or accidental variations of that system. It is drawn for the most part from public sources available to any researcher.

The economists who specialize in monetary theory, including the Fund officials and staff, have erected a mystique around their subject which intimidates even other economists. They represent themselves as highly trained technicians who determine the 'correct' exchange rate and the 'proper' amount of money creation on the basis of complex formulas. They deny the political significance of their work – or perhaps they themselves have been conditioned to believe that there are no real alternatives to the formulas they manipulate. Only a few have ever admitted the political importance of monetary issues, or tried to explain these issues to the public. The task of explanation which I have attempted here has therefore not been easy, but it has proved to be immensely illuminating.

The IMF can best be understood by the study of its effects in the countries forced to accept its advice. For this reason the heart of this book is a collection of case studies which tell the modern history of several countries from the point of view of their foreign exchange needs and resources, their balance of payments crises, and the way in which these crises were resolved.

Two introductory chapters sketch a model of payments crises, alternative methods for their solution, and the political and social effects of the 'solution' favoured by the IMF. Since these two chapters are the key to an understanding of the case studies which follow, readers are urged not to skip over them. Every effort has been made to demystify the technical jargon and to provide clear explanations of these very important concepts.

By following the fate of the external economic relations of the countries which provide our case studies, it is possible to explain a number of events which seem at first to be a matter of internal politics: the military take-overs mentioned above, for example, or the growth of regional inequality in Brazil and Yugoslavia. Naturally this method cannot pretend to give a comprehensive picture of a nation's politics; in such a brief survey the internal factors have to be ignored or slighted. It must be stressed, however, that the internal political evolution of a nation is intimately and structurally connected to its external economic situation. Different groups and classes within a country have different allies or well-wishers outside that country, and the economic strategy which they adopt is likely to benefit both themselves and their foreign allies. Conversely, a revolutionary government will find it necessary not only to restrict its ties with the outside world, but also to repress or destroy those classes which are the allies of its external enemies.

The class basis of a government will determine both its choice of an external economic strategy, and the strength of its will to carry through with its chosen strategy.

The economic situation of a country determines its political structure in the way that the skeleton determines the structure of the human body. The bone structure cannot determine the colour of skin and hair, or the appearance of the flesh, much less the moral and intellectual qualities that make each person unique. But a body cannot grow in defiance of the size and shape of its skeleton.

Similarly, there are economic laws which must be obeyed. If the pro-capitalist interpreters of those laws are accustomed to lie to us, and to deny the alternatives that exist, this makes it all the more urgent for all of us to understand what the real problems, and the possible solutions, are. And if the bone structure has been distorted and deformed by external pressures, it is not surprising that the flesh and spirit may be diseased as well. But for societies, as for bodies, a Procrustean bed is not the solution. Only with the aid of a thorough understanding of what is physically and politically feasible can policy-makers begin to correct the distortions without killing the patient.

The final chapters of this book try to suggest alternatives to the vicious circle of debt and dependence which is described in the major case studies. Since it is difficult to prescribe solutions in the abstract, I have provided some additional case studies of nations which have tried in different ways to break out of the circle. Most such attempts have not been successful. The difficulties should not be underestimated.

In the 1950s it was hoped that countries like India, Yugoslavia, and Indonesia would lead a genuine 'Third World' whose development would avoid both the evils of capitalist exploitation and the hard labour and bitter shortages of socialist autarchy. Today that dream is dead, and all of these nations are more deeply dependent than they were at the time they gained their political independence. This is the story of how that dream was killed.

The IMF is not the real villain of the piece, though it is the agent of the villains. They are the multinational corporations and capitalist governments which are the natural enemies of Third World independence and can usually mobilize the resources to crush it. But this is also the story of the human errors, weaknesses, and corruptibility that give the enemies of independence a 'fifth column' within the body politic of their victims. As Mao Tse-tung warned his cadres as they took power in China in 1949, the 'sugar-coated bullets of the bourgeoisie' are likely to prove more fatal to a revolution than real bullets.

1

The Foreign Exchange Crisis

All nations need to trade with other nations. They may need to import food, either to cover a harvest shortfall and avert a famine or to make up a deficit caused by the fact that their resources are devoted to producing commodities other than food. They may want agricultural products that cannot be grown within their country, or minerals which are not found there. 'Third World' countries – the subject of this book – want to import capital goods and sophisticated technologies in order to raise their own level of production and feel a part of the modern world. Their rich citizens want to import luxuries which other nations produce.

Some items in this list fill genuine needs; others, like the luxury goods, may represent an obvious waste of scarce resources. Capital goods and sophisticated technologies may seem necessary imports to a country that wants to industrialize; but on the other hand they might not be necessary if the country rearranged its priorities or mobilized its own resources more effectively. It is important not to confuse the desire for foreign goods, or even the economic demand for them, with a genuine need. Whatever a nation imports, however, whether luxury or necessity (unless obtained through a 'barter' or 'bilateral' agreement with one other nation), must be paid for with internationally acceptable money or, as it is commonly called, foreign exchange.

In a capitalist economy, individuals and firms buy foreign exchange with their own currency for the transactions which they wish to carry out with foreigners. The price which they have to pay for it is the *exchange rate*. Under the so-called 'Bretton Woods system'* governments are supposed to deter-

---

* At the time of writing this had broken down, due to the inability of the major capitalist nations to keep their currencies steady against one another. See the final chapter on the implications of this for the Third World.

mine the exchange rate for their own national currencies by setting its value in terms of gold, but in practice the exchange rate is usually quoted in dollars. The government is expected to 'defend' the exchange rate by making up the difference between the demand for and the supply of foreign exchange at that exchange rate. The supply of foreign exchange is determined by what the country is earning from its exports or receiving in the form of loans, gifts, and investments; the demand is determined by what people are willing to pay for imports, or send out of the country as investment income or capital flight. Usually supply and demand are not in exact balance at the given exchange rate; then the government has to make up the difference by itself buying or selling its own currency for foreign exchange in order to maintain its value.

If the supply and demand of foreign exchange at the official exchange rate is persistently out of balance, the government's buying or selling operations will encounter serious difficulties. In the case of persistent *deficits* in the balance of payments, which is the problem we are concerned with in this book, the government's own holdings of foreign exchange (its reserves) will be exhausted by the perennial necessity to supply the gap by which demand for foreign exchange exceeds the supply. This is the situation which gives rise to a balance of payments crisis.

Chronic foreign exchange deficits and balance of payments crises are characteristic of those countries of the Third World that are trying to develop under capitalist auspices. (The oil-rich countries of the Middle East are an obvious exception.) The factors contributing to their foreign exchange weaknesses are complex but can probably be summed up by the political and economic weaknesses of these countries, considered individually, vis-à-vis the developed capitalist nations and their 'multinational' corporations. Certainly, highly developed capitalist nations, notably the United States and Britain, may also run chronic balance of payments deficits and have intermittent currency crises, while some underdeveloped countries, such as the major oil exporting countries, have large foreign exchange surpluses. The general rule holds true, however, that poor countries are characterized by foreign exchange shortages.

This situation has evolved historically since the end of the Second World War. During the war, the main combatants, which were also the most highly developed capitalist countries, consumed more than they produced. They had few exports to sell to their traditional markets in Asia, Africa, and Latin America; but their need for imports from them was high. At the end of the war, as a result, many of these countries (most of them at that time still colonies) held huge reserves – claims on the future production of the industrial states which had fought the war.

These reserves were soon dissipated. In many cases, the former colonial power imposed restrictions on the use of these reserves, usually as part of the price of political independence. Despite this external constraint, most of the newly independent ex-colonies and the Latin American nations were eager to spend their reserves on a flood of imports. Most of them, although paying lip service to the desire for economic development, had a criminal ignorance or indifference to the importance of foreign exchange for development. Their reserves were dissipated within two or three years.

Some other countries – India and Yugoslavia are examples from this book – paid much more serious attention to economic development from the start and were not guilty of the consumer spending spree indulged in by countries such as Brazil and the Philippines. They were, however, convinced that heavy import surpluses – more imports than could be paid for by export earnings – were essential to their development efforts; so that, very much like the spendthrift nations, they first ran down their reserves and then ran up foreign debts. For most of these countries, by the late 1950s their foreign exchange reserves had been used up, and repayments of interest and principal began to fall due from the borrowing which had begun earlier in the decade.

How to Read a Balance of Payments Table

On the next page a balance of payments table for Brazil in 1969 is presented, which is adapted from the *Balance of Payments Yearbook* published by the IMF. It is important to understand the principle behind the presentation of balance of payments figures. This is not because this brief explanation will enable one to interpret actual tables; the figures can only be interpreted with any accuracy by specialists working with much more detailed breakdowns than are found even in the IMF yearbooks. Understanding how to read a balance of payments table, however, can give us a good idea of the categories which contribute to a nation's capacity to earn or attract foreign exchange, and those which represent the expenditure or drain on its earnings and holdings of exchange.

Further, by understanding the method of double-entry bookkeeping which is used in balance of payments tables, one becomes aware of the accounting principle which is also an economic fact of life: a nation can spend only as much as the total which it can earn, borrow, or receive as gifts, or has saved (as reserves) from past earnings. Since gifts ('unrequited transfers' in balance of payments terminology) form a very tiny proportion of most countries' income, almost all of a country's imports will have to be paid for by the export of real goods and services, either in the present, by 'current account' earnings; or in the future, to pay off 'capital account' borrowing.

In this illustration, both the double column (debit and credit) system and the single column (net sum) presentations are shown side by side, although most actual tables will use either one or the other. There are advantages to each type: the double column system allows one to see the absolute magnitude of the economic and financial transactions which are entered in the balance of payments; while the single column system provides a quick summary of which items are in surplus or deficit. In the illustration (to anticipate for a moment our discussion of individual items) the right-hand single column shows us that Brazil had a deficit of goods and services in 1969 of $367

4

Balance of payments table

Brazil, 1969

	(in million $'s)		
	Double column presentation		Single column presentation
	Credit	Debit	
Goods and services	*2,601*	*2,968*	*−367*
1. Merchandise	2,311	1,993	318
2. Non-monetary gold	—	—	—
3. Freight and insurance on merchandise	66	119	−53
4. Other transportation	65	151	−86
5. Travel	28	77	−49
6. Investment income	22	366	−344
7. Other government	28	92	−64
8. Other private	81	170	−89
Unrequited transfers	*83*	*52*	*31*
9. Private	61	47	14
10. Government	22	5	17
Capital (excluding reserves and related items)	*1,519*	*697*	*822*
Non-monetary sectors	1,321	473	848
11. Direct investment	218	11	207
12. Other private long-term	526	200	326
13. Other private short-term	134	3	131
14. Local government	24	—	24
15. Central government	419	259	160
Monetary sectors	198	224	−26
16. Private institutions	192	9	183
17. Central bank	6	215	−209
Reserves and related items	*15*	*481*	*−466*
Net errors and omissions		*20*	*−20*
	4,218	4,218	0

million, despite a surplus on merchandise trade of $318 million. Every single item in the 'services' category (numbers 3–8) was in deficit, with the largest outflow by far due to 'investment income'. Brazil received a net flow of $31 million in unrequited transfers – less than one-tenth of the deficit to be covered on goods and services. The capital item, however, shows a huge inflow of investment from abroad, enough to cover the entire goods and services deficit and allow the accumulation of reserves to the amount of $466 million.

These gross figures are instructive, but in many respects they conceal more than they reveal. A closer look at the various component items, and some explanation of what they include or exclude, will be useful. First, however, it is time to give a formal definition of the 'balance of payments'. According to a publication of the IMF:

> The balance of payments is a system of accounts covering a given period that is intended to record systematically (a) flows of real resources, including the services of the original factors of production, between the domestic economy of a country and the rest of the world, (b) changes in the country's foreign assets and liabilities that arise from economic transactions, and (c) unrequited transfers, which are the counterpart of real resources or financial claims provided to, or received from, the rest of the world without requital.[1]

The balance of payments records transactions between residents of the country and the rest of the world, so it is important to understand the definition of 'resident'. The Brazilian subsidiary of a US-based multinational corporation is considered a resident of Brazil for balance of payments purposes. Therefore, goods imported by the subsidiary from its parent company, and the payment made for it, is entered in the balance of payments, but if the subsidiary borrows money from a Brazilian bank this is not. Foreign embassies, consulates, and military establishments are, however, not considered 'residents' of the country in which they are situated, and the transactions between them and the local economy are entered in the balance of payments (line 7 in the illustration).

The first large category, 'goods and services', represents the transfer of real resources between residents of Brazil and the rest of the world during the period covered by the table. It records these transfers at the prices actually charged, which of course does not touch the question of whether these prices were by any definition fair and equitable. Trade in merchandise exports and imports (credits and debits respectively) is by far the largest item in the balance of payments of most countries. From the table we can calculate that Brazil exported in 1969 about 15 per cent more in merchandise than it imported.

Line 2, non-monetary gold, is a category reserved for gold that is mined within a country for export or addition to reserves; it is not applicable in this case. Items 3–8 comprise the 'services' category, in which Brazil is heavily in deficit. Line 3, freight and insurance charges, is closely related to merchandise trade. This item has occasioned bitter debates between poor and rich countries, since the poor countries accuse the rich of monopolizing the supply of these necessary services and charging artificially high prices, particularly for shipping.[2] Other transportation, line 4, comprises mainly payments made for the use of port and navigation facilities from one country to another. Line 5, travel, includes tourism which in some countries, such as Yugoslavia, may be an important surplus item. For most Third World countries, however, tourism receipts are more than offset by the business and study expenses of their own nationals abroad. Other government, line 7, as mentioned above includes embassy and consular expenditures, but especially the upkeep of large military missions and bases abroad. For Brazil this is a deficit item, indicating the absence of any large foreign military presence; but for Vietnam and the Philippines this would be a large surplus category. Line 8, other private services, is a miscellaneous category. The earnings of migrant workers abroad, which is quite an important surplus item for Yugoslavia, would be entered here.

Investment income, line 6, deserves rather more extensive discussion for at least two reasons. The first is that since investment itself is listed elsewhere, in the capital account, it might seem reasonable to include investment income (profits on direct investment and interest on international loans) in the capital account as well. The IMF has decreed, however, that the supply of capital is a service, and that profits and interest payments should be legitimized as a charge for this service. This has a practical significance: when a country accepts the obligations set by the IMF for maintaining the convertibility of its currency, it agrees to put no restrictions on current account payments. Placing investment income firmly in the 'goods and services' section of the balance of payments ensures that restrictions on payments to foreign investors cannot legitimately be imposed under IMF rules, while its inclusion in the capital account would allow them.* Another point to remember about this category is that the amount listed as investment income includes *all* income earned on direct investment, whether it is repatriated to the country of origin or reinvested in the host country. Reinvested income is lumped together with new investment in the capital account section of the balance of payments.

Another reason for paying particular attention to investment income is the sheer size of this category in the balance of payments of most Third World countries, where it should be more accurately termed investment *payments*, since the income goes to other countries. In Brazil in 1969 this category accounted for an outflow of $344 million, which more than

---

*Although this may come as a surprise to many economists, it is clearly the sense of this paragraph from an official Fund publication: 'The treatment that must be accorded income from investment, or depreciation or amortization of an investment, has raised the question in practice that may indicate why the drafters of the Fund agreement specifically included interest and net income as payments for current transactions. Since a member country is free to regulate capital movements and may attach conditions to the inflow of capital, it has sometimes been assumed that it may, as a capital control measure, also require the investor to forego the repatriation of income, amortization, or depreciation as a condition of permitting the capital inflow. This is not so as the terms of Article VI, Section 3 make clear. Such a requirement would clearly be a restriction on the making of payments for current transactions and accordingly prohibited under the Fund agreement.' (James G. Evans, 'Current and Capital Transactions: How the Fund Defines Them', *Finance and Development*, September 1968, p. 34.)

offset the country's surplus on merchandise trade. The drain on poor countries' international reserves which investment payments represents comes out even more strongly when a 'global' balance of payments is prepared for all Third World countries. Angus Maddison, who prepared a summary balance of all Third World countries for 1963, found that investment payments represented the largest individual deficit item, amounting to a total of $5.4 billion* for that one year.[3]

Current account transactions record the transfer of real resources – 'goods and services' – that have taken place during the period covered. The capital account includes all items which will give rise to transfers of real resources in the future, *after* the period covered by the table itself. Another way of saying the same thing is that this category indicates changes in the country's debtor or creditor position. The net inflow of $822 million on capital account indicates that Brazil incurred debts to foreigners to that amount during 1969.

Most Third World countries are heavily in debt already, and their debtor position deepens each year. Whether this is or is not a good thing depends on factors which one cannot read in a balance of payments table; particularly, whether the borrowed money is being invested in enterprises which will enable the country to pay back the debt as it falls due. The subcategories of the capital account in the balance of payments can suggest only a little about the rate at which repayment will fall due.

Line 11, direct investment, refers to the acquisition or installation by foreigners of factories and businesses in Brazil in the expectation of earning profits in future years. Line 12, private, long-term, refers to loans with maturities of more than one year, while short-term capital has maturities of less than one year, e.g. trade credits. If a large proportion of debt is held in short-term liabilities this leaves a country susceptible to a sudden reversal of capital flow, which causes a balance of payments crisis (the 'hot money' phenomenon). In 1969 Brazil's short-term borrowing was modest compared with the inflow of long-term and direct investment, but in following years short-term borrowing increased sharply while the other two cate-

* A 'billion' is equivalent to a thousand million.

9

gories declined – a fact which indicates possible danger to Brazil's current boom (see Chapter Seven). Line 14, local government [foreign] borrowing, is a relatively small item; line 15 is where the official loans, usually called 'foreign aid', would be entered.

The 'monetary sectors' category gives the changes in investment position of private banks and the Central bank, respectively. These transactions are separated from those of the 'non-monetary' sector because almost all Central Bank transactions, and sometimes those of the private banks, are undertaken in order to finance the balance of payments items already discussed. In other words, these are 'accommodating' or 'compensatory' capital movements which take place solely to fill the gap in demand and supply left by the other transactions. In the same way, changes in national reserves also finance the gap between supply and demand for foreign exchange. In the balance of payments, an increase in reserves is entered as a debit, or with a minus sign, while decreases are entered as credits. This is confusing unless one conceptualizes the reserves as something external to the balance of payments itself, into which all surplus must be paid in a manner analogous to a loan to a foreigner, and from which money to finance deficits may be drawn (the balance of payments does not give the *size* of the reserves, but only the net *change* for the period covered). The fact that many Third World countries actually keep their reserves in London or New York should make it easier to visualize. From the table it can be seen that in 1969 the large inflow of capital to the non-monetary sectors and to private banks was able to finance (a) the deficit on goods and services; (b) a fairly large debit item for central bank capital transactions (line 17) which probably represents repayment of old borrowings, and (c) an increase in reserves of $466 million.

'Net errors and omissions' is a standard book-keeping device required by the principle that credits must equal debits in the total balance of payments. In practice, the records and statistics that have to be used in drawing up the table are in many cases only estimates; and large categories of transactions may escape the statistician. Part of the 'errors and omissions' item usually represents capital flight – unrecorded, probably illegal movements of private short-term capital – particularly in the case of Third World countries such as Brazil.

Was Brazil in surplus or deficit in the year 1969? As we have seen, the balance of payments itself must always equal zero: credits equal debits by definition. Surplus or deficit are concepts which refer to only *some* of the items in the table, with the rest considered as 'financing' the surplus or deficit. In practice, however, there is no unanimous agreement as to which statistical categories represent transactions entered into for their own sake ('autonomous' movements) and which represent 'financing' or 'accommodating' movements. Although central bank operations and changes in reserves, for example, are almost universally agreed to be 'financing' operations, the large build-up of Brazil's reserves in 1969 may well represent a conscious goal of the monetary authorities, taken in preference to, say, import liberalization measures. Or, the private capital and loan operations, made in the expectation of profit or interest, may have been induced by government measures aimed at financing a trade deficit.[4] As an IMF official specializing in balance of payments questions admits:

In fact, the determination of balance of payments surplus or deficit is far from being a fully objective exercise. It has the clearly normative aspect of providing a guide for economic policy ... It is not surprising, therefore, that the definition of surplus or deficit is by far the most controversial question in balance of payments methodology. This has been evident at meetings of balance of payments experts which the Fund has held. When these meetings have taken up the concept of a surplus or a deficit, the discussion has become livelier or even emotional. At the same time it has usually been inconclusive, being concerned with something about which reasonable men can forever hold different views.[5]

With this in mind, let us consider some possible interpretations of the table used for illustration. To someone like the author, who is suspicious of the long-term effects of direct investment and loans, whether long- or short-term, on the future balance of payments, the most important measure might be the $336 million deficit on current account (up to line 10). In this perspective, the large surplus on capital account is ominous because it means heavy repayment obligations in the future.

Many countries 'draw the line' under direct and long-term investment capital to obtain what is called the 'basic balance', putting the volatile short-term capital movements below the line as 'financing' flows. In this illustration, lines 14 and 15 are not broken down into long and short term loans. If we draw the line between 12 and 13, however, Brazil had a surplus by the 'basic balance' definition of $266 million.

The IMF recommends the use of an 'official settlements' balance which would include *only* central bank transactions and reserve changes 'below the line' as financing operations, with all short-term capital, plus errors and omissions (which, as noted above, probably represents short-term capital) above the line. By this standard, Brazil had a much larger surplus of $675 million!

Balance of Payments Crises, and Possible Solutions

A balance of payments deficit is not the same thing as a balance of payments *crisis*, although a long succession of deficits will often lead to a crisis. The 'official settlements' balance gives the most immediate clue to the imminence of a payments crisis, but the current transactions balance, studied over a period of years, will show whether the country is chronically consuming more than it earns and therefore building up a heavy debt. And, for the countries we are concerned with, it is usually the debt repayment burden which precipitates a payments crisis.

The typical balance of payments, or foreign exchange, crisis in Third World countries arises when fixed obligations in the exchange budget (a projected balance of payments drawn up to guide government policy) necessitates the earmarking of so much exchange that other parts of the budget – usually imports – would have to be cut back to an unacceptable level. The most important fixed obligation in most Third World countries is the payment of investment income (line 6). In this way chronic deficits on current account in past years may result in an exchange crisis in the present.

The importance of foreign exchange reserves lies in the fact that the larger the reserves, the longer a country can avoid having to take steps to adjust a payments deficit. As long as a nation can continue to draw down its reserves, there is no crisis. For this reason, one useful measure of the adequacy of reserves, or the imminence of a payments crisis, is the relationship between reserve holdings and the current level of imports. A country whose reserves are sufficient to pay for six months' imports has a fairly comfortable reserve 'cushion' against shortfalls in earnings, while one with only two months' worth is in a more precarious situation. Reserves covering only a few weeks' imports signal a crisis. When net reserves are negative, it means that the country's debts due for repayment exceed the amount in the reserves available to pay them off.

The International Monetary Fund was founded in order to supplement each member nation's reserves, so that by drawing on its quota in the Fund a country could have a longer breathing space in which to wait out seasonal or cyclical fluctuations, or to take corrective measures which might not have immediate effect. The purpose of the IMF was to prevent countries temporarily in payments crises from curtailing imports when they were short of liquidity (cash or assets which can be used for making payments), and particularly to prevent them from imposing restrictions on trade in order to deal with payments crises. However, since it was not the Fund's intention to finance large and persistent deficits, a procedure was evolved requiring repayment of loans from the Fund (technically speaking, 're-purchases' of the borrowers' own currency) in three to five years' time. The Fund also developed the practice of imposing progressively more severe conditions as the country borrowed more deeply from its quota. A member nation pays one-quarter of its quota in gold and the remainder in its own currency. If it wants to purchase foreign exchange from the Fund, paying with its own currency, permission is granted almost automatically to the extent of its gold subscription, or 'gold tranche'. Drawings in the next 25 per cent of its quota, called the 'first credit tranche' are conditional on the member 'making reasonable attempts to solve its problems', in the Fund's view. Requests for drawings beyond this proportion of the quota require substantial justification. 'They are likely to be favourably received where the drawings in question are intended to support a sound programme aimed at establishing or maintaining the exchange stability of the member's currency at a realistic rate of exchange ...'[6]

This is reasonable enough, in principle. Countries should not have to adjust their exchange rate or payments system if they are suffering a temporary shortage of foreign exchange which can be expected to correct itself within a year or two; nor should they be allowed to borrow indefinitely if the deficits are persistent and adjustments need to be made. The problem arises from the Fund's bias, which is a reflection of the desires of its most powerful members, in favour of specific measures of adjustment which *do not, in fact, result in a stable, healthy payments balance.* There are several methods of coping with a foreign exchange crisis; it is necessary to consider all the possibilities and their implications in order to understand the significance of the Fund's prescriptions.

In theory, a country with a balance of payments problem might attempt to solve it by changing any given item in the balance of payments, that is by increasing any of the credit items or decreasing any of the debit items. In practice, however, there are many items over which the government has little control; or where any possible changes would be too small to solve the problem. Export earnings cannot be increased with a wave of the wand. Freight and insurance payments represent a relatively small drain on the total budget, and could not, in any case, be reduced without a corresponding, but much larger reduction in the nation's merchandise trade, which is ordinarily the largest item in the payments table.

The item for 'investment income' is however, as we have seen, a very large debit item for most Third World countries. When payments for interest and amortization of the foreign debt absorb a large proportion of export earnings, making it impossible to finance the usual level of imports, it becomes the main cause of the payments crisis and thus a possible focus of change. In the nineteenth century, and in this century before the Second World War, America and many European nations (as well as poorer countries) often chose debt repudiation as a way out of a payments bind. In the contemporary world, however, the sanctions for international bankruptcy are severe; they almost certainly include the breaking of trading links upon which the nation normally relies, the denial of credits which are the lifeblood of trade, and in extreme cases (China after 1949; Cuba after 1960) a deliberate government-enforced trade boycott. Despite these sanctions, the following case studies show that several countries have on occasion flirted with the idea of unilateral repudiation as a way out of payments crises, and a few have attempted it quite seriously.

Alternatively, the payments on debts can be 'rescheduled' or 'refinanced' with the cooperation of the creditor countries – a more common method since it enables the debtor nation to avoid the trade sanctions which repudiation would entail. Creditor nations have proved willing to cooperate, on the assumption that it is better to be paid late than never and that, in any case, the principle of financial responsibility must be upheld, even if this involves granting new credits.

Alternatively, or more usually concurrently, the nation in trouble may try to seek *new* foreign aid or more foreign investment funds in order to solve its problems. However, a crisis arises almost by definition when new sources of financing in the needed amounts are not available: when reserves have been exhausted and no more credit can be obtained *unless significant policy changes are made*. It may well be that a change of course on the part of the government, away from nationalist economic policies and towards measures favouring foreign investment, could attract new loans; but in some countries – Cambodia, Brazil, and Indonesia, of the following case studies – a coup against the existing government was necessary as a precondition for the new policies.

A country wishing to control the outflow of investment income may compel foreign companies to reinvest all or most of their profits in the country. This can prevent, temporarily at

15

least, the drain on foreign reserves caused by unlimited profit remittance. It is likely to scare away new investment, however, and more important, the official loans and credit guarantees that for most countries amount to more than the direct investment they can hope to attract. Nationalization of foreign firms is likely to incur the same severe sanctions in international trade as debt repudiation; most governments are not determined enough, and do not enjoy enough internal support, to withstand this economic pressure successfully. On the other hand, policies designed to attract foreign investment – even when they are successful in their aim, which is by no means always the case – imply a larger burden of profit remittance abroad in the future.

All of the policies discussed so far involve various methods of *financing* to carry a government through a payments crisis. It is, however, often necessary for a government in crisis to make adjustments in the volume and pattern of its production and consumption in order to reduce its import bill and/or enhance its earnings from exports. There are several different methods which it can employ to achieve these goals, all of which have different 'side effects' and various advantages and disadvantages.

Exchange controls are the most direct and immediately effective method of restricting imports and/or payments for invisibles and capital movements. When controls are in effect, individuals and firms cannot obtain foreign exchange except by licence from the Central Bank or other licensing authority, which allocates the available exchange according to administrative determination as to what the country needs from abroad. The advantage of such a system is obvious: when a nation is desperately short of foreign exchange, it makes eminent good sense to control the expenditure of what is available to make sure that essential imports have priority. It is first cousin to the state trading systems of centrally planned (communist) societies, in which exports and imports are determined by the government plan without reference to exchange rates and internal prices, but in capitalist Third World countries an exchange control system functions as a sort of dam, holding back excessive private demand for imports at the point where the foreign exchange to pay for them must be obtained.

In a capitalist economy, the disadvantages in practice of an exchange control system are considerable. Because the demand for foreign exchange exceeds the supply at the given exchange rate, the government is subsidizing the imports it allows by selling exchange to favoured importers at the official rate, which is lower than the free (or black) market rate. This may be justified as a 'subsidy to national industry' if raw materials and capital goods imports to industry are imported at the favoured rate. The system is, however, susceptible to corruption: bribes taken by exchange officials for licensing imports of dubious value, willingly paid by importers who can sell their goods for huge profits on the import-hungry internal market.

Devaluation is an alternative solution, in which an overvalued exchange rate is changed to one closer to what the free market supply and demand for foreign exchange would dictate. A *floating exchange rate* is, in the case of poor countries, an effective devaluation in which no new rate is chosen by the government but market forces alone, in theory, determine the price of exchange. Devaluation is intended to restrict imports by raising the price in domestic currency of *all* imports, and will (in theory) give exports a boost by permitting export producers to lower their selling price in foreign exchange without losing income in domestic prices. A free market exchange rate will get rid of corruption in the distribution of import licences, because there is no longer any subsidy to importers which would justify bribes for licences; indeed, there are no more licences at all. By the same token, however, the government has abdicated all decisions on what should or should not be imported; one could say it has eliminated crime by making everything legal.

Furthermore, devaluation does not necessarily work out as well in practice as theory says it should. Imports for which there is a strong demand will be imported even at the new exchange rate; consumers may not be willing, or able, to buy local products in preference to the imported; local producers may not be able to manufacture import-competitive products at short notice, and some items they may not be able to produce at all. Similarly, it is an empirical fact that in a large proportion of cases, exporters merely pocket a higher profit at the new exchange rate and do not lower their export prices in response to devaluation. Often the exporter is a foreign-owned corporation and the extra profit will eventually be remitted abroad. Further, many primary-product exporting countries have discovered that if the exporters *did* lower their dollar prices, the country would actually lose income, if international buyers are already taking as much as the country can produce at the higher price!

It is partly for these reasons that *multiple exchange rate systems* have been popular with these countries. By setting different exchange rates for various categories of imports and exports, the indiscriminate across-the-board effects of a straight devaluation are avoided. Imports which are important items in the cost of living can be subsidized, and luxuries highly taxed; traditional exports like Brazilian coffee can be taxed and new export lines subsidized, all by varying the price charged or paid for the foreign exchange by the Central Bank. Multiple exchange rate systems can be very simple, with perhaps only two rates used and most transactions carried out at the 'free market' rate; or they can proliferate into highly complicated systems, with half a dozen rates for different types of imports and as many more for exports. In the 'exchange auction' system used by Brazil in the 1950s, the various exchange rates were not set by the government, but by the bids of importers for the limited amounts of exchange allocated by the government to each category of imports. Subsidies and tax rebates can act as *de facto* multiple exchange rates.

Multiple rates allow a government some control over the composition of the country's foreign trade without giving rise to such blatant corruption as exchange controls; furthermore, where the rates are set so as to yield revenue, they can be an important source of government domestic income. Brazil's government obtained about one-third of its total federal revenue in some years from the exchange auctions. But this system is not so immune to corruption as it may seem: the effectiveness of multiple rates in guiding the economy can be no better than the intelligence with which they are devised and the honesty and efficiency of those who enforce them.

Import restrictions are handicaps which make it more difficult to import goods even though exchange may be freely available. Tariffs are the most common form of restriction; prohibitions on the import of certain goods or quotas and import licensing systems which limit the total amount which can be imported are another. When deposits in advance are required from importers purchasing foreign exchange, this is effectively a forced, no-interest loan which raises the cost of the imports and limits the total demand. A tax on the sale of foreign exchange will make it more expensive and is therefore functionally equivalent to a devaluation on the demand side.

Finally, a government may follow *deflationary monetary and fiscal policies* in an effort to limit the demand for foreign exchange indirectly. If a country's residents are to be permitted to purchase foreign exchange freely at a fixed price, then the level of demand *within* the country must not be allowed to expand without limit. If there are no controls on domestic demand, the import bill may exceed the foreign exchange available to pay for it, which will strain the government's ability to support the exchange rate. Since governments create new money via budget deficits, i.e. by spending more than they take in taxation, and printing money to pay for the rest, a *deflationary fiscal policy* means the reduction of the deficit through an increase in taxes, or a decrease in government spending and subsidies, or both. Since government spending is considered an important instrument both of economic development and of social justice or income redistribution in Third World countries, a restraint on these functions is extremely unpopular with nationalists. It is also very likely to cause political problems for the government that has to turn down the demands of various social classes for a share of budget expenditure.

The other source of new demand is the power of banks to create additional credit through lending. A *deflationary mone-*

tary policy is one by which the government limits credit creation by raising the interest rate which banks must charge, or the amount of reserves they must hold against their deposits. Since business depends on credit to finance current operations, a deflationary monetary policy is always bad for the domestic businesses that depend on local sources of credit; it is likely to cause unemployment and, if severe, business failures. The consequences of deflationary fiscal and monetary policies may be so damaging to the domestic economy that nationalists consider the price too high to pay for the marginal effect that such policies are likely to have on the demand for foreign exchange.

In real life, one will seldom find only one of these policies used in a particular case of exchange crisis. If the whole burden of adjustment were put on any one measure, that measure would have to be applied to such an extreme that its side effects would be intolerable. The standard prescription of the IMF for a payments crisis is for a combination of devaluation with deflationary monetary and fiscal policies; further, if the prescription is followed the country is usually rewarded with more generous extension of new credits and, where needed, a rescheduling of the old ones. Therefore, in the IMF package, certain measures for adjustment of the exchange imbalance are combined with new possibilities for financing the deficit.

Exchange controls, on the other hand, are usually employed as an alternative to devaluation and deflation. Controls, by suspending the operation of the foreign exchange market, relieve the pressure for exchange rate adjustment and for the control of inflationary trends. They are normally dismantled only when the country's desire for more foreign financing runs up against the creditors' dislike for exchange controls, although they may also be attacked politically by importers shut out of the system and exporters offended by the exchange rate tax on their earnings. When exchange controls are removed, the other methods for controlling imports: devaluation, deflation, and import restrictions, have to be beefed up to curb the effects of the reintroduced market forces.

The case studies in this book are chiefly a history of exchange crises viewed as turning points for the country in question. The importance of the choice of method, or combination of methods, for meeting a crisis cannot be stated too strongly.

2

The IMF and the New Style of Aid-giving

The International Monetary Fund and its 'twin' institution, the World Bank* were designed at a conference held at Bretton Woods, in the New Hampshire mountains, in 1944. The United States, which was inevitably to be the most rich and powerful nation in the immediate post-war era, had for that reason the controlling voice in designing the institution. Britain's J. M. Keynes argued vigorously the cause of the European nations, who were bound in the short term to be debtors to the Fund. Problems of the economic development of the Third World were scarcely contemplated at Bretton Woods; most of the Third World, apart from the Latin American nations, was at that time still under colonial rule. Nevertheless, it is not possible to understand the present role of the IMF in the Third World without considering its origins and its constitution.

In the late nineteenth and early twentieth century the major trading nations of the world had all tied their currencies to the value of gold. These currencies were therefore stable in relation to each other. Balance of payments deficits corrected themselves automatically, because money to pay for the deficit left the country, and the contracted money supply depressed the prices of goods and labour which therefore became cheaper and more competitive on the world market, attracting capital and export orders. Allowing the vicissitudes of international trade to control the domestic money supply soon became intolerable to national governments, however – especially to the more democratic ones, which were under pressure from their electorates to maintain a minimum wage. The depressions which resulted from this automatic adjustment mechanism became politically and economically intolerable.

The Great Depression of the 1930s saw the final abandonment

* See appendix I on the relationship between the IMF and the World Bank.

of the international gold standard. In the attempt to salvage something from the collapse of international trade, the major trading nations devalued their currencies (i.e. set their own price for them, independent of gold values) in an effort to win back export markets by lowering the international price of their products. The poor nations and colonies, no longer able to pay for their imports with exports, stopped importing because of their lack of funds and began to produce import substitutes at home. Or, they entered into bilateral trading agreements in which imports from one trading partner could be paid for by exports to that country, without the expenditure of scarce gold (since their own currencies were no longer as good as gold).

No one was quite so alarmed at this state of affairs as the US government, since that country had just become powerful enough to challenge Great Britain for domination of international trade. American exports were being undercut by the currency devaluations of trading rivals – or shut out altogether by exchange and import controls. Germany's aggressive use of exchange restrictions and bilateral trading agreements was a major cause of the frictions leading to war.

The Second World War itself gave the *coup de grâce* not only to Germany's imperial pretensions but also to Great Britain's one-time pre-eminence in world trade and finance. As the war drew to a close, the American leaders, who identified the national interest with a world economy open to their trade and investment, tried to devise a system which would reconcile the exchange rate stability of the 'golden age' of international trade with the insistence of nation-states on managing their own economies so as to minimize the possibilities of depression and unemployment. The system which was fashioned at Bretton Woods, to be enforced by the International Monetary Fund, was called the *par value* system, of 'fixed but adjustable' exchange rates.

The fundamental law of the Fund, its Articles of Agreement, expressed its hostility to the trade and exchange practices of the Depression. Two articles are important for our purposes. Article VIII provides that:

no member may, without the approval of the Fund, impose restrictions on the making of payments or transfers for current international transactions, or engage in discriminatory currency arrangements or multiple currency practices ...[1]

The Fund recognized that many countries were not in a position to abolish exchange restrictions and make their currency convertible immediately, so Article XIV provided for a transitional period, during which members which were not able to abide by the standards of Article VIII were nevertheless obliged to do what they could to move towards convertibility.

Competitive devaluations were to be prevented by making the IMF the arbiter of the proper level of exchange rates. Each member was to establish a 'par value' for its currency, expressed in gold, in consultation with the Fund. Changes in the par value (after an initial 10 per cent) were to be proposed by the member and subject to approval by the Fund.

The Fund, therefore, has a definite constitutional bias against both exchange restrictions and unstable exchange rates as a means for correcting payments imbalances. To back up its recommendations, it holds about $29 billion in the currencies of member countries which it can 'sell' to members in payments difficulties. It was the intent of its founders that by providing in this fashion an extension to the reserves of member countries, it would make expedients such as devaluation or exchange controls less necessary. The Fund's pool of currencies has provided in practice a kind of bribe in favour of international multilateral trade, and against nationalist or bilateral solutions to payments difficulties.

The IMF has never played a deciding role in the adjustment of exchange rates and trade practices among the wealthy developed nations, despite the large sums it has made available for the defence of their currencies. The gigantic speculative crises of recent years have shown that the Fund can be, at most, a forum for negotiations; it cannot dictate policies when there are fundamental disagreements among the titans of international finance. It is rather the weaker nations which are subjected to the full force of IMF principles, for the rich nations (the US, Japan, and major European countries) can agree sufficiently to present a united front in the IMF to the poor countries which look to the Fund, and the rich countries, for credit.*

The poor, raw-material-exporting countries of the world, first those of Latin America and then the newly independent ex-colonies in Asia and Africa, began to request drawings from the IMF after their reserves were spent, the Korean War boom in raw materials prices collapsed, and they found themselves short of funds with which to purchase the imports they had become accustomed to. The Fund, noting that in their pursuit of development these countries were using exchange controls, multiple exchange rates, and other restrictions which were frowned upon by the Fund's articles, used these requests as an opportunity to press these countries to liberalize their trade and payments. Throughout the decade of the 1950s the technique of the 'stand-by arrangement' was developed in connection with loans† to several Latin American countries. The stand-by arrangement was a line of credit which the Fund made available to a member, with the release of the money made conditional on the observance by the member of certain specified economic and financial targets over the period of the arrangement.

During the same decade the Fund produced an ideology of development which was in harmony with its philosophy of economic liberalism. This *laissez-faire* outlook reflected the free trade ideology of its most powerful member, the United States, which at that time thought it would benefit most if the barriers to movement of goods and capital into other countries could be torn down. The Fund's philosophy called for the widest possible freedom of play for market forces and frowned on many kinds of government intervention, such as price subsidies, rationing, or protection of domestic industries, as 'distortions' of free market relations. 'Distortion' is, however,

---

*For a discussion of formal and informal decision-making power in the Fund, see appendix II.

† Strictly speaking, these are not loans but 'purchases' by the member of needed foreign currencies with its own currency. Functionally they are virtually the same as loans.

a loaded word which has no meaning apart from the model one chooses to use, and in any case the inequality of power relationships meant that the Fund could do nothing about market 'distortions' (such as trade protection) which were practised by the rich countries.

Since the Fund's orthodox economic ideas soon came under attack from nationalist economists (particularly the Latin American school known as the 'structuralists') the Fund had to admit that 'monetary stability has little attraction as a policy if it is presented as an alternative to economic development. It may, however, be accepted as a desirable policy if it can be shown that it will assist in the more effective achievement of that objective.' In a series of articles published in the *International Monetary Fund Staff Papers*[2] they developed the theme that the Fund was the real champion of the development of poor countries, thanks not only to the money which was made available, but also to the conditions under which it was lent. This self-congratulatory attitude has persisted,[3] despite the profound and nearly universal scepticism of the supposed beneficiaries, who tolerate IMF 'technical assistance' only because it is the condition for large amounts of aid.

'Foreign Aid' – The Change of Emphasis

It is not possible to discuss IMF programmes for Third World countries without an understanding of the role of foreign aid. 'Foreign aid' is an over-used and inaccurate term that will be used in this work only because any alternative terminology is likely to prove cumbersome and distracting. It is essential, therefore, to define what is meant by foreign aid in this discussion. Here the term will be used to cover financing transactions *made* or *guaranteed* by one government (the creditor) to another government (the debtor). These financial transactions may be in the form of gifts (a small proportion of the total); they may be government-to-government loans on terms of any degree of 'hardness' up to, but not including, the commercial; and they may include government guarantees to cover payments due to private exporters. They *do not* include private capital movements, whether loans or direct investments, that are not guaranteed by the creditor's government. One might say that foreign aid includes all financing transactions that would not have taken place in the absence of government action, although in the case of export credit guarantees there is a good probability that exporters might take the risk upon themselves if they were not able to foist it off on their governments.

For about a dozen years after the end of the Second World War the United States was the main source of foreign aid. As the only significant creditor country of the era, the US found the IMF and World Bank inadequate instruments for the redistribution of its own huge resources, which was the condition for the rehabilitation of international trade. It therefore instituted bilateral aid programmes which served both to redistribute dollars which enabled other countries to buy US exports, and to purchase military, political, and economic advantages around the world for the US. In the beginning, this aid was 'untied' – that is, there was no requirement that aid money be spent on US goods – first, because US products were most in demand so most likely to be purchased anyway, and second, because even if the money was spent in a third country it would still serve to redistribute the embarrassingly large US reserves.

In those years European countries received most of the balance of payments support.[4] Aid to poor countries for economic development was extended mainly for concrete, conspicuous projects – a dam, a factory, a school, etc. The programmes were haphazard and experimental, and not very well coordinated. The US aid programme went through a confusing series of reorganizations and titles: Economic Cooperation Administration, Mutual Security Agency, International Cooperation Agency, Foreign Operations Administration.

Towards the end of the 1950s, a number of circumstances contributed to a major shift of emphasis and mode of operation in aid-giving, a change so significant that its results could be called the new style of aid-giving. The major components of this new style were:

 (a) the growth of the practice of 'tied aid';

 (b) a shift in emphasis from 'project' to 'programme' aid;

 (c) the development of the 'consortium' technique in order to coordinate policies of several different aid-givers, and to encourage more countries to 'share the aid burden' with the United States;

 (d) the decision to rely on IMF stand-by arrangements as a 'pilot' for other aid programmes;

 (e) an increase of more than 50 per cent in IMF quotas, and therefore lending power;

 (f) the formation of the International Development Association (IDA), an affiliate of the World Bank which could administer lending of 'soft' loans (loans on terms very much easier than commercial).

The architect of the new style was an American official, C. Douglas Dillon, the Deputy Secretary of State for Economic Affairs. The impetus for the change was the fact that the international situation had fundamentally changed since the early post-war years.

The resurgence of the European economies, including the defeated Axis powers, meant that they were becoming capable of competing successfully in export markets with the United States. The consortium technique was discovered by accident, when India was at the point of defaulting payment for orders placed in several different countries, and the only way of rescheduling payment terms (since each creditor would refuse debt relief unless the others extended the same terms) proved to be an international conference of the creditor countries.

At the same time, the United States government discovered with some chagrin that its once overwhelming surplus in international trade was reversing to a deepening deficit, while it was by no means ready to give up the military bases and economic and political leverage which its overseas spending policy had purchased for over a decade. It seized upon the consortium technique as a means of putting pressure on the newly rich states of Europe and Japan to finance their own exports to the so-called 'developing' countries, which it called 'sharing the aid burden'.

At present, when almost all aid funds are 'tied' to purchases in the creditor country, the term 'burden' may seem strange, but it was real to the US by the late 1950s. In the fiscal year 1960, only 41 per cent of American aid (exclusive of surplus agricultural products furnished under P. L. 480, and Export–Import Bank financing which was tied, by definition, to US exports) was spent on American goods. As the US implemented the practice of aid-tying, the proportion rose to 79 per cent in 1963, and to 94 per cent in early 1965.[5] One example will show the situation the US wished to extricate itself from:

[In the 1950s] the Turkish government was able to extract large quantities of soft aid from the United States, the availability of which was what enabled it to go on eagerly accepting the suppliers' credits that the European countries found themselves compelled to make available in increasing quantities in order to maintain the flow of their exports ... From 1956 to 1958, US grants were in effect financing Turkey's repayment of debt.[6]

Not surprisingly, one of the first consortia formed was that for Turkey. The technique has been widely applied in the 1960s, although the word consortium has been abandoned for the term 'consultative group'. Most of these groups have been organized by the World Bank.

Aid-tying by the US eventually resulted in the Europeans and the Japanese adopting the practice themselves in self-defence. The result is that today, more than ever, aid seems to be merely another name for the financing of one's own country's exports. The terms of each country's aid differ according to the commercial competitiveness of the exports; the United States makes its relatively high-priced exports more attractive by offering softer credit terms, while Japan, whose exports are today likely to capture any untied aid still around (see the chapter on Indochina) is least likely to offer concessional credit terms.

The large increase in the IMF quota and the formation of the soft-loan World Bank affiliate, the IDA, were both proposed by US President Eisenhower in August 1958. His Deputy Secretary of State for Economic Affairs, C. Douglas Dillon, was determined to expand lending to Third World countries, for reasons which were spelled out by the *Financial Times* of London:

> ... the main immediate cause of current international payments stresses [and thus the need for more liquidity through the IMF and other sources] is the tendency for primary producing countries to restrict purchases of both consumer and capital goods because their export earnings have been heavily reduced by the tumble in world commodity prices ...[7]

It is likely that this tendency was viewed with as much alarm by the suppliers of the goods as by the impecunious customers. The spectre of the 1930s – of nations turning away from international trade and adopting inward-looking protectionist policies – was raising its head once again. Western policymakers perceived that expanded aid must supplement contracting trade as a means of financing their exports.

The shift in emphasis from 'project' aid to 'programme' aid, also known as budget support or balance of payments support, was a gradual change, and there is still much 'project' aid at the present. The shift, however, fitted integrally into the new, rationalized style of aid-giving which was being promoted by the United States. The problem with 'project' aid, from the US point of view, was that it gave the donor too little leverage over the economic policies of the recipient country. This disadvantage was especially pronounced if the project itself was dearer to the heart of the aid-giver than to that of the recipient. The aided country would accept the project, and then spend the rest of its budget on items which might not be 'rational' in the eyes of the donor. The switch to 'programme' aid, which was not tied to the importation of equipment for a specific project (though still tied to procurement in the donor country) could give the donor leverage over the entire economic programme of the recipient. It was in fact very similar to an IMF stand-by arrangement, in that disbursements could be tied to specified performance criteria, which were sometimes identical to IMF conditions. Furthermore, in sufficient volume it could prop up a government that was not capable of supporting itself through taxation. Like an IMF stand-by, *it was a means to support a government and ensure its obedient behaviour at the same time.*

The International Monetary Fund was given a key role in this grand strategy. It was included in the membership of each consortium or consultative group as they were formed, and it was given the responsibility of deciding whether the country in question was credit-worthy, and thus whether the other countries (the most important of which was, of course, the US) should aid its government. The consortium would coordinate and, in effect, monopolize aid flows from the entire capitalist world; and the IMF 'good housekeeping seal' was the precondition for this aid. The Fund had become a super credit agency.

In a statement before the House Banking and Currency Committee on 4 March 1959, which was considering the expansion of IMF quotas, the chief architect of the strategy, Douglas Dillon, explained:

In country after country the Monetary Fund has assisted it (sic) to carry out sound financial policies in a spirit of cooperation with fellow members. As an international organization it is better able to advise sovereign governments on sensitive matters of financial policy, or to insist on appropriate corrective measures in return for credits, than are other sovereign governments. This, I think, deserves to be underlined. In the delicate area of fiscal and monetary policy, governments find it much easier to accept the counsel of an objective, impartial, and highly competent international organization than the advice of other governments, no matter how good or well-intentioned.

Of course the US government was not really ceding control to another body, since it was able to control all important decisions of the Fund through its dominant voting power and informal influence (see Appendix II). The illusion of multilateralism was useful, however, not only with the targets of the 'advice' but also with the newly rich European nations which the US hoped to draw into the aid business as partners rather than rivals.

An editorial in the *Manchester Guardian* spelt out the new strategy explicitly:

The Fund and Bank, it is faintly hoped, may be able to impose some financial prudence on the Latin Americans more successfully than any United States Government body has been able to do. A pilot operation along this line is the recent IMF advance to Brazil. If this succeeds, the Fund may be further used as an instrument for creating 'safe' lending conditions. The Export–Import Bank and the Development Loan Fund would then come in with large amounts but in conditions made safe by the pilot.[8]

Although this particular operation in Kubitschek's Brazil was one of the more spectacular failures of the IMF's disciplinary powers (see Chapter 7) the US adopted the general practice of following the lead of the IMF. To the present, the IMF has served as the bell-wether of Western aid programmes.

The IMF Stand-by Arrangement and Stabilization Programme: A Model

A stand-by arrangement with the IMF is negotiated by the affected country's top financial officials (usually the Minister of Finance and the Governor of the Central Bank) and a team of IMF staff members visiting that country. These negotiations are often hard-fought and bitter – a far cry from the image which the IMF would like to project of its highly competent staff dispensing impartial expert advice to grateful country officials. The IMF mission members have consulted before leaving Washington with all the Executive Directors most concerned with that particular country, including always the US director. They are *de facto* empowered to negotiate on behalf of the Fund, and their decisions are seldom if ever overruled in Washington. Once negotiations are concluded, they assist the borrowing country's officials to draft a Letter of Intent which sets forth the promises which have been made in order to qualify for the Fund's assistance. Items covered by the Letter of Intent include exchange rate practices, import regulations, control of the domestic budget deficit, bank credit controls, and policies towards foreign investment. It often contains very specific quantitative commitments for many of these items; it is understood that if the government fails to keep the commitments in its Letter of Intent, its right to borrow under the stand-by arrangement will be suspended.

Although the details of each programme will vary, the IMF standard of a desirable economic policy is uniform and predictable enough to allow us to sketch a model of it here. The basic components of any such programme are the following:

(1) Abolition or liberalization of foreign exchange and import controls.

(2) Devaluation of the exchange rate.

(3) Domestic anti-inflationary programmes, including:

    (a) control of bank credit; higher interest rates and perhaps higher reserve requirements;

    (b) control of the government deficit: curbs on spending; increases in taxes and in prices charged by public enterprises; abolition of consumer subsidies;

    (c) control of wage rises, so far as within the government's power;

    (d) dismantling of price controls.

(4) Greater hospitality to foreign investment.

Most academic criticism of IMF programmes has focused on the anti-inflationary policies listed under number three. While these policies certainly have very undesirable effects on business activity and welfare programmes, the issues become less technical and more comprehensible if we start our discussion with number one. 'Liberalization' of exchange and import controls means, quite simply, the dismantling of controls that have been erected to save foreign exchange. This is a curious requirement to impose upon a country already suffering from a shortage of foreign exchange, since it can predictably and logically be expected to worsen that shortage. It is, however – as we have seen – a basic objective of the Fund, written into its Articles of Agreement. It is absolutely fundamental, and – despite the tortuous justifications in Fund ideology of the benefits of liberalization for development – it is a measure which benefits the country's trading partners rather than itself. The Fund, it must be remembered, *must* promote the international flow of trade and investment, not modes of development which require a restriction of this flow.

The next item on the list, the setting of a 'realistic' exchange rate, should be understood as a corollary to liberalization. If all, or some, exchange and import controls are to be dismantled, then to compensate for the heavier demand for foreign exchange, its price must go up (devaluation). The ideal policies which the Fund might like to see adopted are often economically or politically out of reach of the government; so the Fund is usually prepared, realistically, to accept progress *in the direction of its ultimate goal*. To illustrate, the continuum of the Fund's exchange rate preferences seems to be the following, with the Fund's ideal at the top and its anathema, state trading, at the bottom:

(1) Stable, unitary exchange rate; devaluation when necessary but infrequently;
(2) 'floating' or 'crawling peg' exchange rates (permitted where a stable rate could not be maintained without tightening controls);
(3) simple multiple exchange rates: perhaps only two rates, with the majority of transactions at the 'free market' rate;
(4) complex multiple exchange rate systems;
(5) exchange controls;
(6) state trading, as in centrally planned economies where the exchange rate has no effect on trading decisions.

It is only with the concept of progress along a continuum that we can understand why the Fund was delighted when Yugoslavia adopted multiple exchange rates in the 1950s (moving from 6 to 4) but frowned on their use in Brazil and Indonesia during the same period. The Fund's scale of preferences has altered somewhat over the years; it used to tolerate multiple exchange rate systems as a 'least worst' expedient much more than it does now; while on the other hand 'floating' exchange rates have risen in its favour as it was realized that the alternative to them might often be tighter administrative controls. Although the IMF is often accused of rigidity, it is in fact more pragmatic than it is given credit for.

We have seen that one of the purposes for which the Fund was established was to prevent devaluations which give the devaluing country's exports an unfair price advantage (in the opinion of its trade rivals). It is paradoxical that under post-war conditions the Fund has more often had to compel devaluation than to object to it. As an IMF official has pointed out, 'the Fund has no power to compel or even formally to propose the devaluation of an overvalued currency'. The means by which it nevertheless does compel devaluation is worth quoting at length:

> Overvaluation, as such, is harmful to the country practising it rather than to other countries. *What is harmful to other countries is the reduction of imports, and perhaps of capital outflows, which the country having an overvalued currency is obliged to bring about in order to obviate a chronic payments deficit that would exhaust its reserves.* And so far as outright restrictions on current payments and imports, at any rate, are concerned, the Fund and GATT between them are, as we shall see, empowered to object to, and in some circumstances to prohibit, their application. Moreover, the Fund frequently expresses views concerning the desirability, where appropriate, of adjusting the exchange rate of the country's currency to a more realistic level as an essential step towards the removal of objectionable restrictions ...[9]

The Fund itself is formally concerned only with exchange rates and exchange restrictions. Trade policies, however, have such an intimate connection with exchange rate policies that the Fund has assumed authority not only over exchange restrictions, but 'restrictions maintained for balance of payments reasons' which may include import restrictions and even protective tariffs.[10] Therefore stipulations for the liberalization of trade may be included in the terms of a stand-by arrangement.

Legally and formally, the Fund has no power to dictate changes in a country's internal policies. In practice, it does this in the case of most drawings made beyond the first credit tranche. The anti-inflationary policies which it insists upon touch the very heart of national sovereignty by affecting government spending, taxation, and credit policy; in fact, because of its anti-inflation emphasis the entire Fund package is usually called a 'stabilization programme'.

Critics of the Fund's stabilization programmes usually miss their mark, however, because they ignore two facts. The first is that the anti-inflationary policy is the necessary corollary of exchange liberalization and exchange stability, which represent the Fund's *raison d'être*. Just as the absence of exchange controls necessarily implies the setting of an exchange rate which will mediate supply and demand without the aid of controls, so if that exchange rate, once achieved through devaluation, is to be maintained without further devaluations *ad infinitum*, then the government must keep domestic demand relatively stable so that the exchange rate may stay stable.

Though the Fund is not entitled to object to a proposed devaluation because it is rendered necessary, for example, by a too inflationary domestic policy, this does not mean that the international system authorized by the Fund Articles is one in which countries are free to pursue whatever internal financial policy they please so long as they refrain from imposing restrictions but keep their external accounts in balance by continually devaluing their rates of exchange. On the contrary, as I pointed out earlier, it is an explicit purpose of the Fund not only to eliminate exchange restrictions but also to promote exchange stability. These two objectives, however, cannot be simultaneously attained unless countries so conduct their fiscal and monetary policies as to maintain a reasonable degree of internal financial stability.[11]

Criticism of the Fund's stabilization policies has also been somewhat off the mark because of a confusion between two ways of viewing inflation – what we might call the 'macro' and the 'micro' view. In the 'micro' view of inflation, which is that of the common citizen as consumer and wage-earner, the Fund policies certainly make things worse rather than better. When wages are held down but the price of utilities and government services and taxes are raised, this seems like a very curious attack on inflation, since all of these measures depress the real income of the ordinary citizen. This paradoxical situation has been called 'inflationary deflation' by Eshag and Thorp.[12]

In the 'macro' monetary theory of the IMF, however, inflation is defined as an imbalance between the supply of money and the volume of goods and services in the country. Since the money supply expands because of government deficit spending and the creation of credit by banks, these must be restrained to put a halt to inflation. This view is not only indifferent to the welfare of the man in the street; it views as a positive necessity a rise in taxes and prices which will take money out of citizens' hands and put it at the disposal of the government. This philosophy, which has been labelled 'orthodox' and 'monetarist' and roundly criticized by economists of opposing schools, is perfectly logical and correct within its own terms of reference. As we have seen, stabilization is essential *if* one accepts the parameters of exchange freedom and stability within which the IMF has to work. This view is, however, indifferent to human needs (despite the efforts of Fund ideologists to identify its aims with popular hostility to inflation), and such programmes often prove politically impossible.

The Fund's hostility to inflation is strongly influenced by the effect of inflation on foreign investors. This was spelled out explicitly by the Chief of the Finance Division of the IMF in *Finance and Development*, in which the Fund and Bank explain their activities to the lay public:

One of the differences between stable and inflationary economies is that investors can make reasonable estimates of future money costs and money receipts in the stable countries, while this is impossible once inflation is well underway. Further, this uncertainty bears most heavily on foreign investors. All the chances in the lottery are stacked against them. International investment is in any event likely to be more hazardous than domestic investment. With inflation, the hazards involved in movements of international capital are increased by the unpredictability of exchange rates. Not only are the net returns on investment in the developing country's currency unknown, but the returns in terms of the investor's currency are even more speculative. So it is not surprising that foreign investors tend to shy away from countries with extreme inflation, and that such countries tend to cut themselves off from access to resources from abroad.[13]

While a strong inflation by itself is thus likely to frighten capital away from a developing country, the policies frequently adopted by governments to ease the burdens of rising prices may have an effect that is even greater in discouraging national progress. As suggested above, strong inflation usually leads to the adoption of payments restrictions. Among the first candidates for restriction are payments on foreign capital. Even if assurances are given that foreign investors will be favourably treated, experience has taught these investors to be wary of restrictive systems, which usually contain considerable scope for administrative arbitrariness. Thus the almost inevitable exchange restrictions brought by strong inflation do more than discourage capital from fostering development. They so frighten capital away, and even encourage repatriation, that measures designed to conserve foreign exchange may in fact dry up a country's resources and dissipate its reserves.[14]

This brings us to the final component of the typical IMF stabilization programme: greater hospitality to foreign investment. This item is in a sense redundant, since we have seen that the entire complex of stabilization policies is designed to ensure that the country can manage its foreign exchange policies with the minimum recourse to restrictions on payments, which would damage primarily foreign investors and suppliers of that country's imports.

Nevertheless, conditions relating explicitly to foreign investment may be included in the Letter of Intent which accompanies a stand-by arrangement. When in 1970 the newly elected government of Mrs Sirimavo Bandaranaike in Ceylon published the letters of intent submitted by the previous government to the IMF, the letter of July 1965 included the provision 'to review the moratorium on remittances and take steps to improve the climate for the inflow of foreign official and private capital into Ceylon'.[15]

The Fund's enthusiasm for private capital as an aid to the balance of payments follows naturally from its position as a defender of international trade and payments and the fact that it is under the control of capital-investing countries. It is less easy to square with the Fund's assumed posture as adviser on balance of payments problems to poor countries, since present investments will represent balance of payments burdens, in the form of profit repatriation, in the future.

The Role of Aid in the Stabilization Package

The Fund takes a similar attitude to foreign aid, although the loans which benefit the balance of payments this year will give rise to a burden of repayment in years ahead. Foreign debt is the dark reverse side of foreign aid; only grants, which are a very small part of the total, are completely free of repayment obligations. The Fund, however, while deploring the huge debt burden now weighing down the balance of payments of most Third World countries, simultaneously continues to regard foreign aid as a normal and desirable way to bridge payments gaps, even to the point of considering aid inflows as an above-the-line transaction in the balance of payments.

For, unlike the post-war economic aid received by the European countries, aid to developing countries constitutes a continuous source of financing. In general, therefore, the recipient countries are not expected to adjust their balance of payments to do without the aid as were the European countries during the immediate post-war period.[16]

Aid is, in fact, an integral part of the IMF stabilization package – both as the *quid pro quo* to encourage the borrowing country to stick to the agreed conditions, and as a necessary condition for the success of the package itself. The reason goes back, yet again, to the exchange and trade liberalization which are the heart of the programme. As we have seen, dismantling controls designed to save foreign exchange at a time of payments crisis seems a rather counterproductive 'solution'. In fact most countries could not possibly afford it, even with the panoply of devaluation and stabilization policies designed to control demand indirectly. Typically, aid is given for the purpose of financing these 'liberalized' imports; conversely, liberalization is the price of aid. The gamble taken by the borrowing country is that the aid received will exceed its costs in additional, probably nonessential, imports. Many hard-pressed governments have believed the gamble was worth taking; the case studies in this book suggest they were guilty of misjudgement. The aid, in either case, must eventually be repaid.

Aid also supports the domestic budget of the borrowing government, since private importers have to pay the government in local currency for the privilege of selling aid-financed goods. In this respect aid has the same effect as a tax programme which brings in the same amount of money, but permits the government to avoid making enemies through new taxes. The aid thus finances government expenditures by providing additional goods to sop up excess currency in the country and channelling the proceeds to the government, which is thus allowed to spend more than it collects in taxes. Without the aid, government expenditures would have to be cut by the amount of aid, or there would be an inflationary increase in the money supply. Thus, although it often preaches austerity when pushing its stabilization programmes, the Fund actually presides over a system in which governments that follow the prescribed trade and investment promoting policies are systematically encouraged to consume more than they earn – with the bill presented a few years later.

To recapitulate: liberalization of exchange and import controls is the heart of each IMF stabilization programme, as required by its Articles of Agreement. All of the other components of the package: exchange rate adjustment, stabilization measures, and foreign aid financing of the deficit, are measures which are necessary to counteract the predictable adverse effect of liberalization on the balance of payments. All of them are necessary, in the sense that the absence of any one of them would necessitate a much more severe application of the others: if domestic anti-inflationary measures were not implemented, then the devaluation would have to be much sharper and/or a much larger amount of aid would be necessary to cover the deficit, and so with the other items *pari passu*. The system is logically interdependent and consistent with the basic aims of the Fund. Effective criticism of it must take into account not only its social, political, and developmental consequences, but those basic aims as well.

The View from Below: Social and Political Consequences

Thus far we have discussed the components of a typical IMF stabilization programme as a consistent whole, growing logically out of the Fund's constitutional commitment to promote freedom of trade, exchange, and investment. What is good for international corporations may not, however, be very good for the citizens of the affected country, so it is now time to sketch briefly the political and social effects of these programmes. The case studies which follow will provide illustrations.

The programmes result, typically, in the take-over of domestically owned businesses by their foreign competitors. The stabilization programme puts the squeeze on domestic capitalists in several ways. The depression which it causes cuts deeply into their sales. Devaluation raises the costs, in local currency, of all imports needed for their business, and of all the unpaid debts resulting from past imports. This, a severe blow in itself, is compounded by the fact that the contraction of bank credit makes it more difficult than before to get the loans they need to carry on operations. Finally, the liberalization of imports robs them of the protected markets they had enjoyed before.

Liberalization of imports tends to benefit the foreign-owned firms, which are dependent on foreign inputs – raw materials, machinery, and spare parts – imported from another branch of the same multi-national corporation. The price charged for these inputs often does not represent the real cost of the merchandise, but may be set much higher than cost in order to transfer profits out of the country (especially where there are controls on profit remittance) in the guise of payment for 'essential' imports. If foreign exchange for imports is rationed and licensed, this practice of 'transfer pricing' will be affected, and the foreign-owned factories may have to cut down production for lack of their usual inputs.[17]

The locally-owned firms, suffering from an IMF-induced depression, may go bankrupt, or curtail operations and fire employees; they are ripe for take-over by a foreign firm. The

41

foreign business, which is likely to be more successful in the competition for scarce credit because it is backed up by the resources of its parent company, may even effect the take-over without bringing in foreign money, by borrowing from the domestic banking system. Even if new money is brought in from abroad, it should be noted that this type of investment does not represent the creation of new productive power, or the transfer of resources from rich countries to poor, but rather the transfer of resources within the poor countries from domestic to foreign ownership. And while it may provide, like foreign aid, some temporary relief to the balance of payments, in the long run it adds to the burden as profits are remitted to the investing country and loans must be repaid with interest.

The local entrepreneur forced to sell out to a foreign firm is, however, not the most lamentable victim of the stabilization programme; he is very likely given an executive position and a fat salary in his own former enterprise. The poorer consumers and wage-earners are the real losers. The failure of businesses throws many people out of work; and the wage restraints which are a key part of any IMF programme will reduce the real income of those who do not lose their jobs. The elimination of multiple exchange rates, where they exist, means that devaluation will raise the local price of essential imported commodities as well as luxuries. If devaluation is successful in its aim of stimulating exports, then the price of local products, particularly food, which can be exported will rise on the domestic market because less will be available for local consumption. *It is an explicit and basic aim of IMF programmes to discourage local consumption in order to free resources for export.*

Another way in which the stabilization programme hits consumers with the paradoxical 'inflationary deflation' is the end to consumer subsidies and the freeing of administered prices. Public utility rates, if they have been below the level considered 'economical' by the IMF, will have to go up; public transportation usually becomes more costly. In Ceylon, the free rice ration for every citizen supplied by the government was a major target of the IMF's deficit-cutting operation; it has been reduced, though not yet abolished.

Because such subsidies, and in fact almost any interference with market forces (except of course the special incentives offered to foreign investors!) are branded as undesirable 'distortions' by the IMF, the effect is to make impossible any attempt at a moderate social revolution by vetoing the very measures which might ameliorate the lot of the majority of the people, short of a real revolution. It should be remarked. however, that the Fund seems to be much more lenient in this respect with some governments than with others. This cannot be explained by reference to differences among the various area departments of the IMF, for there are wide variations within the areas themselves, but there is a plausible political hypothesis: where the most powerful opposition to the government in power is rightist and friendly to the US (as in Brazil, Argentina, and Indonesia before their respective military coups) the government is likely to receive more severe treatment from the IMF when it tries to support social reform measures than in countries where the chief rival to the government's power is left nationalism. This hypothesis could explain why the IMF has seemed more sympathetic to governments such as Eduardo Frei's in Chile (which nevertheless did not prevent the electorate from choosing the Marxist Allende in 1970), and to successive governments in Ceylon, where the army is very weak and pressure on the government comes more from the left.

The Fund's Fifth Column: Internal Allies

Although the majority of a country's citizens may suffer from the effects of an IMF programme, the Fund has important allies within most countries. The most enthusiastic allies are the exporters, whose profits will rise if the currency is devalued. Although exporters are often foreign-owned corporations, where there is a strong domestic class of exporters (i.e. the sugar barons in the Philippines) this class will form a fifth column inside the country lobbying for the IMF sponsored reforms.

Government officials have conflicting interests, and are often divided among themselves about the desirability of accepting the conditions attached to IMF loans. The unpopularity of the loan conditions will make their job of dissent management much more difficult – a problem that will have special weight in a democracy but cannot be ignored even in an authoritarian system. On balance, however, the attraction of the funds to which the IMF is the key will usually be decisive, since the method of dispensing aid supports the government budget and relieves it of the necessity of raising new taxes. This conflict of interest explains why government officials will negotiate fiercely about the terms of a stand-by arrangement but will very rarely break off negotiations in earnest.

A special subcategory of government officials are the Western-educated economists called 'technocrats' who return to their native country to occupy important posts in the Ministries of Finance and Trade, and on the special commissions for economic planning and development. These technocrats have been indoctrinated with the Western liberal ideology of development, and tend to support IMF diagnoses and prescriptions. The Fund itself runs an institute for the training of Central Bank and Finance Ministry officials, and disperses its graduates, indoctrinated with the Fund ideology, throughout the Third World where they form an 'old boy' network of support for Fund principles.

Democracy, Military Coups, and the IMF

The intimate relationship between IMF programmes and military coups is a major theme of this book. Too much nonsense has been spoken and written about the 'immaturity' of democratic systems of government and the absence of democratic attitudes in the Third World, and too little recognition has been given to the fundamental contradiction between a government's responsibility to the citizens who elected it, and the obedience to the demands of foreign creditors expressed in the IMF stabilization programmes. IMF programmes are politically unpopular, for the very good concrete reasons that they hurt local business and depress the real income of the electorate. A government which attempts to carry out the conditions in its Letter of Intent to the IMF is likely to find itself voted out of office. A government which does not carry out the conditions, or make an agreement at all, is likely to find its international credit for imports cut off, which puts it into a popularity bind of a different variety and makes a rightist coup likely.

Brazil provides a classic illustration of the contribution of IMF programmes, combined with promises of foreign aid, to the overthrow of a democratic government which was, perhaps, all too responsive to the will of the electorate. The coups in Turkey (1960), Argentina (1966), and the Philippines (1972) provide other examples; no doubt readers could add to the list.

In Ceylon (now Sri Lanka) the Bandaranaike government has reneged on promises made during its campaign for office, when it won votes by attacking the previous government's subservience to the IMF and World Bank. Once in office, however, the new government proved not committed enough to carry through a go-it-alone austerity programme, and soon went crawling back to the IMF to clean up its credit rating. The popular disillusionment with the broken campaign promises climaxed in the abortive radical insurrection of April 1971, and the sequel has been increasing repression and militarism. Watch the next elections, in 1975 – if they are held.

The 1973 military coup against Allende's government in Chile is the best-known recent example which falls into this pattern. Chile's electorate, like Ceylon's, is acknowledged as one of the most politicized, sophisticated, and literate in the Third World; that nation was no 'banana republic' but a democracy which took its constitution and its elections very seriously. Chile's experience is described in chapter 9.

Debt and Dependency

The IMF may claim that all these deleterious social and political effects we have described are really 'not its department', since it pretends to be a politically neutral, technical advisory service on balance of payments problems. The ever-increasing debt burden of most Third World countries, which is the immediate cause of most payments crises, cannot be dismissed in the same way. The Fund displays an obtuse indifference, curious for a body which claims the position of balance of payments adviser, to the fact that this year's aid is the debt repayment burden of future years. It even assumes, as we have seen, that the recipients can plan on receiving large amounts of aid into an indefinite future. Therefore, the Fund does not advise nations on how to reduce their imports and stand on their own feet economically, but coaches them on how to qualify for increased quantities of new credit.

Equally ominous is the effect of devaluation in increasing the income of producers of traditional raw materials exports, whether minerals or plantation products. The countries concerned are thrown back into the very economic pattern they were trying to escape from; in fact, the Fund, the Bank, and the developed capitalist world implicitly define development as the intensification and rationalization of that very pattern. When the export producers are foreign, their increased profits are eventually remitted out of the country; where they are nationals, the effect is the political and economic reinforcement of the most reactionary social classes, the natural allies of foreign traders and investors.

Thus the government which, willingly or reluctantly, submits to IMF policy prescriptions is rewarded not with a healthy and diversified economy and a better life for its citizens, but with temporary relief for immediate payments difficulties. When a country is in crisis due to an impossibly heavy schedule of repayments of foreign debts, the Fund takes a sympathetic attitude and convenes a debt rescheduling conference if the country concerned proves it is penitent and submissive by agreeing to let the IMF dictate its economic policies in the future. To the debtor country, debt rescheduling is 'better than new aid' in the sense that the money they do not have to pay back this year is released for any other purposes for which it is needed, while new aid is usually tied to purchases in the donor country, which discounts from its nominal value. However, the rescheduled debt will still have to be paid back in the future, with interest charged on the deferred payment. The potential for repeated payments crises and 'rescue operations' stretches into the indefinite future in a vicious circle: an IMF programme is made the condition for further debt relief, but the IMF programme perpetuates the colonial economic pattern and the 'aid' can never be fully paid back. The poor countries will have to run faster and faster just to stay in the same place.

It is true that the Fund and its twin institution, the World Bank, are declared opponents of one kind of debt, the suppliers' credits. As the name indicates, these are credits which are extended by the exporter eager to make a sale, and often guaranteed by the exporters' government which is just as eager to promote national exports. These credits are often called 'short-term suppliers' credits', but they may have maturities as long as five or ten years, and are thus short-term not for balance of payments accounting purposes, but in the sense that often the loan will have to be paid back before the project it finances is producing. The Fund and Bank object to this type of credit, they say, because of the burden that high interest rates and bunched repayments represent to the balance of payments. It is certainly true that most of the payments crises of the late 1950s and 1960s were due largely to repayments of suppliers' credits falling due. The irresponsible accumulation of heavy debts of this type threatens to bring the entire aid/debt/dependency system crashing down from its own weight, which probably accounts for the alarm of the Fund and the Bank (see section on Ghana in Chapter 9).

It may be suspected, however, that one reason this type of credit is so objectionable to these institutions is that it has, in the past, made it possible for some governments to evade IMF requirements. For example, in 1958 both Brazil and the Philippines rejected IMF programmes while obtaining private credits from Western countries. In Ghana:

Western official aid after the 1966 coup tended to be for less directly productive investments, primarily infrastructure. This meant that for many of the industries that the Ghana government wanted to initiate through state corporations, essentially the only form of finance available would be either private credits from Western countries on rather onerous terms, or official credits from Eastern European countries. Therefore, in the absence of a buoyant foreign exchange situation, the establishment of a larger industrial sector virtually dictated the type of foreign credits that would be available.[18]

An IMF official has admitted, disapprovingly, that 'some developing countries have regarded these credits as more convenient than the financing of projects by long-term loans from governmental and multilateral institutions. The substitute financing avoids the scrutiny associated with these long-term loans, but at the cost of a rapid increase in debt service . . .'[19]

Thus the so-called developing countries are caught in a double bind. If they seek official help on softer than commercial terms, they have to accept outside scrutiny, give up projects that they may sincerely believe essential to their national welfare, and accept conditions which doom their efforts at industrial, diversified development. If they accept suppliers' credits on commercial terms in order to go through with their cherished projects, they are caught anyway when the payments come due before they are able to meet them. It cannot be stressed too strongly that long-term official aid is not necessarily 'development' aid just because it is so labelled, and its terms are somewhat softer. Nor, for that matter, are suppliers' credits necessarily evil just because they are not made on concessional terms. Either loan could be put to wasteful and unnecessary uses; both types have to be paid back eventually.

If the Western governments were genuinely concerned about the effects of the debt burden on development, they could declare the debts forgiven, or at least, as Laurence Whitehead has suggested, refrain from vindictive sanctions when the suffering debtor finally repudiates the debts.[20] The fact that forgiveness of debts is never considered in the contemporary world indicates that the much-deplored debts are in fact serving a useful function above and beyond the money to be repaid. They help to keep the potentially rebellious borrower in line.

The system can be compared point by point with peonage on

an individual scale. In the peonage, or debt slavery, system the worker is unable to use his nominal freedom to leave the service of his employer, because the latter supplies him with credit (for overpriced goods in the company store) necessary to supplement his meagre wages. The aim of the employer/creditor/merchant is neither to collect the debt once and for all, nor to starve the employee to death, but rather to keep the labourer permanently indentured through his debt to the employer. The worker cannot run away, for other employers and the state recognize the legality of his debt; nor has he any hope of earning his freedom with his low wages, which do not keep pace with what he consumes, let alone the true value of what he produces for his master.

Precisely the same system operates on the international level. Nominally independent countries find that their debts, and their constant inability to finance current needs out of imports, keep them tied by a tight leash to their creditors. The IMF orders them, in effect, to continue labouring on the plantation, while it refuses to finance their efforts to set up in business for themselves. It is debt slavery on an international scale. If they remain within the system, the debtor countries are doomed to perpetual underdevelopment, or rather to development of their exports at the service of multinational enterprises, at the expense of development for the needs of their own citizens.

3

Exchange Controls and National Capitalism: The Philippines Experience

At the end of the Second World War, two circumstances offered the Philippines a precious potential opportunity to rebuild its economy along diversified industrial lines and thus to break the vicious circle of poverty and dependence which is characteristic of the Third World.

The first was the fact that the Japanese occupation had severed the umbilical cord of free trade which had tied the Philippines to the United States since 1909 and had tailored the output and the consumption of the Philippine economy to American markets and American supplies. The effect of thirty years as an American colony had been the creation of the classical colonial relationship, with the Philippines supplying raw materials, mostly agricultural – sugar, coconut products, hemp, cordage – and importing industrial products from the mother country. The Japanese occupation had broken this connection and destroyed much of the economic structure it had created: the sugar plantations, in particular, had declined into ruin during the war years. Rehabilitation of the economy was imperative, but the very fact of the destruction offered the opportunity of constructing something more than had existed under the structure of colonial preferential trade.

The second factor was the relatively strong foreign exchange position which the country enjoyed in the immediate post-war period. Unlike most war-ravaged countries at that time, the Philippines had a hard currency, bound by treaty to the US dollar at the rate of 2:1, and no lack of dollar exchange. During the late 1940s, the country enjoyed windfall dollar receipts which were far in excess of its capacity to earn through exports, in the form of spending by American soldiers, US government disbursements for salaries of local personnel, veterans' payments to Philippine soldiers, war damage payments, etc.[1]

Taken together and intelligently planned, the large foreign exchange holdings and receipts could have been used to finance the rehabilitation of the Philippine economy along more diversified and autonomous lines. The opportunity was squandered, however; most of the windfall income went into private pockets and the foreign exchange was used to finance massive imports of consumer goods which contributed nothing to the development of the economy. This happened not only because Philippine officials were more corrupt and less far-sighted than they should have been, but because the United States, in granting the country its political independence in 1946, was careful not to give it economic independence.

The instrument of US control over the nominally independent former colony was the Philippine Trade Act of 1946, commonly known as the Bell Trade Act. This bill, which has determined the course of the country's post-war economic policy, was drafted and debated in the US Congress, and designed to conform to the needs of *American* interests, during the last few months before the scheduled grant of independence to the Philippines. The provisions of the Act were also discussed, debated, and finally accepted by the Philippine Congress, but in a quite different context as the country was offered the bill only on a take-it-or-leave-it basis in the form dictated by the US. Although there were strong feelings against the Bell Act in the Philippines (the Huk-supported Democratic Alliance representatives had to be ousted from the seats to which they had been elected, to ensure passage of the Act by the Philippine Congress) it was voted through in the end. Passage of the Act in the Philippines was made possible not only by the genuine support of the pre-war exporting interests, which would benefit from the reconstruction of the old economy, but also by a considerable element of bribery, since release of funds from the US Rehabilitation Act was made conditional upon Philippine acceptance of the Trade Act. A number of legislators who were not happy with the Bell Act nevertheless campaigned and voted for it because of their belief that the country was in desperate need of the funds which would flow into the country under the Rehabilitation Act. In retrospect, it may be questioned whether they sold their independence birthright for a short-lived spree spending unearned dollars.

The most important provisions of the Bell Act were those which restored pre-war trade preferences and restricted Philippine currency autonomy. The parity provision, which gave US citizens equal rights with Filipinos in the ownership and exploitation of national resources, was in practice much less important, although it drew more hostile attention from nationalists.

The Bell Act restored the pre-war trade preferences between the Philippines and the US and thus closed off the option of reconstructing the economy along more protectionist and autonomous lines. General Carlos P. Romulo, a supporter of the bill, admitted that it would 'to a very great extent, tend to restore the status quo as it existed before the war'.[2] Another Filipino economist and businessman commented in 1950:

> The war broke our trade relations with America and destroyed most of the industries depending on free trade. Consequently, after liberation, before the pre-war industries dependent on free trade had been rehabilitated, I was in favour of abandoning entirely our free trade arrangement with the United States to start a new economy for the Philippines. We lost in the fight against the Bell Act, and now our Philippine economy is in the process of rehabilitation, as it had existed before the war, with sugar, coconut oil, cordage and cigars again depending on their free entry into the American market ...
>
> Our experience for the past three years, I believe, has shown that free trade means the preservation of the status quo, inimical to the creation of new industries that are necessary to replace the ones that are to be destroyed with the gradual cessation of free trade.[3]

The Bell Act also provided for continuing US control over the exchange rate policy of the Philippines, a more serious infringement of sovereignty than the notorious parity clause (which required amendment of the Philippine constitution). The relevant provision of the Act (Title III, Section 342) reads:

> The value of the Philippine currency in relation to the United States dollar shall not be changed, and no restrictions shall be

imposed on the transfer of funds from the Philippines to the United States, except by agreement with the President of the United States.

In contrast to the situation in recent years, when the Philippines has had devaluation, or *de facto* devaluation in the form of the 'floating rate' forced upon it, the provision for a fixed parity prohibited the country from devaluing its currency without the approval of the US President. The purpose of this clause, according to Rep. Wilbur D. Mills, was:

to safeguard the value of capital that may go from the United States to the Philippines ... so that when the capital decides to revert to the United States it may come to the United States without depreciation.[4]

The prohibitions against restrictions on convertibility and transfer of funds also meant that the Philippine government could not, without US permission, put an end to the wastage of resources which the orgy of post-war imports of consumer goods represented.

The pattern of reconstruction set by the Bell Act, and the limitations it imposed on currency sovereignty, made something of a mockery of the report of the Joint Philippine–American Finance Commission a year after independence, in 1947. This report said:

The Commission regards the next few years as a period of national emergency; not in the sense that survival is at stake, but in the sense that emergency measures and an emergency national psychology will be required if the country is to grasp the opportunity for rapid economic development which is presented.[5]

The opportunity referred to was the foreign exchange windfall. The Commission, trying to work within the 'letter and spirit' of the Trade Act, could not recommend direct controls on the expenditure of this dollar exchange, which it correctly foresaw was likely to be dissipated without any lasting benefit to the economy, but it did recommend limiting non-essential imports and introducing import licensing procedures. The commission, however, had no power to enforce acceptance of its recommendation, and the opportunity was not grasped. As the then Central Bank Governor commented:

> Few steps were taken to put the economy on a sounder basis and to encourage the establishment of new industries because the windfall dollar profits were not spent on productive investment. When they started to decline, therefore, the country was faced with a serious payments situation.[6]

The dollar windfall dried up in 1949, but the demand for imports which it had primed remained high. Dollar expenditures had been outrunning dollar receipts throughout the post-war years, but by 1949 income declined so sharply that the Philippines found itself in an exchange crisis. The government acted by imposing sweeping controls on all transactions in gold and foreign exchange. Under the new procedures, no foreign payment could be made without the permission of the Central Bank. Private firms were prohibited from accepting foreign credits.

The consent of the US President to these exchange controls was secured on the grounds that this was an emergency measure necessary to sustain the value of the peso.[7] A mission of the International Monetary Fund, which was studying Philippine finance at the time, agreed that under the circumstances, exchange controls were 'unavoidable'. Similarly, the U.S. Economic Survey (Bell) Mission which went to the Philippines in 1950 recommended that 'as a safety measure, the present exchange and import controls be retained but that their administration be simplified and liberalized and the full remittance of current earnings be permitted'.

The introduction of exchange and import controls ushered in a twelve-year period of development which ended when controls were abolished in 1962. This period is considered by some to be the golden age of both industrialization and 'filipinization' of the Philippine economy; others remember it as a nightmare of corruption and windfall profits for the politically favoured few. It is important to consider both aspects.

Exchange controls can serve two important functions. Controls, properly administered, provide a tool for stopping the haemorrhage of foreign exchange leaving the country as re-mittance of earnings, profits and dividends, repatriation of foreign capital, payments for imports, etc. In other words, they provide a direct and immediate solution to foreign exchange crises. However, controls also provide policymakers with a powerful tool for directing the course of economic development, since foreign exchange must be rationed and conscious de-cisions have to be made on the question of which imports are essential and which superfluous, which industries shall be con-sidered vital enough to be allowed to import raw materials, etc. The mere existence of controls does not, of course, ensure that they will be administered wisely, or even in conformity with national economic policy, rather than political or private motives. Without any doubt, the administration of controls did become corrupted by private interests – no one familiar with the Philippine political system could question that. Neverthe-less, some measurable and significant progress was made in the manufacturing sector, which stirred to life after generations of discouragement from the competition of duty-free imports from the United States.

The manufacturing sector expanded vigorously in the 1950s, under the régime of controls, with a growth rate of 10-12 per cent per year. Income originating in manufacturing increased from 8 per cent of national income in 1949 to 18 per cent in 1965.[7] According to a publication of the First National City Bank in Manila:

The exchange control system helped set in motion a radical alter-ation of the country's economic structure. Stimulated by an effective barrier against foreign products and by preferential access to foreign exchange ... an entire spectrum of new or expanded local industries came into existence. The traditional trading-in-finished-goods orientation of the non-agricultural sector soon changed into packaging, assembly, and light manufacture.

During the control period, real gross national product rose by 6·5 per cent a year – a performance acknowledged by the World Bank as 'one of the more impressive records of economic gain among the less developed countries'. By 1959, real gross national product totalled P11 billion compared with P6 billion in 1950. This

83 per cent improvement in real terms reflected the sustained stability of the value of money. Between 1950 and 1959, the Manila consumer price index was kept to a remarkable increase of only 2 per cent.[8]

This 'remarkable stability' in the price index was made possible by the combination of conservative fiscal policy with rapid expansion in output.[9] Although this price stability seems enviable in retrospect – as the country has suffered a 20 per cent yearly inflation since 1970 – some economists maintain that the nation's growth rate could have reached even higher levels during the 1950s were it not for the Central Bank's rigid insistence on limitation of the money and credit supply.

Along with the rapid growth of the manufacturing sector and the resultant diversification of the economy came an increase in the participation of domestic capital in the expansion process. In 1949, Filipino capital constituted only 55 per cent of the investments in new enterprises in the country. By 1961 the Filipino proportion had risen to 88 per cent. From 1949 to 1961, Filipinos invested a total of P1,400 million in new enterprises; Chinese accounted for P435 million; Americans (despite parity) invested only P31 million.[10]

The traditional export sectors found themselves at a relative disadvantage during this period, since manufacturing expansion was favoured by the exchange policy, but even so, export earnings expanded 59 per cent from 1949 to 1953.[11] During the period of controls, however, individual and corporate exporters were not allowed to keep their dollar earnings, but had to turn them over to the Central Bank for pesos at a disadvantageous rate of exchange. It is probably for this reason that by the time controls were abolished, substantial filipinization of the export sector had taken place as foreign owners divested themselves of these less profitable holdings. For example, foreign-owned sugar centrals accounted for less than 8 per cent of the average annual production by 1962.[12]

The position of US investment during these years is worth examining in some detail, particularly because the parity clause, granting American firms equal treatment with Philippine-owned business within the Philippines, was in effect throughout the period. There was no legal favouritism of indigenous capital over American capital. Rather, the exchange control mechanism itself, even when applied impartially to foreign and local firms according to a development formula, inherently favoured the local firms.

Both Filipinos and foreigners seek lower costs, tax advantages, security of life and property, tariff protection, freedom from government competition and from expropriation, consistency in government policies. But foreign capital seeks, in addition, guarantees of the right to remit profits and repatriate earnings; here their interests may clash with those of Filipino entrepreneurs, who, in times of foreign exchange shortage, may need foreign exchange for raw materials or capital equipment.[13]

A blatant example of US government intervention on this account is recalled by Central Bank Governor Miguel Cuaderno in his memoirs. Cuaderno relates that Eugene Clay, assistant to US Ambassador Myron Cowen in Manila, threatened Cuaderno in the latter's office that he would recommend withdrawal of President Truman's approval of the institution of exchange controls if 'we did not agree to relax the application of the controls on certain American business firms in the Philippines'.[14]

What happened to American investment during the period of controls? Different sources vary on the amount of investment involved, but are in general agreement on the pattern.

First, American firms were welcome to, and did participate in the expansion of the manufacturing sector. 'American investment in manufacturing and commerce proved relatively acceptable to the Philippine society and was attractive to Americans because it helped to ensure access to the highly protected and lucrative internal Philippine market.'[15]

The fastest growing sector of US direct investment was manufacturing (including petroleum refining) which increased from $23 million to at least $190 million. Close behind was commerce; $30 million to $150 million ... This pattern directly reflects the system of indigenism which maintained powerful incentives to foreigners to invest in manufacturing for the domestic market and in final processing and distribution facilities in order to get inside the wall of protection that was integral to the system.[16]

57

In public utilities and natural resource industries, and in export agriculture, on the other hand, a number of American firms sold out their holdings to Philippine owners; net disinvestment took place.

Another point to remember is that during this period the largest share of new American investment was not brought into the country, but was the result of ploughing back earnings which had been blocked by the exchange controls and could not be taken out of the country. From 1950 to 1961, new foreign investment brought into the country was estimated to amount to only $17 million, but re-invested earnings came to $500 million.

In 1954, the Philippine government sent a mission headed by Senator Jose P. Laurel to Washington to negotiate a revision of the Bell Trade Act. (The US team was chaired by James Langley; the product of the negotiations is known as the Laurel–Langley Agreement.) Central Bank Governor Cuaderno, a member of the Philippine mission, was determined to secure the abrogation of Article V of the Agreement, which contained the provision limiting the control of the Philippine government over its own currency and requiring approval of the US President for any changes. Cuaderno has left his account of these negotiations in his memoirs:

Despite the brief which I prepared and read before the plenary meeting of both panels clearly indicating the inconsistency of a free country's currency being controlled by another country, the member of the American panel representing the State Department made a last-minute attempt to have us reconsider our decision that Article V should be eliminated; he wanted us to agree, instead, to the inclusion of a provision which would require prior consultation ... It was only after I threatened to vote against the draft of the revised Agreement and left the room that Mr Langley, against the stand of his two colleagues, agreed to let our previous understanding eliminating Article V of the old Agreement stand.[17]

So the Philippine government had finally obtained control over its own currency and exchange rate policies. Or had it? In ironically prophetic words Cuaderno added, 'The United

States should be satisfied that, as a member of the International Monetary Fund, any major exchange policy which the Philippines might wish to adopt would have to be passed upon by the Fund.'[18]

Why, if controls contributed to industrial diversification, filipinization, and price stability, were they abandoned in 1962? Liberalization in this case was *not* the result of an exchange crisis which forced the country to submit to the demands of the International Monetary Fund. There was such a crisis in 1958 which the IMF tried to use as a lever to require decontrol and devaluation, but they were rebuffed by the Philippine negotiators, including Cuaderno who has left an account of these negotiations also.

Cuaderno's resistance to the IMF demands is remarkable because of his long and friendly association with that institution, which had been climaxed by his election in 1956 as Chairman of the Board of Governors of the World Bank, IMF, and IFC; and because of his firm agreement with IMF orthodoxy on the importance of a stable currency.

When Cuaderno went to Washington seeking a loan that would permit the Philippines to meet its exchange crisis and continue importing the materials needed by its industry, he knew that the Fund would grant the loan only if the Philippines presented an acceptable stabilization plan. Cuaderno's plan rejected suggestions for a devaluation of the peso and proposed instead a tax of 25 per cent on the sale of foreign exchange – effectively a 'one-sided' devaluation. A similar tax which had been in effect before 1954 was abolished at the insistence of the United States in the Laurel–Langley Agreement.

Cuaderno discovered that although several of the officials and experts of the IMF were sympathetic to his proposal, US government pressure on the Managing Director prevented the Fund from extending the loan he sought.

When we discussed the matter with the Fund's Managing Director, this official would have supported the plan had not the American member of the Fund informed him that the US government did not think the Philippine government could re-impose a foreign exchange tax under the Laurel–Langley Agreement. I was furnished a copy of an opinion to this effect written by a law clerk of the State Department.

When the Managing Director of the Fund learned of the views of the State Department, he refused to discuss the matter further with us ... I felt very deeply the refusal of Managing Director Per Jacobsson to have his staff discuss our stabilization programme with our mission when he learned that the State Department did not favour it. I thought it was not good policy for an international organization such as the International Monetary Fund to allow itself to be influenced by any member country.[19]

Instead of the exchange tax, the Managing Director of the Fund suggested the alternative of devaluing the peso and removing exchange controls. 'We had a feeling', Cuaderno reminisced, that this was 'what the US government officials liked us to do.'[20] Cuaderno, feeling very strongly that such measures would not work in a poor country like the Philippines, refused to submit to the pressure. He was supported by Edward Bernstein, at that time chief economic researcher of the IMF, who wrote a paper in support of Cuaderno's plan.

Cuaderno refused to accede to the US–IMF conditions for a stabilization loan and succeeded in borrowing the short-term funds needed to tide over the crisis from private banks in New York where he had friends. According to his own assessment, the success of his management of the crisis vindicated his refusal to devalue and decontrol.

The Fund mission which came to Manila [in 1959] found out that the conditions of the economy, particularly the exchange reserves of the country, had improved and that the outlook for the year was better ... The mission did not mention devaluation at all. The Fund officials must have been surprised to see that our plan was a success, despite the fact that we did not secure a stabilization loan as other countries had done in the past ... the country's payments position had so improved that we were able to pay the outstanding balance of short-term loans secured from US private banks aggregating $35 million, US bankers' acceptances of about $27 million, advances secured in 1955 and 1956 from the International Monetary Fund, and about $9 million for additional subscription to the capital of the Fund and the International Bank ...

The country had an international reserve of \$162·9 million on 31 December 1959.[21]

The Philippine government's successful defiance of the Fund on this occasion punctures the Fund's claim to a monopoly of wisdom on the handling of exchange difficulties. The country's experience in weathering the crisis of the late 1950s compares favourably with its deepening economic difficulties as an obedient pupil of the Fund in the 1960s.

This episode illustrates a fundamental shift in the US attitude towards exchange controls and exchange rate stability which had taken place at some time between the passage of the Bell Trade Act in 1946 and the negotiations of 1958. Apparently the US authorities had come to the view that exchange controls were more harmful to US business interests than repeated and sizeable devaluations of currency would be – that it was more important, from the standpoint of foreign investors, to be able to take profits out of a country than to guarantee a constant value to the capital invested there. Ever since this shift in attitude occurred, both the United States and the IMF have been consistent advocates of devaluation and opponents of exchange controls.

Why, then, did the Philippines abandon exchange controls, if they were not forced to do so by the pressure of an exchange crisis? Some economists have suggested in retrospect that decontrol was the only rational decision by 1962 because import controls and import substitution had succeeded in eliminating consumer goods from the import list, so that 'virtually all imports were by now essential in some sense. Any further tightening of import controls would be likely to depress output and employment because of the dependence ... on imported inputs.'[22] This is, however, a patently ridiculous rationalization, for when all imports are in some degree essential, it must be even more imperative to set priorities, and it makes no sense at all to decontrol, which would permit some of the exchange to go for non-essential imports once again.

But if the necessity of economic development cannot explain the decision, there is a hypothesis based on class interest which fits the known facts better. During its twelve-year existence, the control programme had created powerful enemies within Philippine society and government. To what extent these internal forces had active support from the US Embassy for their campaign against controls is difficult to prove, but many Filipinos believed there was outside orchestration of the campaign. Certainly the American Chamber of Commerce in the Philippines made clear its hostility to exchange control.

The control programme was vulnerable to public criticism because of problems in its administration, which given the thoroughly capitalist orientation of the Philippine government were probably inevitable. The economic development of the 1950s was not an unqualified success story. The 'import substitution' industries which had mushroomed under the protective umbrella of controls were for the most part assembly and packaging industries which had been built up, not as part of a comprehensive industrialization plan, but in order to take advantage of the protected market to make high profits. These industries were dependent on imported raw materials and thus represented a continuing heavy claim on the foreign exchange resources of the country. 'Import substitution' had not resulted in any lessening of dependence on imports, only in a shift in their composition.

In the political milieu of the Philippines, corruption and favouritism were inevitable concomitants of the creation of an artificially protected economy. The scandals which surrounded the granting of exchange and import licences could be used by economic interest groups who were hurt by the controls to turn public opinion against the programme.

Two kinds of domestic business interests were opposed to controls. The first group were the 'outs', the enterprises which suffered from favouritism in the administration of controls because they were not able to profit by it. Their argument, although self-interested, did have the merit of fairness: if controls were dismantled, political favourites would be deprived of their windfall profits and free-for-all competition would presumably take the place of graft.

The second powerful group was that of the exporters, who

also felt themselves disadvantaged by the system of controls because it favoured manufacturing. These exporters were not permitted to keep the dollar earnings of their foreign sales, but had to turn them over to the Central Bank in exchange for pesos. This made sense from the national point of view, as one industrialist explained:

Under our monetary system no producer earns dollars; it is the country that earns dollars; and it is the government that should distribute these dollars and allocate them to producers, importers, etc., as the interests of the country and the people demand. To do otherwise will be discriminatory, because there is no reason why a producer of rice, our staple food for example, should be treated differently from a producer of sugar or coconut when they are all important to the national economy.[23]

The export producers did not take such a high-minded view of the situation, however, and chafed because they were not permitted to keep their dollar earnings. In 1955 they succeeded in pushing a No-Dollar Import Law, or barter law, through the Congress. Although in many countries barter transactions are permitted as a means of saving scarce foreign exchange, in this case the law had the opposite purpose – that of allowing exporters to evade exchange and import controls in order to make large profits. Cuaderno explained the mechanism in a memorandum to President Magsaysay, which urged him to veto the bill:

This particular provision of the Bill would allow the barter of any export product (for which the country now receives dollars) for all categories of goods when authorized by the Secretary of Commerce and Industry. In all cases of barter transactions which have heretofore been presented to the Central Bank, the Philippine exporters almost always preferred to barter Philippine products (which could be sold for dollars) with luxury items or [items] which are not essential, and because of the high profits obtained from luxury and non-essential goods in the Philippines, the exporters in barter transactions sell Philippine products at much lower prices than what they are being sold for.[24]

The bill became law, and from that time on represented a continuing leakage of foreign exchange receipts to the private benefit of exporters (mainly in sugar and logging) that otherwise could have been applied to national development. This loophole also gave rise to a significant trade in fictional 'new' exports such as 'rice bran'.[25]

After this partial victory, the anti-control lobby continued its campaign, arousing public indignation on the issue of graft and corruption in the administration of controls. This became a serious problem during the presidential term of Carlos Garcia (1957–61) who, not having the personal magnetism of his deceased predecessor Magsaysay, used the indiscriminate distribution of exchange permits to bolster his political position. Corruption is certainly a difficult (and chronic) problem in the Philippines, but to attempt to solve the problem by abolishing controls seemed like throwing the baby out with the bathwater. As a Manila columnist complained, satirizing the arguments of the decontrol faction:

> What we could not understand is why controls had to be eliminated just because graft and corruption had become associated with them ... If any office or institution affected by graft and corruption had to be abolished ... we would have to exterminate perhaps our whole government ... But no one ever thought of abolishing the entire executive department or precipitating a political decontrol programme in order that no more widespread graft and corruption could be associated with the administration, and so that our people can be given unrestricted freedom of movement for the purpose of finding realistically the level of social and political order they are capable of maintaining by themselves without supervision and control from a government.[26]

Nevertheless, under the banner of fighting corruption, the anti-control bloc in Congress won a major victory in 1959 when, in passing the law providing for a tax on foreign exchange, they ordered the administration to draw up and begin to implement a programme for the abolition of exchange controls. Under this mandate, Central Bank Governor Cuaderno prepared a four-year plan for stage-by-stage decontrol. Although he was probably not personally convinced of the wisdom of such a step, the success of his policies during the 1950s gave him some confidence that, provided the necessary complementary measures were taken, it might be possible to dismantle controls gradually. He wrote,

I had to be sure, also, that in the initial implementation of the plan neither the cost of living of the masses nor the operation of infant industries producing essential goods would be affected adversely. Besides, there was the policy of giving Filipinos every opportunity to have a larger share in the country's economic activities.[27]

If this programme of gradual lifting of controls was to be a success, it was imperative that the Government approve the complementary measures indicated in the programme, and that the Monetary Board take a firm stand against any demand to modify or in any way change whatever decisions the Board had taken with respect to the implementation of the decontrol programme.[28]

The new Filipino industrial class, represented organizationally by the Philippine Chamber of Industries, viewed the decontrol programme with considerable unease and commented, in its Annual Report for 1960:

The sudden announcement by the Central Bank of the adoption and effectivity of the four-year programme of gradual decontrol caught many industrialists by surprise ... Despite the representations of the PCI, however, the Central Bank deemed it wise to start the decontrol programme on the premise that R. A. 2609 made it mandatory for the Central Bank to take this step ... All told, the year under review saw an economic climate somewhat discouraging to the growth and expansion of industry in the Philippines. While hoping these sacrifices were only temporary in nature, many members of the Chamber at the same time braced for the possibility of greater trials.

They were not mistaken, for the Central Bank's gradualist programme did not satisfy the enemies of controls, who continued to attack the programme and agitate for total decontrol. Cuaderno warned:

Perhaps the most dangerous substitute for the gradual decontrol ... was the immediate lifting of controls. If we found it very difficult to draw up the plan of decontrol, it was because we had to make very sure that during the interim period of two to three years, the cost of living of the common man would not be seriously

affected; that the operations of essential infant industries would not
be unduly disturbed; and that the use of free-market exchange
would not result in nullifying the efforts being exerted by the
Government to render all possible assistance to Filipinos to acquire
a dominant position in the economic affairs of the country. It
should be obvious to our leaders that all these would be impossible
to achieve if exchange and import controls were suddenly lifted.[29]

The practice of allocating exchange permits for political
reasons reached the point of absurdity in the election year of
1961. To compound the evil, the lame-duck Garcia administration handed out exchange permits indiscriminately to its cronies
after its electoral defeat, regardless of the actual availability of
exchange. The Central Bank would have been $280 million in
the red if all the exchange permits were honoured. This problem could have been taken care of by cancelling all outstanding permits and starting over again, but since the new President,
Macapagal, was in any case ideologically committed to
liberalization, he chose to abolish controls immediately, despite
Cuaderno's warning.

This act won the enthusiastic blessing of the IMF and of the
US Government, which immediately loaned the Philippines
$300 million to support liberalization. Without such a credit,
decontrol would have plunged the Philippines abruptly into a
foreign exchange crisis. Decontrol meant that now individuals
and firms who could obtain dollars could spend them abroad
in any way they pleased, without supervision by the government
and without regard to whether the expenditures would benefit
the economy as a whole. The stabilization loan initiated a
vicious circle of borrowing to pay for unnecessary imports.

The decontrol system was popularly billed as a progressive
departure from the system of foreign exchange controls then in
force. It was, in truth, much more than that. *The programme was
a repudiation of any and all forms of direct management over the
use of our foreign exchange assets. It was a solemn commitment by
our government that, under no circumstances, and whatever the
social cost, will it intervene in the utilization of a scarce national
asset vital and indispensable to our development.*[30]

The unlimited imports which decontrol permitted, coupled with the massive outflow of capital funds remitted under our invisibles account resulted in chronic deficits in our international payments. These deficits were made up for by external borrowings. What this meant, in effect, was that, under the decontrol programme, our government committed itself to make dollars available to anyone who can afford to pay for them, for virtually any purpose whatsoever, *even if this meant borrowing dollars abroad to effectively fulfil such a commitment.*

Our Central Bank, in short, incurred foreign debts in order to be able to finance transactions that sabotage our economy. We incurred liabilities, not to build up our productive capacities, but to cripple and weaken our own economy.[31]

A number of complementary measures were introduced simultaneously with decontrol, to facilitate its operation and partially mitigate its effects. Because foreign exchange was no longer rationed, the exchange rate was freed to be determined by supply and demand. This meant a *de facto* devaluation which made imports more expensive (in 1965 the devaluation was made official and the exchange rate set at 3·9 pesos to the dollar). Tight credit restrictions helped limit the demand for imports, and a new tariff structure went into effect. Higher tariffs on most products were intended to limit demand and protect local industry, but on a few basic items tariffs were lowered to soften the inflationary effects of the floating exchange rate. The $300 million credit from the US helped to finance the increased demand for imports.[32]

This policy package had profound consequences for the Philippine economy and society. The consumer and wage-earner were made to pay for new windfall profits to the already wealthy land-owning and exporting class, while the young entrepreneurial class was driven out of business or into the arms of foreign competitors. These changes need to be examined carefully.

The exporting interests had been the most enthusiastic advocates of decontrol, for obvious reasons. Previously they had had to surrender all their dollar earnings for pesos at the 2:1 exchange rate; after decontrol only 20 per cent had to be changed at the old rate while the rest was exchanged at the much more favourable free market rate. One thousand dollars of export earnings would exchange for only 2,000 pesos before decontrol; while exactly the same amount of dollars brought 3,520 pesos under the new formula of 3·9 pesos to the dollar for 80 per cent and 2 : 1 for 20 per cent. It has been computed that in this fashion decontrol resulted in a windfall to exporters of P800,000,000, the equivalent of $20,500,000 at the new exchange rate. The exporting classes were, however, traditionally the wealthiest class in the nation – the so-called oligarchs – so this effect was highly regressive in terms of income distribution and economic development.

There is no evidence that any of these windfall gains trickled down to the impoverished rural classes, the oligarchs' tenants and day labourers. The incentive effect which this devaluation had on export production and earnings does not seem to have been commensurate with its social costs. Sugar exports, about one-quarter of the total, depended totally on artificially high prices paid by the US, and a change in the exchange rate had no effect on those prices or the size of the US quota for Philippine sugar. A Central Bank official permitted himself a public expression of sarcasm when the sugar growers became alarmed by fears they might lose this protected market:

It is ironic that this industry, which has so long and so loudly called for a return to market forces and market prices for everybody else, should now have to battle against the introduction of market prices for itself. Its spokesmen have long decried distortions in resource allocation by non-market forces. The bystander may be pardoned a sardonic smile at the spectacle of current efforts to maintain this oldest major distortion in the Philippine economy.[33]

With the one exception of iron ore, the improvement in the exchange rate resulted in no new export development. The ten most important exports, virtually all in the agricultural and extractive sectors, contributed the same 86 per cent of export earnings in 1968 as in 1962.[34] The total volume of exports did rise, however, which with the improved exchange rate meant that the exporters' real income more than doubled.

The devaluation apparently did cause a measurable shift in

agricultural land use, away from food production for the local market in favour of the production of plantation crops for export.[35] This was in turn a major determinant of the price inflation, to which the devaluation contributed directly as well as indirectly. The index of real wages declined about 10 per cent between 1962 and 1964 because of the inflation.[36] Though accurate figures are impossible to obtain, employment declined as well, which is not surprising in the light of difficulties suffered by the industrial sector.

Filipino entrepreneurs of the new import substitution industries lost ground as a result of the new situation. Tight money policies checked not only the demand for imports, but working and investment capital for the rest of the economy as well. One Filipino businessman explained why this credit shortage favoured foreign firms to the disadvantage of local ones:

If any Filipino company is manufacturing some goods and his competitor is a branch office of some giant corporation, whether in Germany or Italy, the United States or England, the resources of the parent company – especially after decontrol – are so unlimited that the Filipino company has a very slim chance to survive. The foreign competitor can just keep giving better terms until the Filipino company finds itself floundering. By the same token, unlimited resources of the foreign, parent company enable it to cut down the price and take losses for a period of time, looking to the long pull to either capture the market or control a substantial slice of it. But the Filipino is limited in his resources; he can take only one, two, three, or perhaps four years of losses; after that he becomes so anaemic that you can almost just push him aside because he is no longer competitive, you see.[37]

The answer, according to this capitalist, was for the Filipino to agree to a joint venture, becoming the local partner of his competitor.

Local firms were harmed by increased competition from imported goods as well as tight credit. High tariffs had little effect when importers could bribe customs officials to overlook their cargoes, which were often invoiced as falsely as the 'rice bran' exports of the 1950s had been. This tactic, known as 'technical smuggling', was made easier by the absence of any foreign ex-

69

change control, which had acted as a double check against illegal imports. The corruption which had plagued the administration of exchange controls did not disappear when they were abolished, but was simply displaced to the administration of tariffs. By 1965 it was estimated that as much as one-third of all imported products on sale in the Philippines had been smuggled into the country, with a total value in excess of $350 million.[38]

All these factors had the effect of changing both the structure and the ownership of the Philippine economy. Reversing the trend of the 1950s, manufacturing declined in importance while the traditional export industries, plantation agriculture and mining, registered the largest gains.

The most direct effect of decontrol was a sharp rise in the rate of imports, particularly consumer goods such as automobiles, TV sets, and electrical appliances. Between 1963 and 1967 the volume of imports rose by 68 per cent while exports increased by only 7 per cent.[39] Invisibles expenditure, including loan repayments and capital flight, soared even more dramatically. The Philippines was a net capital exporter in the 1960s as decontrol allowed foreign investors to take out 2·5 dollars for every one they brought in.

The outflow of dollars was financed by foreign borrowing, as both official aid and private credits. Before decontrol, the Philippines' external debt was only $275 million. Eight years later, by the end of Ferdinand Marcos' first term of office as President, the total had jumped to $1,880 million.

Balance of payments crises are closely correlated with election years in the Philippines, since huge amounts of money, both pesos and foreign exchange, are distributed in attempts to control the voting. The 1969 campaign was worse than previous ones in this respect, as Marcos was determined to become the first President of the Philippines to win re-election. By the time the election was over, the country's immediate foreign exchange liabilities totalled about four and a half times the amount available to cover them in the reserves. But election spending was merely the last straw which precipitated crisis, not its fundamental cause. The truth was that the Philippines had run a persistent trade and payments deficit ever since decontrol, and the repayment obligations for the loans which had financed those deficits were beginning to fall due.

The nation was virtually bankrupt. There were predictions that another devaluation was inevitable, but Marcos had campaigned with a pledge of no devaluation. He affirmed just after winning the election that 'we have no intention of devaluing the peso because we would be hitting our low income groups, especially daily wage-earners and employees with monthly salaries'. The solution to the crisis, the President announced confidently, was that bank consortia were to be organized in America, Europe, and Japan under World Bank sponsorship to lend the Philippines still more money by supplying trade credits which, the President affirmed, would permit the Philippines to import needed goods without dollars.

But if Marcos was depending on new credits from consortia sponsored by the World Bank, he would have to eat his campaign promises of no devaluation. A World Bank spokesman warned publicly, 'Whether it is decided to go ahead [with the sponsorship of a creditors' club] will depend on discussions going on between the Philippines, the International Monetary Fund, and with us.' The Fund and the Bank wanted devaluation, and the abolition of the new exchange controls which had crept back in as a means of alleviating pressure on the exchange rate. The government was forced to negotiate with the IMF. During these talks, the Philippine officials argued against devaluation, warning of the social and political dangers of another rise in prices and a further worsening of income distribution. The government, however, had virtually no alternative to acceptance of the IMF programme other than repudiation of its debts, and it did not have the social backing or political courage to face the consequences of a cut-off of aid and trading credits which that course would involve.

In February 1970 the peso rate was freed to 'float', a euphemism for devaluation. The economic and social effects of the 'floating rate' of 1970 repeated those of 1962. Industries, finding the cost of repaying their foreign borrowing had increased by nearly 50 per cent, collapsed or were taken over by foreign-owned competitors. The inflationary consequences, which were more severe in 1970 than in 1962, were so quickly observable that 'floating rate' has become the popular byword for inflation. The official price index had risen annually by at least 20 per cent per year for the past three years.

According to a survey by a Philippine research organization, the 1970 devaluation brought hardship to 81 per cent of Filipinos, and hit the poor harder than the rich. Although it is a popular myth that no one starves in the Philippines, where the land is fruitful and aiding poor relatives is a family responsibility, nutritionists were alarmed that scrimping on food would widen the already perilous 'protein gap' in the average Filipino's diet. Unemployment is high, has risen over the past ten years, and can be correlated with the government's tight money policies and the difficulties of local businesses. In the sectors where labour is organized, strikes had become frequent and militant prior to the declaration of martial law in September 1972.

Adoption of the floating rate by no means solved the foreign exchange crisis. For the past four years, the country has faced such crippling debt obligations that the major task of the Central Bank has been negotiating debt extensions and roll-overs. Fully $770 million in repayment obligations fell due in 1970 alone, which amounted to 75 per cent of merchandise export earnings for that year. Central Bank governor Licaros, admitting the country could not possibly pay that sum, stated that the Philippines' creditors 'who are interested in continuing to do business here' would not press collection, knowing the government could pay in the future. But as one American banker remarked cynically, 'We didn't really have any choice. After all you can't put the Philippines into Chapter XI' (referring to a section of the American bankruptcy laws).

The World Bank kept its promise and convened an 'Aid Philippines' group in late 1970. However, although new credits for the country totalled $311·4 million the following year, this was not even sufficient to cover the debt amortization and interest payments due the same year, which totalled $388 million. The point is that the nation, thanks to 'decontrol', the careless contraction of foreign debt (most of it during the Marcos presidency), and IMF dictation, is in a chronically desperate crisis in which it has to run ever faster just to keep from going broke. There can be no doubt that this crisis, combined with Marcos' personal ambitions, made martial law almost inevitable within the limits of the government's options.

The relationship of the foreign exchange crisis to the suspension of genuine (if highly corrupt) elections should be underlined, for they are related in at least three respects. First, given the constraints under which the economy is now labouring, it could not possibly afford the extensive vote-buying which has characterized previous campaigns, but Marcos was by 1972 so unpopular he could not hope to influence the result otherwise. His 1969 performance is non-repeatable.

Second, devaluation has become very unpopular with the voting public. But if the Philippines is to stay in the good graces of its foreign creditors, more devaluations will be inevitable. In fact, the peso seems to be 'floating' gradually downwards in a series of unannounced mini-devaluations which avoid unfavourable publicity.

Third, the relatively non-corrupt elements and areas of the Philippine electorate, notably in the Manila metropolitan area, have tended in recent years to register their protest against the government by electing economic nationalists to Congress and to the Constitutional Convention in 1971. These persons have provided articulate leadership to other opposition groups, and had succeeded both in blocking administration programmes and in creating uncertainty about the ultimate direction of Philippine politics. In 1966 Marcos had to proclaim an administrative order containing guarantees to foreign investors, since he despaired of getting such a law through the Congress. Before September 1972 the Constitutional Convention was in the process of writing many nationalistic provisions into the new constitution, but when martial law was declared that draft was scrapped and the constitution was rewritten by the President's office.

The independent judiciary in the Philippines has also frightened the administration, and foreign investors, by questioning the legality of certain lucrative foreign business activities. Just one month before the declaration of martial law the Supreme Court caused a sensation by ruling (in the Quasha decision) that property owned by Americans as a consequence of their exercise of 'parity' rights was illegally acquired and might be subject to confiscation without compensation.

Martial law has made possible the solution of some of these problems by permitting the arrest of the most prominent opposition figures and frightening the rest. The first wave of arrests, which took place the night martial law was declared, included most of the prominent economic nationalists among Congressmen, judiciary, and Constitutional Convention delegates. Though many have since been released, the effect of the arrests has been to silence public debate on economic, as well as other, issues. Prominent labour leaders have been arrested in an obvious attempt to intimidate workers' struggles for better pay.

With Congress suspended and the judiciary rendered powerless, Marcos has hastened to assure foreign corporations that he can now guarantee them a friendly climate. He has promised better incentives for foreign oil exploration (the Philippines is near Indonesia and hopes to share in the area's oil bonanza), and has reassured Americans that the Quasha decision of the Supreme Court and other decisions limiting their powers and profits in the Philippines will not be implemented.

Although authoritarian measures to cope with the crisis are now possible, the crisis will continue. During the next three to four years payments due on the external debt will require about $400 million yearly. The Marcos government is banking on more aid and investment to bridge the gap, but these will only create more and larger obligations in the future.

4

Indonesia: A 'Success Story'

Indonesia, although endowed with enough natural and human resources to make it one of the richest countries on earth, is in fact one of the poorest in so far as the livelihood of its people is concerned. The economic structure imposed by Dutch colonialism and the exploitative nature of international economic relations in the post-colonial era have combined to keep Indonesia one of the least industrialized nations in the world, heavily dependent on exports of raw materials for its earnings in the world market.

The failure to develop has been commonly attributed in the Western press to the disastrous economic policies pursued in the era of 'Guided Democracy' (1959–65) under President Sukarno's leadership. There is some truth to this charge, but it must be seen in perspective. During its first decade of independence, Indonesia laboured under the necessity of repaying huge debts to the Netherlands – obligations which it had been forced to accept as the price of independence; and its major businesses, which were mostly export-oriented, remained under Dutch ownership and thus outside the effective control of the Indonesian government.

The Dutch debts were unilaterally repudiated by Indonesia in 1956 and the Dutch firms nationalized in 1958, but the island nation remained vulnerable to world economic conditions over which it had no control. The price of natural rubber, Indonesia's major foreign exchange earner at that time, fell drastically from 38·5 cents per pound in 1960 to only 25·7 cents per pound in 1965.[1] This drop of 33 per cent in the price of a commodity which provided 60 per cent of Indonesia's total export value contributed to the economic crisis as surely as did the government's policies.

It is nevertheless true that Sukarno failed to recognize Indonesia's critical economic situation and to employ his political gifts in finding a permanent way out of the crisis. Rather than make hard political decisions about the distribution of the country's resources, he chose to finesse the problem by allowing unrestrained government spending which caused the severe inflation of the mid-1960s. Acting, apparently, on the belief that the world owed the Indonesian consumer a living (which may be morally defensible but was certainly economically and politically naïve), he obtained loans from both the communist and capitalist world which continue to haunt his successors in the form of billion-dollar debts.

As Sukarno squandered foreign loans on consumption goods, prestige projects, and armaments, so he wasted the nation's dwindling foreign exchange earnings from exports. Indonesia had inherited from the Dutch colonial government a system of absolute control of foreign exchange. Exporters were required to deposit all foreign exchange earnings with the government and received in return payment in the national currency, rupiahs, at a rate of exchange determined by the government. The government then sold that exchange in excess of its own needs to importers at a higher rate of exchange, and kept the difference in rupiah proceeds as its own revenue. After independence this system became extremely complex, with rates set at many different levels to encourage or discourage selected categories of exports and imports. The effect of this system was to tax exporters via the overvalued exchange rate, to the benefit of both government revenues and those importers privileged enough to obtain the scarce foreign exchange permits.

The government eventually obtained the major part of its revenue from this multiple exchange rate system. The problem was that exchange controls were less and less effective as a means of conserving and allocating scarce foreign exchange as the government became more dependent upon them for revenue. In the later years of the Sukarno era the government began to sell so-called 'free' foreign exchange which could be used for luxury imports (i.e. outside the regular régime of controls which prohibited such imports) to obtain more revenue. Although Sukarno *seemed* to be moving in the direction of state control of the economy, in this critical sector he countenanced 'a denial of economic planning and a return to an intrinsically *laissez-faire* method of allocating precious foreign exchange'.[2]

Sukarno's success in playing off communist and capitalist aid-givers against each other lasted only a few short years, and by 1963 he found himself pressured by both sides to choose between them. Although his bombastic anti-Western statements and threats to nationalize Western-owned oil companies in Indonesia provoked the US Congress into banning economic and military aid,[3] the State Department and AID remained very interested in using Western aid to steer Indonesia towards economic policies favourable to the Western bloc.

In a striking 'dress rehearsal' for the events of 1966–7, the United States used the IMF as an intermediary between itself, the Indonesian government, and a prospective consortium of Western aid donors. An Economic Survey Team from the United States visited Indonesia and issued a report in November 1962, recommending a five-year $390 million aid programme to which the United States would contribute $233 million. These amounts are miniscule compared to the sums Indonesia has obtained in aid in recent years, but at the time the promise of a long-term aid commitment seemed very attractive.

The aid, however, was contingent on Indonesia's cooperation with the IMF in the matters of devaluation of the rupiah and budgetary restraint. An IMF mission went to Djakarta to help the government devise a stabilization programme. In March 1963 the US offered a ten-year loan of $17 million to finance imports needed for the stabilization programme.[4] In May the Indonesian government announced a series of regulations which amounted to a *de facto* devaluation of the rupiah and the elimination of many government price controls and subsidies. In June a consortium of prospective aid donors met under the auspices of the Development Assistance Council of the Organization for Economic Cooperation and Development,* in an

*The OECD, which is composed of the rich capitalist nations interested in financing their exports by foreign aid, took the lead in organizing a few of the early consortia, particularly that for Turkey. The World Bank contested this initiative, however, and the OECD has subsided into relative impotence.

attempt to raise $400 million to help Indonesia cover its balance of payments gap. The US strategy was for the US, the World Bank, and the IMF to contribute about half of that amount and the other four members of the consortium – Britain, France, West Germany, and Japan – to raise the rest of it.[5] In August Indonesia entered into a stand-by arrangement with the IMF, reportedly signed 'under US initiative', which would enable it to draw up to $50 million over the coming year.[6]

In September, however, Sukarno's anger at the proposed federation of Malaysia led him to seize British-owned businesses in Indonesia. Almost immediately, the United States and the IMF announced the cancellation of their recently concluded aid arrangements.

At this point Sukarno began to realize the political price he would have to pay for future economic aid and to make his famous 'To hell with your aid' statements. In his National Day address on 17 August, 1964, Sukarno expressed admiration for the self-reliant economic policies followed by Kim Il Sung in North Korea,* saying that Korea had completely solved her problem of food and clothing 'enabling her both politically and culturally not to depend on anybody at all'. He added, 'Indonesia does not want to stay behind.'[7]

The year 1965, the last year of Sukarno's reign, saw mounting hostility to foreign investment and looming economic disaster due to the lack of foreign exchange for consumption imports, for factory spare parts, and for payments due on foreign debts. In early 1965 most remaining foreign-owned enterprises in Indonesia, with the exception of the oil companies, were nationalized. On 27 May the law guaranteeing foreign investments was repealed. The trade unions and the Indonesian Communist Party (PKI) pressed the government to take over the oil companies too, and the government obliged half-way by placing the companies under government supervision 'without prejudice to property rights' of the companies. The government announced plans to take control of the foreign trade sector.

In his National Day speech in August Sukarno announced Indonesia's withdrawal from the IMF and the World Bank

* See chapter 9 and appendix IV.

and declared that the coming year would be 'A Year of Self-Reliance.' According to the speech, this meant an austerity programme tailored to the necessity of conserving foreign exchange and preserving the nation's political independence, which would entail cutting imports to a minimum, stressing domestic investment and home production of import substitutes, and accepting only those foreign credits which did not prejudice national control of the economy. It meant 'the acceptance of hardship as the price of revolutionary achievement'.[8]

There is reason to doubt that Sukarno had the determination, or the comprehension of economics, necessary to carry through such a politically difficult programme. The mere threat, however, must have alarmed many vested interests both inside and outside the country. In the event, Sukarno did not hold on to his power throughout the year, so his policy of self-reliance was never put to the test. The events leading to his ouster as the nation's leader – the murder of six Army generals, with alleged communist collusion; the subsequent decimation of the PKI and the massacres, under Army sponsorship, of hundreds of thousands of Indonesians; the March 1966 order in which Sukarno was forced to transfer most of his executive powers to General Suharto – all had their logic in the tense internal politics of Indonesia, but were intimately related as well to the foreign exchange crisis and the belief of the Army and other conservative elements that foreign aid was essential for its solution.

One month after the March 1966 transfer of power the new Minister of Finance announced the reversal of Sukarno's policy of hostility towards private enterprise and foreign investment. Six days later the US offered an $8·2 million credit for the purchase of rice, and this gesture was followed by offers from the UK and Japan.

Despite this tentative indication of support, the new leaders found that the Americans did not automatically rush to support the anti-communist régime. Instead, the formula chosen closely resembled that of the abortive 1963 stabilization programme. The US wanted to see evidence of specific new economic policies before pledging support, and backed the IMF (which Suharto's government hastened to rejoin) as the adviser and referee of those new policies. Indonesia was persuaded to accept a consortium of all the creditor countries as the instrument for negotiation of debt rescheduling, and for badly needed new credits.[9]

In the late summer of 1966 (half a year before the country formally rejoined the IMF in February 1967) an IMF mission arrived in Indonesia to work out a new stabilization programme, and soon the effects of IMF advice became apparent in new government policies. One of the most important of these was the shift of most foreign exchange transactions from the control of the Central Bank to the open market on 3 October 1966, the first major step in the decontrol of foreign exchange. The government abdicated its function of allocating scarce foreign exchange (which it admittedly had handled badly in the past) to market forces of supply and demand. A weak economy could not afford to take such a step without a massive new injection of foreign aid, but this was the promised quid pro quo for the decontrol measures.

The IMF advisers also worked out a familiar package of anti-inflationary measures as the necessary complement to the decontrol of foreign exchange: a balanced budget, limitation of government expenditures to no more than 10 per cent of national income, improvement in the tax collection system, a 'realistic' exchange rate, an end to subsidies, a review of the pricing policies of state enterprises, reductions in the number of government employees, and severe limitations on the creation of bank credit.[10]

The government also hastened to give substance to its promise of a friendlier climate for foreign investment. A new Foreign Investment Bill guaranteed prospective investments against nationalization for a period of twenty years (thirty in the case of agricultural estates), promised reasonable compensation in the event of nationalization after the stated periods, assured freedom to remit profits and to repatriate capital, and provided generous tax concessions. In December, three days before a crucial meeting of foreign creditors, the government announced its intention of restoring the foreign-owned companies nationalized under Sukarno to their former owners.

The Western nations responded to these proofs of obedience by offering $174 million in *ad hoc* credits to get Indonesia through its annual crisis for 1966, and by arranging for debt rescheduling. The need for rescheduling was acute because fully $534 million in repayments were falling due or in arrears by 1967, which represented 69 per cent of anticipated export earnings for that year. Unless some of the payments were deferred, any new credits extended to Indonesia would simply go down the drain of debt repayment, leaving the new anti-communist government just as economically vulnerable as Sukarno's had been. Therefore, when the Western creditor nations met in Paris in December 1966 they agreed to a moratorium until 1971 on repayments of all principal and interest on long-term debts contracted before June 1966. After 1971, Indonesia was to repay her debts in eight instalments: 5 per cent in 1971, 10 per cent per year 1972–4; 15 per cent in the three following years, and 20 per cent in the last year, 1978. Similar terms had been negotiated separately by the Soviet Union and the other communist bloc creditors (except China), who had not been invited to the first capitalist creditors' meeting in September.

Members of the 'Paris Club' creditors' consortium were the US, Britain, Japan, Australia, France, West Germany, Italy, Netherlands, the World Bank, the OECD, and the IMF. The Fund, with US pressure clearly discernible behind its efforts, vigorously supported lenient terms for the debt rescheduling and pressed for the creation of an aid consortium which would mobilize new credits for Indonesia.

The Inter-Governmental Group on Indonesia (IGGI) was formed in early 1967. Similar 'country groups' have been favoured by the United States in recent years as a means for persuading other capitalist nations to assume a share of the aid 'burden' proportionate to the benefits in investment and trade which the latter derive from the Pax Americana. In the case of Indonesia, the major target of the US share-the-burden campaign was Japan, whose large and growing economic stake in the rest of Asia still depended on US determination to preserve the security of the area.

The IGGI has regularly met twice a year in the Netherlands (the former colonial power in Indonesia). At the first meeting, late in the calendar year, Indonesia, supported by the IMF, presents the aid donors with its estimates of the aid needed to finance its deficit (balance-of-payments and budget) in the coming fiscal year. The following spring, after the Indonesian government has presented its budget and the IMF has renewed its stand-by arrangement, the consortium members meet again and agree among themselves who is to supply the needed credits. In the pattern which has by now become well-established, the United States leads the bidding with an offer of one-third of the needed sum, in the expectation that Japan will supply another third and the rest of the consortium will provide the remainder. In 1968 the US refused to put up its one-third until Japan did the same, which resulted in a six-month delay of aid deliveries and serious difficulties for the Indonesian government.[11]

It is probably significant that the aid pattern matches precisely the proportions of actual and intended foreign investment in Indonesia from 1967 to 1971, with the US and Japan (if the nominally Philippine investment is attributed to Japan, the real source of capital for the Philippine logging companies) both supplying one-third of the investment capital.[12]*

The debt rescheduling formula of 1966 had only postponed the problem, and as 1971 approached, when payments on the Sukarno debts were due to resume, the Paris Club commissioned West German financier Hermann Abs to study the Indonesian debt problem. His recommendation, that the pre-1966 debts be repaid in thirty instalments between 1970 and 1999, was approved by the creditors in April 1970. It is by a wide margin

---

* Japan's reliance on imports from Indonesia expanded sharply in the 1960s. In the first nine months of 1971 Japanese imports amounted to $611·8 million, compared with only $161·7 going from Indonesia to the US. The corresponding export statistics for the same period were $210·2 from the US to Indonesia and $305·9 from Japan. (IMF and IBRD statistics in *Direction of Trade*, February 1972.)

the most lenient debt settlement which has been voluntarily granted to a Third World government by its creditors. The agreement included a 'most favoured nation' clause which prevented Indonesia from repaying the Soviet bloc countries at a faster rate than the Western creditors.

Significantly, this generous deferment closely followed an exchange reform and devaluation promoted by the IMF, which left Indonesia with one of the 'freest' exchange systems in the world. The last vestige of the multiple rate system was abolished in April 1970, and the unitary exchange rate means that imports designated as 'essential' no longer enjoy a preferential exchange rate, but must compete in profitability on the open market with all other categories of imports, including luxury goods. Without the deferment of debt repayment and the record $600 million of *new* loans agreed to by the IGGI in the same month, Indonesia's balance of payments could not have tolerated such a liberalization. It should not have been done at all in terms of development priorities, but that is a problem related to the type of 'development' which is sponsored in Indonesia by the IMF and the IGGI.

The Suharto régime and its supporters talk constantly of the economic miracle which has brought Indonesia out of the Sukarnoist dark ages, but on closer examination the real miracles appear to be a result of accounting, public relations, and the ever-mounting annual IGGI credits, rather than of any substantial reforms. Apart from the expansion of exports (discussed below), the main claims to success are based on three achievements: control of inflation, a balanced budget, and the stable external value of the rupiah.

The truth is, however, that all three 'achievements' have been possible only because the IGGI has so far been willing to provide the enormous loans necessary to support the budget and the balance of payments. It works in this way: the IGGI credits finance hundreds of millions of dollars of imports each year which Indonesia would not be able to pay for with its foreign exchange earnings.* The country's foreign payments

* In fact, the dollar values for imports and exports of goods have been roughly in balance ever since independence. It would be just as accurate

are thus 'balanced' by foreign loans, and the debts continue to mount.

At IMF insistence, the IGGI donors agreed that their aid credits would be handled in an unprecedented manner: the government sells the aid (in the form of import credits) on the free market to importers *without any specification as to use of the money*, and uses the sale proceeds ('counterpart funds') as budget revenue. Thus, not only did the government relinquish its right to control its foreign exchange *earnings* by the decontrol measures of 1966 and 1970, but it auctions its government-to-government *aid* on the free market as well, while the aid donors have relinquished the right to specify which imports they are willing to finance* Finally, the aid-financed imports control inflation by absorbing the excess currency generated by the budget deficit.

Thus annual doses of substantial aid produce three 'miracles' simultaneously – miracles which have nothing to do with real development which would promote the country's economic in-

---

to say the aid is financing 'invisible' and 'unrequited' payments: debt repayment, repatriation of profits to foreign investors, etc. Consider this abbreviated table from information in the IMF Annual Report for 1971 (Table 76, pp. 200–1):

(Figures in US $ million)	1969	1970
Exports	955	1,181
Imports	−993	−1,139
Balance of merchandise trade	2	42
Services ('invisibles') and private unrequited transfers	−363	−443
Balance on current account	−361	−401
Capital inflow (aid and investments)	279	361

* This system is similar to the stabilization funds in Laos and Cambodia (see next chapter) but aid to Indonesia is still 'country-tied', i.e. each donor specifies that it is granting credits for its own exports only. This has resulted in an ironic breach in the unitary exchange rate, since credits for imports from high-cost countries must be sold at a discount in order to find buyers.

dependence, but on the contrary make Indonesia far *more* dependent on continued injections of aid. In 1967, when IGGI aid totalled only $200 million, this aid financed 28 per cent of all imports; and·the import credits, sold by the government to private importers, generated more than 30 per cent of government revenue. Since 1967 the annual doses of aid have risen steadily; by 1970 the figure was $600 million, three times the 1967 amount and more than 50 per cent of imports. For the fiscal year 1973–4 the IGGI agreed to supply $876·6 million. The government claims that its 'regular' budget is now completely financed by its own revenues and that aid funds all go into the 'development budget', but this is no more than an accounting trick to divert attention from the steadily mounting aid totals. The so-called development budget includes such items as the refurbishing of government offices and acquisition of official cars, which is described as 'infrastructure development'.

The Suharto government points to the new foreign investments and the expansion of exports since 1967 as proof of the efficacy of its economic policies. The major export growth has occurred in the same two commodities – petroleum and timber – which have attracted the lion's share of new foreign investment. In fact, the government's future hopes of foreign exchange earnings, from which the massive old and new debts will eventually have to be repaid, rest squarely on the fate of its extractive and raw materials exports, mainly petroleum. Many economists doubt that prospective earnings will in fact cover the nation's future foreign exchange obligations. Apart from that, the nation's precious natural resources are being dissipated, with massive profits to investors, and substantial revenues to the government and its officials, but little or no investment in a diversified economy for the future.

Petroleum is the most important export commodity of Indonesia. The benefits of oil export earnings are shared out among three groups: the foreign corporations, the Indonesian state monopoly 'Pertamina', and the Indonesian government. In return for a cut of the profits (the petroleum sector contributed 30 per cent of domestic government revenues in 1971 and a climb to 40 per cent was anticipated for 1972) the government has relinquished any pretensions to control the earnings of the other two groups. The foreign corporations extracting petroleum are exempted from the normal foreign exchange regulations and operate as a *de facto* free trade area. They are allowed to utilize their foreign exchange earnings directly for imports, salaries of foreign personnel, and profit remittance. A substantial proportion of their profits (estimated as 60–65 per cent) are paid as royalties to Pertamina, which the Indonesian army controls and 'milks' as a source of finance independent of the government budget. The profits from petroleum are large, but they are applied to the repression, not the enrichment, of the mass of the population.[13]

More than one-third of all foreign capital investment in Indonesia is in the timber industry. Timber exports, which amounted to only $10 million in 1966, have expanded to a rate of $160 million a year in the first quarter of 1971. But the cost to the country is high. Indonesia's rich timber stands are falling victim to the same wasteful and exploitative cutting which has denuded the Philippine islands, threatening its water resources and agricultural land as well as the forests – and at the hands of the same American, Japanese, and Philippine logging companies which have destroyed the ecological balance in the Philippines.

There is no systematic plan for industrial development. Domestic producers suffered bitterly, and predictably, from the effects of the IMF-sponsored stabilization programme, particularly the contraction of bank credit and competition from the avalanche of aid-financed imports and other goods made available under the liberalized foreign exchange system. One report claimed that 9,517 Indonesian firms collapsed between 1964 and 1970.[14] The local textile industry was left demoralized by the use of foreign credits to import huge amounts of finished textiles, and equipment for competing synthetic fibre plants, while their own factories stood idle for lack of working capital.[15] Thus the cost of a stable price index and increased government revenue was a drastic slowdown of domestic production, which in the long run could only perpetuate the chronic economic crisis. The IMF, however, was particularly pleased with the results of Indonesian stabilization, not least because this was a drastic, rather than a gradual, programme.[16]

While domestic entrepreneurs were forced out of business by competition from imports, foreign owners of industrial plants (which had been denationalized) received special protection from the Indonesian government. When the Goodyear tyre factory at Bogor stopped production in September 1968, blaming its problems on excessive tyre imports, the government thoughtfully removed tyres from the list of imports which could be bought at a favourable exchange rate, reduced the sales tax on home-produced tyres, and banned tyre imports by government agencies.[17] The automobile assembly industry similarly flourishes under the protection of prohibitive tariffs and taxes on the importation of assembled automobiles, although the man who was Minister of Trade for much of the post-1966 period admitted that 'the foreign exchange required to import components [for assembly plants] will frequently exceed that required to import complete items'.[18] In his reasoning, the foreign exchange wastage is justified by the creation of employment opportunities – a strange argument since the government could create absolutely useless jobs more cheaply, and in any case a few thousand more jobs will scarcely touch Indonesia's unemployment problem. In 1968 the Ministry of Industries closed some manufacturing sectors to *new* foreign investment, but the effect was only to protect the existing foreign-owned factories. The foreign investor in Indonesia today enjoys more privileges and immunities than his native competitor.

Despite these inducements, there has been little new foreign investment in manufacturing industries. The nation's population, although numerically large, is still too poor on the whole to make an attractive market, and imported goods pre-empt the opportunities that do exist. Djakarta has, however, been blessed with two new soft drink factories; and the Surabaja Investment Information Office reports that potential investors are interested in night clubs, bars, steambaths, massage parlours, restaurants and bowling alleys, but not in more productive investments.[19]

Indonesia has also put out the welcome mat for foreign banks. Under World Bank sponsorship, new development banking facilities and a private development finance corporation are being set up. This can be called foreign investment only in an ironic sense, as the intent is to mobilize local rupiah savings and put them at the disposal of the foreign investors, who do not want to bring in their own money if they can borrow funds locally.[20]

Mass dismissals of employees by the government and by private firms were a logical consequence of the IMF austerity programme and have added to an already staggering unemployment problem. The rate of unemployment was estimated at 13–15 per cent in 1967, and no one claims that any solution is yet in sight. Foreign investment projects, existing or contemplated, are not labour intensive and any employment which they provide can be only a drop in the bucket compared to what is needed.

Suharto's government has continued Sukarno's policy of holding rice prices down by direct controls as well as massive imports, since rice is an important component of the closely watched cost-of-living index; but the policy has depressed the earnings of the rice-producing peasantry. Other consumer subsidies, however, have been ended; the prices of gasoline products, for example, were raised sharply in 1966, 1968, and 1970; and fuel prices are an important component, through transportation and energy costs, of the prices of most basic goods. The lack of significant public protest over the removal of these subsidies, as well as the remarkable docility of the labour force in the face of adverse conditions, can be attributed to the annihilation of the PKI which had provided leadership on these issues in the Sukarno era.

Apart from the changes discussed above, the remarkable thing about Suharto's so-called New Order is the number of problems which have remained unsolved, or worsened, since Sukarno was ousted. Corruption and income inequality are much more blatant than before, as the generals hobnob with foreign oil magnates. Despite much fanfare about tax reform, there has been no basic restructuring; most of the improvement in government finance can be attributed to expansion of the oil industry, to foreign aid, and to taxes on imports and exports, which are politically and technically the easiest to collect.

Indonesia remains one of the least industrialized countries of the world, almost totally dependent on a few raw materials exports for its international earnings. In 1970 petroleum and rubber accounted for 60 per cent of the total exports by value, with lumber, tin, and coffee adding another 20 per cent and the remainder contributed by various other raw materials. Despite the extremely low level of wages, none of Indonesia's manufactures show prospects of being competitive on the world market.

The most significant irony, however, is that the much-maligned 'Sukarno debts' are rapidly paling into insignificance relative to the debts that the Suharto government is blithely incurring with IMF support and approval. Sukarno left a legacy of over $2 billion in debts; but the *new* debts of the Suharto régime, plus projected foreign financing of the remainder of the Five-Year Plan to 1974, add up to *more than $4 billion.* The annual rate of new credits has expanded from $175 million in 1966 to $876·6 million in the fiscal year 1973–4.[21]

Although at the urging of the IMF the donors are supplying loans on the most favourable terms which are available to any borrowing country, there is continuing uncertainty about the debt burden which the post-1966 aid will represent in the future. So far the IGGI has provided all the aid that Indonesia, with IMF backing, has requested; whether its members can continue to do so indefinitely at an ever-expanding rate, even to protect their old loans and their valuable petroleum, timber, tin, copper, and bauxite holdings, is an interesting question.[22]

There can be no question, however, that Indonesia stands virtually no chance of climbing out from under her debt burden by any means other than repudiation. It may well be rescheduled again and again, at intervals of perhaps a decade, but it will not be paid off – quite the contrary – if present trends continue. Indonesia's vast natural resources are mortgaged for an indefinite future to subsidize an oppressive military dictatorship and to pay for imports which support the lavish life-style of the generals in Djakarta.

Indonesia is considered one of the great 'success stories' of the IMF and Western aid, but that success has nothing to do with a rational balance on its international payments accounts; still less does it refer to the welfare of the peasantry of Java or the urban proletariat of Djakarta. The success is that of the great multinational corporations, who have through the IMF cadged their governments into financing the balance of payments deficits which their profits have caused; and of Japan, who has secured through IMF policies the assurance that Indonesia will continue to export its petroleum and timber to serve the needs of the Japanese economy rather than its own.

5

Money to Burn: At War in Indochina

The war waged by the United States against the peoples of
Vietnam, Laos, and Cambodia has become the prime contemporary symbol of the clash between the forces of change and
self-determination, and those of repression and the status quo.
The presence of the IMF – missions, advisers, resident representatives – fools no one about the fact that this is an American
war; people neither know nor care that the IMF is there at all.
An exposé in this sense would be superfluous.

There are nevertheless very good reasons for scrutinizing the
role of the IMF in Indochina. For one, it demonstrates the
astonishing length to which the IMF will go in subordinating
itself to the political and military aims of the US government,
while it abandons in the process any pretence of aiding the
growth of a balanced economy. Similarly it reveals the cynical
US use of IMF advice and support as a fig-leaf of multilateralism for programmes which are in execution almost purely
American.

Also, an understanding of the monetary mechanisms recommended by the Fund in Indochina reveals, as much or more
than any other method, the corruption and cynicism of the conduct of the war. For the fact is that the so-called nations which
the West claims to be 'aiding' in Indochina are not nations at
all, nor even governments in the usual sense. They are unable
to collect taxes from the population nominally under their control, who are in fact paying them, willingly or reluctantly, to
the genuine governments of the liberation forces. The so-called
pro-western governments are merely parasitic cliques, families,
and classes created and nourished artificially by massive in-
fusions of aid from outside.

There is yet another reason. The role of foreign aid, and the
IMF, in Indochina is clearly not the same as in countries such
as Indonesia and Brazil, where the governments recognized

and supported by the West are still by and large in control of their territory. In the latter, the business of economic exploitation can be placed at the head of the agenda while a cautious eye is kept on dissident elements. In Indochina, however, the exploitation of the country's raw materials is less important to the capitalist West than the strategic and symbolic importance of defeating the insurrection, and must in any case be postponed until security can be ensured. Therefore the economic aid programmes, and IMF recommendations, show instructive variations from the norm for more stable countries. The Indochina programmes should not be considered aberrations, however; rather they are extreme cases, the study of which can give us valuable lessons about the purposes of similar programmes in many other countries, for many of the same principles and mechanisms are used in all of them.

Indochina is not a poor territory. French planters and business houses took out huge profits under the colonial régime. Even after Indochina was divided into four different political units (North and South Vietnam, Laos and Cambodia) which were given legal independence in 1954, the problem of the newly created states was *not* a need for foreign exchange to sustain essential imports. The great majority of the population of Laos were providing their own subsistence. The same is true of Cambodia, which imported only moderate amounts of foreign goods before the US–South Vietnam invasions of 1970 brought war to the country. The problem – and it was a US problem – was how to encourage weak and greedy aristocrats to maintain a semblance of national government; and how to finance armies and government services out of proportion to population and resources in order to combat the revolutionaries. Essentially two devices have been used to channel aid money for these purposes: commodity import programmes (CIP) and IMF-sponsored stabilization funds. We will consider Laos first because that tiny country has experienced both forms in turn and in combination since 1955.

A subcommittee of the US Congress reported in 1971 that 'since the beginning of its independence in 1955, Laos has been unable to support its small population of less than three million people by either internal production or sufficient exports to earn foreign exchange to pay for the consumable goods required by the Lao people'.[1] This is not true, for in reality most of the Laotian population were living outside the monetized economy. What the small country could not support on its own resources was the large Royal Laotian Army which the US desired it to maintain, not as a fighting force, but as a decoy, a 'trip wire' which the US hoped would dramatize communist attacks and thus justify US intervention.[2] To take a large number of men away from productive activities to serve in the army, paying their wages in kip (the Laotian currency) from the government printing presses, would have caused a serious inflation in the absence of external subsidies. The first method by which external dollar aid was translated into kip for payment of the army and government budget was described by Roger Hilsman in his memoirs of the Kennedy administration:

The solution was for the United States to send commodities – rice, consumer goods, and so on – to Laos as part of the American aid programme. The Lao government would then sell the goods to merchants for kip which could be used to pay the army. The goods made available in this way would match the money supply, and inflation would be avoided. The soldiers, through US financing, in effect earned foreign exchange to pay for imports of goods and food that would sop up the excess currencies their own pay generated.[3]

The amount and type of aid-financed imports were not determined by the economy's need for imports, but by the need to 'sop up' the government's budget deficit in kip. The result was the creation of completely artificial needs for consumer goods imports, and even the import of vegetables and foodstuffs in large quantities (which Laos should have been able to produce internally) from nearby Thailand for the urban regions of Vientiane and Savannakhet. The flood of imported commodities which displaced domestic production gave rise to the quip that 'Laos used to have an economy but now she has an aid programme.'[4] A corollary was the development of a class of Laotian importers, whose fortunes were made on the aid-financed goods. The exchange rate which applied to the import of these commodities was so overvalued that it was immensely profitable to re-export goods the Laotians could not use, such as television sets, and resell them in the larger markets of Thailand. 'The transactions eventually became so blatant,' wrote Hilsman, 'that rather than shipping the goods to Laos and then reshipping them out again, the merchants merely arranged for a customs official in Laos to issue a receipt for the goods, which really never left Bangkok.' Since so many goods never even reached the country, the programme did not serve its purpose of controlling inflation very well: the price of rice, for example, doubled between 1955 and 1957.[5]

The shifting alliances of Laotian politics are extremely confusing, and can be mentioned only briefly here.[6] The essential point is that although over the years there have constantly been so-called left, right, and neutralist factions, the only division that counted was between the Pathet Lao revolutionaries and the United States military and financial power. The so-called neutralists have in fact always been in alliance with one or another of the main protagonists, as the one-time split between 'left-leaning neutralists' and 'pro-Western neutralists' illustrates. From 1959 until shortly before the Geneva peace conference on Laos in 1962, the Pathet Lao, allied with Prince Souvanna Phouma's 'neutralist' faction, seemed headed for a clear military victory over the isolated right faction backed by the United States. During this period of military disturbance, the United States was forced to supplement its commodity import programme with direct cash grants in order to offset the budgetary deficits and keep the kip stable. This system, as an AID economist noted, 'proved expensive to the United States, as the grants were closely tied to the level of the ever increasing budgetary deficits'.[7] Then in January 1962 the US realized it was backing the losing side, and suspended aid in order to force its erstwhile rightist protégés to the bargaining table in Geneva.

After a temporary truce was arranged in Geneva, the US worked to realize Averell Harriman's suggestion that 'we must be sure the break comes between the communists and the neutralists rather than having the two of them teamed up as before'.[8] Aid was reduced to a trickle* for fourteen months, until Souvanna showed signs of redefining his neutralism in favour of the US. During the time US aid was suspended, the unsupported budget deficits resulted in a runaway inflation in Laos.

When the United States decided to resume aid payments in 1963, making up the budget deficit and stabilizing prices were the main objects as before. The Commodity Import Programme, however, was not considered optimum for the purpose. For one thing, the anomalies and corruption to which it had given rise had attracted unfavourable publicity; the re-export of television sets had become notorious. There was a more serious limitation, however. The CIP programme was, by US law, limited to the import of 'essential goods' and, no matter how the definition was stretched, the market for 'essential' goods was limited in Laos. The proviso that all goods had to be of US origin unless a waiver were obtained constricted possible imports even further.[9] Even at a special preferential exchange rate for US aid-financed imports, the tiny Laotian market couldn't absorb enough 'essentials' to finance the government's huge deficit, even though it was estimated about this time that Laos was importing 40 times the value of its exports.

What was needed, from the point of view of US officials in Vientiane, was a mechanism that would absorb the kip created by the Laotian government deficit by translating it into *external* demand. Since the demand for essential imports could not fill the gap, then Laotians should be encouraged to trade their kip for foreign exchange which could be used for any purpose whatever: imports of all kinds, from Japan, Thailand, France, or even China; trips and study tours abroad; even the transfer of foreign exchange out of the country into Swiss bank accounts. Only in this way, which meant glutting the tiny monetized part of the economy with all of the dollars it could absorb, could the deficit be covered and prices and the exchange rate remain stable. The problem of the Laotians was not that of con-

---

* Although throughout this period – since the expensive Royal Laotian Army was worthless as a fighting force – the Americans assembled and trained a secret army of minority tribesmen and foreign mercenaries.

serving foreign exchange but of stretching their imaginations for ways of spending it.

It was in these circumstances that the Laotian government invited the International Montary Fund to make a survey of their exchange problems. The IMF recommended the establishment of a multilaterally supported Foreign Exchange Operations Fund (FEOF), which went into operation on 1 January 1964. FEOF corresponded so well with the ideas of US officials, and with US willingness to provide the lion's share of the funds, that we may raise the question as to who was advising whom in this process, but certainly the cooperation of the Fund and of the other nations contributing to FEOF (Britain, France, Japan, and Australia) gave it an aura of international respectability which the US found extremely valuable. In the first year's pledging the US offered $4 million and the other four donors a total of $3·8 million to support FEOF; the IMF appointed the administrator who would oversee FEOF's operations.

There was no pretence that this foreign aid would contribute to the emergence of a balanced economy in Laos. As an AID official who helped devise the policy recalled,

> Nor was there any hope of [sic] pretence that this exchange stabilization fund would help eliminate or even substantially reduce this disequilibrium in the balance of payments. It was clear, on the contrary, that the stabilization fund would have to be renewed periodically without much hope of reduced funding requirements and that the resources of the fund would have to come entirely from aid grants, with the United States aid programme providing at least half the requirement; it was also clear that some portion of this exchange would inevitably be utilized to finance the importation of luxury goods as well as the export of capital since the fund was to sell its exchange in the free market without any controls placed on the disposition which purchasers could make of the exchange acquired from the fund.[10]

The FEOF in operation was simplicity itself. Anyone with Laotian currency could walk into its office and purchase foreign exchange at the rate of 505 kip to the dollar. This rate, suggested by the IMF at the time FEOF was established, remained stable for nearly eight years – a feat which seemed truly incredible for such a poor, tiny state fighting a civil war. The feat was not incredible, however, but tautological, since the exchange rate remained fixed because the contributors to FEOF, particularly the US, were willing to supply foreign exchange indefinitely at that rate, to match the Lao government deficits.

No questions were asked of the persons presenting kip for dollars concerning their origin, political allegiance, or the use to be made of the dollars: the kip was perfectly convertible. Importers could acquire dollars for use on any kind of import from anywhere in the world. Presumably the Pathet Lao also tapped the fund for dollars. And the money could be sent out of the country to rest in foreign bank accounts. The FEOF office itself provided a telegraphic transfer service to facilitate this, until outraged US congressmen questioned the practice as contributing to 'capital flight'. At that time the service was terminated, without apology, as 'not essential to FEOF's stabilization function'.[11]

The outraged congressmen were a cross the AID officials had to bear, since it was not permissible to admit that the purpose of the fund was not the conservation and proper use of US taxpayers' money, but of getting Laotians to spend it by any means possible so as to absorb useless kip. In fact, the use of FEOF proceeds to cover the budget deficits gave rise among US AID officials to the colourful phrase, 'burning the kip'. The currency was not actually burnt, however. Harold Whittington, a staff investigator for the congressional committee looking into the operations of the fund, explained that it was an accounting procedure:

The physical currency itself is not the stabilizing factor. The way it actually works in Laos is that the Laotian government writes rubber cheques against its account. The bank honours these cheques and pays out local currency. That puts the currency into circulation. We then provide the dollars, whereby whoever has the currency can bring it in and exchange it for dollars. The hard currency is then expended for their import needs and also for capital flight and that sort of thing. The local currency coming back is put back into the banking drawers to be utilized to pay out on the next rubber cheque, thus, the same currency is constantly in circulation.

97

At the end of the year, the Laotian government bank account shows a huge red balance, the FEOF bank account shows a huge black balance, and we authorize the transfer of our portion of the FEOF arrangements to cover the Laotion red balance . . .[12]

To USAID officials, FEOF had several advantages over CIP as a device for 'burning' kip. As already mentioned, FEOF sales had much greater potential since the money was not tied to US procurement rules or limited to essential commodities, or limited to commodities at all. Further, it abolished the possibilities of corruption because there were no rules at all to be evaded. As an AID official in Washington told the congressional investigating committee, 'the essence of it is that any Laotian that has kip can buy foreign exchange at a fixed rate ... so he can be a crook, a corrupter, or an honest man and he will get exactly the same rate. So there is no incentive to be a crook.'[13] Finally, since FEOF dollars were sold at a rate of 505 to 1, while AID commodities had to be given the preferential 240:1 exchange rate, FEOF was more 'efficient' in soaking up kip in terms of dollar costs. In 1964, the combined CIPs of US and other donor nations removed about 2·4 billion kip from circulation through the sale of $10 million aid goods; while $6·8 million sales through FEOF of untied dollars mopped up 3·4 billion kip.[14]

Because of these advantages, USAID shifted the emphasis of its stabilization programme to FEOF on 1 September 1965. After that date CIP remained responsible for only four categories of imports: rice, petroleum, oil and lubricants, and machinery and utility vehicles. All other goods previously imported under CIP would henceforth have to be imported at the 505:1 FEOF exchange rate. The United States agreed to augment the resources of FEOF by a sufficient amount to absorb the diverted demand which would result from this rechannelling of imports.[15]

So the United States, with half-hearted assistance from the other FEOF contributors and with the benevolent advice and assistance of a resident representative of the IMF, poured foreign exchange into Laos in amounts which were limited only by the restraints which it could enforce on a steadily growing government deficit. FEOF started with the sum of $7·8 million for 1964, with a little over half contributed by the US; by the late 1960s total contributions averaged more than $20 million per year, with the US providing 72·1 per cent of the total.[16] It was the highest per capita aid programme in the world, but the proportions become even more astonishing when it is realized that FEOF benefited, at most, only about half a million people who lived in the monetized sector of Laos.[17] In fact, an operation such as FEOF is possible only for a very small economy like that of Laos because of its extremely high per capita expense; it has never been tried in South Vietnam, which has six times the population of Laos.[18]

International support for FEOF has been lukewarm at best, even from Japan which benefits through a $6 million yearly trade surplus with Laos from the untied foreign exchange pumped in through the fund. A US congressional investigating committee reported sourly in 1971:

> It is relatively obvious that our partners have never really bought the FEOF stabilization programme. As the costs of the Foreign Exchange Operations Fund skyrocketed, our partners have not been willing to increase their contributions; the US taxpayers picked up the tab for the additional input into the fund ...
>
> ... France, for all practical purposes, has been using FEOF to acquire the kip needed for its local expenses in Laos. Japan has reserved its kip being acquired through FEOF for future uses and has indicated that it will not increase its contributions to FEOF. Australia and the United Kingdom are – in all probability – also looking for ways to gracefully rid themselves of FEOF ...[19]

The Japanese and French practice of reserving their kip for their own use meant that in practice their contributions were useless for the purpose of 'burning' kip. Their kip purchases were merely 'sterilized', or made unavailable for use for one year, and then could be poured back into the economy, to be sopped up by the other contributors' FEOF donations.

For nearly eight years FEOF performed the 'miracle' of maintaining a stable and fully convertible kip in a nation that had virtually no independent foreign exchange earnings aside from its exports of opium.[20] By 1969, however, the system was showing signs of breaking down as the Laotian government began to run deficits in excess of the amount agreed to by FEOF donors. By 1971 government revenues covered only 30 per cent of disbursements and the year's deficit exceeded 15 billion kips, of which only 8·8 billion could be absorbed by the dollars in FEOF.[21] The shortfall was met by an emergency supplement from the US of $4 million. Then, in an effort to adjust demand to supply, the US Embassy (sic!) devalued the kip by 20 per cent in November 1971, to the rate of 605 to 1.[22] This was followed in a few weeks by the devaluation of the US dollar itself, and with it the kip, in relation to other currencies.

The effect of the devaluations on the Lao trading and speculating class, who had assumed that the exchange rate was immutable, was to trigger a panic of capital flight and dollar buying. This resulted in a 'run' on FEOF, which was forced to suspend operations for a few days in March 1972. Due to this currency crisis, the signing of the annual FEOF donors' agreement was delayed by ten weeks, during which time the US provided an interim subsidy of $7 million. When the agreement was signed, for a total of $24 million, the US was found to be supplying $16·1 million and, indirectly, the $2 million 'first-time' contribution from the Royal Laotian Government. The kip continues to burn.

*

Cambodia would most likely have become an artificial dependency of the US like Laos when both countries became independent in 1955, except for the stubborn conviction of its reigning monarch, Prince Norodom Sihanouk, that the small country could best survive by remaining neutral and non-aligned. About $350 million in US aid was received by Cambodia between 1955 and 1963. According to Sihanouk, it was 'the major source of our foreign currency' in the first years of independence, but the annual sums were declining towards the end of that period, and relations between the Prince and the militantly anti-communist US State Department were never very warm.

The nature of US aid to Cambodia, more than its relatively modest dimensions, was a source of dissatisfaction to Cambodians. The US gave some loans to small private industry, but resisted Cambodian requests for aid in building larger, state-owned industrial facilities which would permit the country to reduce its imports. The military aid programme was an even more serious source of contention. Sihanouk suspected that the obsolete war equipment that was shipped to Phnom Penh, coupled with a prohibition against obtaining aid from any other source, was actually intended to keep his military force small and ineffectual rather than to strengthen it. The Americans, however, made it clear that they would do no more until Phnom Penh came around to the belief that 'application of the principle of collective security will better assure its independence' – or, in blunter words, until Sihanouk abandoned neutralism.[24]

The major concern of the Prince was not the ideological threat of the communists but the territorial ambitions of Thailand to the west and Vietnam to the east, both traditional predators of Cambodia. He was disquieted by the massive military aid which the US was funnelling to the enthusiastically anti-communist régimes in Bangkok and Saigon, since he feared that it might be used against Cambodia rather than its intended target. Disquiet turned to alarm in June 1958 when two South Vietnamese battalions reportedly invaded a frontier village in Stung Treng province and moved the border markers to favour South Vietnam before withdrawing. Sihanouk's government protested to the United States, on the assumption that the Americans had sufficient power to restrain their protégés; but they received no satisfaction from the indifferent US reply to their alarm. The following month Cambodia initiated diplomatic relations with the People's Republic of China, having come to the conclusion that some counterbalance to American power would be necessary to safeguard their independence. Washington was infuriated by this move and reportedly considered a threat to suspend aid payments in an attempt either to bring Sihanouk to heel or to encourage his overthrow – a move which the US Ambassador in Phnom Penh succeeded in blocking.[25]

Tensions increased and aid funds declined in the following years. Sihanouk became convinced that the United States was supporting rightist Khmer Serei opponents who were plotting to overthrow him from neighbouring Thailand and South Vietnam. He was also displeased by the social changes in Cambodian society which US aid had fostered, at the same time as he pondered the danger to himself if the US should suddenly cut off its aid. To Sihanouk, the assassination of South Vietnamese Premier Ngo Dinh Diem in October 1963 was a brutal object lesson in the perils of dependence, as the US had encouraged the coup by suspension of aid payments and by forcing Diem to give up his personal guard.

Shortly after the assassination, therefore, the Prince announced a series of startling policy changes. He unilaterally renounced United States military aid from 1 January 1964, and ordered all French and American troops to leave the country. Simultaneously he proclaimed an economic plan which he called 'Khmer socialism' which entailed the immediate nationalization of import and export businesses, and the nationalization of Cambodian banks by the end of the following June. Such measures would probably have provoked a cut-off of American aid in any case, and Sihanouk, recognizing this, had finessed their revenge.

The consternation in Washington which this announcement provoked showed which government was most dependent on the aid programme. Sihanouk himself appeared positively euphoric at having taken the decision, and his speeches and press conferences explaining the move show that it was not an arbitrary or impulsive one:

Contrary to what some think, it is not the actions of the Khmer Serei or their insulting broadcasts which are at the origin of that decision which has been maturely reflected and prepared since 1958. Western circles are very wrong in believing me naïve, choleric, impulsive, etc. The changes in our internal system which have just been decided have profound causes.

In the first place I would cite the prospect of the withdrawal of American aid, aid which has more and more irritated not only myself but above all Cambodian circles of all tendencies, from progressives to nationalists of the right, for once in agreement. I must admit that the withdrawal of this aid will be an immense relief for

us. For one thing, we won't have to hear any more talk of that aid as indispensable for our survival. For another, we will be obliged to devote infinitely more energy to the development of production.
... Everyone agrees, above all the foreign residents in Cambodia, that the rich are amassing fortunes at an inadmissable speed while the standard of living of the great majority of the population is improving only very slowly.[26]

Our liberalism which shows itself in every sphere, is enjoyed to an excessive degree by the private capitalist sector which inevitably abuses it and deprives the State of important revenues and other benefits.[27]

To our great regret, the Khmer people have come to feel that American military aid was less and less intended to permit Cambodia to defend – if not effectively, at least with dignity – its territorial integrity and its neutrality and that, therefore, it was becoming a kind of encouragement to the annexationist aims of Thailand and South Vietnam, to the detriment of Cambodia.[28]

We will be poorer, but more independent.[29]

A large part of American economic aid is frankly detrimental to our interests. That is the case for example with the allocation of foreign exchange to the private sector. It would be preferable to do without this aid which, in the long run, will poison us just as opium poisons the human organism.[30]

Sihanouk also had a realistic idea of what the nation would have to do if it was to give up American aid. He predicted that the new austerity programme would mean a shortage of cement, iron, gasoline, automobiles, and luxury products of all types. He suggested also that the state would reduce the allocation of foreign exchange for the purpose of tourism.[31] The relatively modest amount of American aid had been financing only about 15 per cent of Cambodia's imports, so the fat could be cut out of the programme without causing an economic disaster; Cambodia had substantial foreign exchange reserves of about $80 million.[32] The Cambodian government itself picked up the tab for the 6 per cent of its annual budget and the army payment allowances which had previously been covered by aid-generated counterpart funds. A year and a half later, a magazine article reported from Phnom Penh that 'according to some observers here, only the new urban-based middle class which

103

had sprung up on profits from US aid has seriously suffered from [its suspension]'.[33]

This class of aid parasites represented the most serious internal threat to Sihanouk's policy of independence and neutrality. Looking back after his deposition, from exile in Peking Sihanouk laments,

> In accepting their 'aid', we were infecting ourselves with a virus which poisoned the national bloodstream ... It was like an insidious, paralysis-type illness – and by the time the symptoms appeared it was too late to do much about it. Even after I cut off aid altogether, the poison continued its work. Top level 'dollar addicts' in our government were prepared to commit treason and maybe to undermine my stop-gap measures, in order to get the dollars flowing in again.[34]

Sihanouk described the process by which the US cultivated allies within Cambodian society:

> As a means of penetrating the economy and the politics of the country, one American cynic was heard to boast that the 'counterpart fund' was the 'greatest invention since the wheel'! Fund administrators consciously developed a sort of comprador class with a vested interest in pushing US policies; a class which had no interest in building up our economy. Trafficking would come to an end if we started producing, from our own factories, the goods they were supposed to be importing.[35]
>
> Within a couple of years, and exclusively through manipulations of dollar 'aid', the US had created a powerful internal lobby in our country, a political fifth column working to scrap neutrality and place Cambodia under the SEATO umbrella.[36]

This class did not appreciate the fact that Sihanouk was performing a double miracle for his small country. It remained an island of peace while war raged in the neighbouring states of South Vietnam and Laos, and was relatively free as well from internal disturbances. And, despite the loss of the balance-of-payments and budget support which had been supplied by American aid, the economy suffered no serious disruptions. As even a high American AID official was forced to admit, there was virtually no price inflation nor balance of payments and budgetary deficits.[37]

Despite this impressive record, the Cambodian middle classes who resented the loss of their import profits and foreign luxuries had a common interest with the United States in promoting the view that Cambodia was in economic crisis, and newspaper and magazine articles spread that impression. According to the *Far Eastern Economic Review*, 'industrialization had almost stopped; foreign exchange reserves were gradually declining and the implementation of the five-year plan was a slow process because of lack of cash'.[38] An article purporting to explain the overthrow of Sihanouk in terms of an economic crisis blamed corruption on the part of Sihanouk's relatives in their management of SONEXIM, the state trading firm, for excessive imports.[39] Although this was probably true it indicated that Sihanouk's austerity plan was being subverted, not that it was wrong in principle.

'National foreign exchange reserves as of February 1970 totalled only 3,814,000,000 riels ($69,345,454)' according to the same source.[40] When we compare this figure with the one given on the same page for total imports in 1969, $76,863,636, there is a surprise. Foreign exchange reserves had dwindled, but by a very modest amount, since aid stopped in 1963; and even calculated at the purportedly excessive import level of the last year of Sihanouk's leadership, Cambodia's exchange reserves were sufficient to cover nearly eleven months' import needs. Since a six month's supply is considered very comfortable and some nations teeter along with reserves equal to only a few weeks' import needs, Cambodia was actually in fine shape. Similarly, in 1969 Cambodia's debt service payments amounted to a modest 8·7 per cent of estimated receipts from merchandise exports in the previous year.[41] If there was in fact a 'shortage of cash' and little industrialization, it could only be due to a very conservative management of the foreign debt and foreign exchange reserves. And if Cambodia was not industrializing very rapidly, neighbouring Laos with its FEOF cornucopia was not industrializing at all.

Sihanouk nevertheless began to waver and, under rightist pressure, invited Lon Nol and Sirik Matak to form a 'Government of National Salvation' in 1969. This new government reportedly 'hoped both to encourage local production and to discourage the import of unnecessary luxury goods – or excessive amounts of non-luxury items such as petroleum and automobiles'.[42] The means which they chose to achieve this were to join the IMF and the World Bank, devalue the riel on the advice of the former, and partially denationalize foreign trade – all policies which were very unlikely to contribute to their professed goals.[43] The last step was taken on the assumption that it was better to legalize diversion of foreign exchange to the entire class of importers than to suffer some leakage through personal corrupt practices! Sihanouk wavered between support of the new policies and antagonism to them – until Lon Nol and Sirik Matak took the opportunity of Sihanouk's absence from the country to overthrow him in March 1970.

The coup must be understood in relation to both domestic discontent within Cambodia and the international context of the Indochina War. Internally, the class which had once enriched itself from US aid still pined for its resumption. Externally, the war had been pressing dangerously at the fragile shell of Cambodian neutrality for a year or two, as the US blamed Sihanouk for allowing Vietnamese National Liberation Front troops to use so-called 'sanctuaries' in Cambodia just across the border from Vietnam. US and South Vietnam military commanders were complaining that the war would end quickly if only they could 'wipe out' the 'sanctuaries'. Whether or not there were any explicit contacts between American military or CIA authorities and the Cambodians who engineered the coup, the recent histories of South Vietnam, Laos, Indonesia, and other neighbouring countries were proof enough that the United States would rush to the support of a Phnom Penh government that would swing the country firmly into the American camp. The US did just that, recognizing the coup makers immediately and sending them dollar aid. Within a few weeks, on 1 May, American and South Vietnamese troops crossed the border in search of the 'communist sanctuaries'.

The end of the Cambodian political and economic miracle can be dated precisely from the overthrow of Sihanouk. The country was engulfed immediately in a brutal war with both civil and international aspects. The economic decline was equally precipitous. Before the war broke out, rice and rubber together had earned about 70 per cent of Cambodia's foreign exchange. In 1969 the country exported 180,000 tons of rice; but production declined and transportation was disrupted when fighting began, and for 1972 American officials estimated that as much as 200,000 tons might have to be *imported* if people were not to starve.[44] Rubber exports dropped from 45,000 tons in 1969 to zero in 1971. The rubber plantations were located close to the Vietnam border and thus in the direct path of the US–South Vietnamese invasion. Out of a total of 51,000 hectares planted to rubber, 7,000 hectares of plants were destroyed by chemical defoliants; and the destruction of buildings and processing equipment brought every plantation to a standstill. French planters charged that the South Vietnamese deliberately destroyed the plantations with air strikes.[45]

Racist attacks on Vietnamese traders and merchants frightened the prosperous Chinese into sending their capital out of the country (the less fortunate Vietnamese were either massacred or deported without their possessions). This capital flight was facilitated by the liberalization of exchange restrictions that the US and IMF immediately urged upon Phnom Penh. The Chinese demand for hard currency was said to be responsible for the sharp rise in the black market price of the riel, from 120 to the dollar to 250 : 1 within a few weeks.[46]

The government budget also ballooned rapidly as a massive expansion of the army – from 35,000 to 185,000 within a year – and the creation of a militia of 143,000 men was planned. By 1971 defence took 60 per cent of the national budget. The money supply rose in the first year of war from 6 billion riels to 15 billion; and it was predicted to reach 25 billion by the end of 1971.[47]

To the American sponsors of the new régime in Phnom Penh the production problem and the budget deficit problem could to some extent cancel each other out. That is, if the Cambodian populace were now forced to buy rice from imported American stocks supplied under the aid programme, rather than locally grown rice, the counterpart receipts would absorb a portion of the runaway money supply caused by the government deficit; in effect, it would channel riels that would ordinarily have gone to Cambodian rice producers to the Cambodian government instead. Cambodia was quickly given a Commodity Import Programme similar to those already operating in Laos and South Vietnam, with the same purpose of propping up the government via AID imports.

Concurrently, the Phnom Penh government invited the IMF to send a mission to survey the economic situation and make recommendations.[48] Its first major recommendation was for a typical stabilization-cum-devaluation programme which included a 'floating' riel, increased taxes on luxury imports, substantial increases in bank rates, reduced controls for agricultural prices, and – crucially – the elimination of most import controls so that the dollar could be made freely available to importers. Shortly before the reforms were announced, Lon Nol suspended the National Assembly and announced that the government would henceforth rule by ordinance, a move which the US embassy hoped would smooth the path for adoption of the economic reforms which they had been urging.[49]

The Cambodian government made history of a sort that month by announcing devaluation a week before it was to go into effect, 'so people will have a chance to get used to it', as they explained. American and IMF advisers writhed in their chairs at the press conference where this announcement was made, but the Fund's representative Gunnar Tómasson (who had previously managed IMF operations in Indonesia) recovered enough to commend the government to the press for 'a courageous effort to attack inflation at its source'.[50] The US showed its approval by supplying a $20 million credit to finance the newly liberalized imports.

There was a unanimity of opinion among the Phnom Penh government, the IMF, and US officials in Cambodia that all Cambodia needed was massive or unlimited supplies of US aid. The IMF, in its report and recommendations, repeated the disingenuous argument which we have met in other cases that the solution to crime is to abolish laws:

Black market operations are especially undesirable at times of war because of the opportunities provided for a few individuals to make large profits on illegal transactions, while the population as a whole is being called upon to make sacrifices. A black market for foreign exchange arises only when there are restrictions on official foreign exchange transactions. The best method of preventing black market operations, therefore, is to remove the restrictions which give rise to the black market in the first place. In the case of Cambodia, this implies that no restrictions should be placed on the access of private importers to official foreign exchange for their import requirements.

It is recognized, of course, that the establishment of a liberal foreign exchange system in Cambodia can only be effected if sufficient exchange resources become available through external assistance.[51]

When questioned by a congressional investigator about what action the Cambodian government was taking to control its budget deficit, 'Cambodian officials replied flatly that Cambodia would be forced to depend on aid from friendly countries to cover the entire budget deficit.'

The position of Cambodia is that its reserves, the exchange rate, the budget deficit must be maintained intact, and that the 'friendly countries', that is, the United States, should make up the difference, preferably in cash grants but possibly in a commercial import programme.[52]

The congressional investigator expressed his doubt

that US officials in Phnom Penh ever truly accepted the view that US economic grants to Cambodia should be tied to US source commodities. US officials in Phnom Penh strongly pressed for establishment of an 'economic support fund' for Cambodia pattern [sic] somewhat after the 'Foreign Exchange Operations Fund' in Laos.[53]

Not surprisingly, the IMF recommended the establishment of an 'Exchange Stabilization Fund' (ESF) for Cambodia which closely resembled FEOF in Laos. Again the United States and the IMF busied themselves organizing multilateral contributions, this time with considerable backing from Japan whose exports stood to benefit the most from untied aid and the liberal import policy. A preliminary conference for ESF was held in Paris in November 1971, and a pledging session met in Phnom Penh the following January. Three days before the pledging was announced, the American columnist Jack Anderson charged that the US had drafted a fill-in-the-blank fund-raising form letter for Cambodian officials to circulate to prospective donors. Anderson also published the text of a State Department message sent with the form which said: 'We understand that [the] Japanese will then move out and actively lobby for participation in the ESF. We can, on a selective basis, do some lobbying here, especially with UK and Australia.'[54] Anderson also supplied figures which, according to him, the State Department had suggested as a proper contribution from each country. It is instructive to compare Anderson's figures with the actual pledging, as such a comparison tends to confirm the accuracy of his information and also suggests the relative degree of each donor's enthusiasm.

Aside from the United States and Britain, only Japan and Thailand, whose exports would profit most from the ESF, contributed as much as 50 per cent of what was requested. Multilateral support had become very strained. Cambodia re-

Contributions to Cambodia's exchange stabilization fund

	Actual pledging[55]	US wanted, according to Anderson
United States	$12,500,000	$12,500,000
Japan	5,000,000	7,500,000
Australia	1,000,000	3,000,000
Britain	500,000	500,000
Thailand	250,000	250,000
New Zealand	112,000	300,000
Malaysia	100,000	250,000
Indonesia	0	250,000
Singapore	0	250,000
Philippines	0	250,000
Total	19,462,000	25,050,000

dundantly chipped in $8,750,000 of its own reserves, plus a dubiously justified compensatory finance drawing of $6,250,000 from the IMF.* The ESF went into operation on 1 March 1972, managed by an official selected by the IMF. He was in fact the same man who had been managing the FEOF in Laos, a former Bank of England employee named Edward Fillingham.[56]

The Cambodian ESF is supposed to differ from FEOF in two respects. Having learned from their experience in Laos the difficulties and dangers of supporting a fixed exchange rate, the US and IMF insisted on a floating rate in Cambodia in order to avoid crises like the one which was blowing up in Laos at that very moment. (Nevertheless, the eventual cost of the fund in its first year of operation climbed to $34,500,000, eighty per cent more than the initial contribution.) And, to please congressional watchdogs, the AID officials had to pretend that some controls would be placed on the use of ESF funds. Foreign exchange would be sold to purchase items on a free commodity import list, and other non-commodity expenditures to be agreed upon by the donors each year, such as Cambodian Embassy expenditures, official travel, students resident abroad, etc. Transfers of capital, debt repayment, and military expenditures would not be eligible.[57]

The ESF is, however, fundamentally the same system as FEOF, with the identical purpose of supporting a top-heavy government and military by flooding the economy with otherwise unneeded imports. The staff investigator who compiled a report on aid to Cambodia (by that time renamed the Khmer Republic) wrote, 'Nowhere did I note even a hint of AID's attempting to determine what commodities are actually needed by the Khmer people.'[58] ESF had to be introduced because, as in Laos, imports of 'essential goods' – even when this was stretched to include air conditioners, television sets, colour

---

* Drawings under the IMF's compensatory finance facility are intended to make up shortfalls in export earnings which occur for reasons beyond the control of the borrowing government. Although it was true that Cambodian exports had fallen disastrously as a result of the war, it is undeniable that the coup leaders had invited the war!

111

plumbing fixtures, and soft drink bottling machinery[59] – could not be sold fast enough to burn up the government's paper riels at the necessary rate. Although one AID official testified that the ESF 'is not in any way, shape or form tied to public budget deficits', this was a lie, as other testimony proved.[60]* When the investigating subcommittee queried AID about end-use monitoring to ensure that only appropriate commodities are imported, the answer it received from AID was: 'The ESF manager is responsible for ensuring effective administration of the ESF, including the prohibition against military items or goods reserved for CIP financing.'[61] Apparently the controls are meant to function against the 'essentials' reserved for CIP financing rather than against luxuries of any definition.

The class of importers dependent on American aid has been revived and strengthened, and forms a local prop for the shaky and corrupt Phnom Penh government. The US Embassy had, in early 1972, 'quietly let it be known' that if Lon Nol were overthrown, American aid would stop.[62] Lon Nol has recipro-cated this support by distributing concessions to Cambodia's potential offshore oil wealth and eight other commercially val-uable minerals to international corporations, though the firms may not be able to exploit the concessions if the Lon Nol government cannot ensure order.[63]

Less than one year after US aid was resumed in 1970, Cam-bodia 'seemed to have entered a new era of economic depend-ence with no end in sight'.[64] In such a brief period a small, poor, but proud, independent, and tranquil nation reached depths of corruption which had been the norm in South Vietnam and Laos for many years. In retrospect, Sihanouk's biggest mistake seems to have been to underestimate the cupidity of those whom he had deprived of the aid porkbarrel for a few years.

*

We will not consider South Vietnam at length, but a few

* An official statement of AID found on page 113 of the same report explains that '. . . counterpart generated from the US contribution to the ESF will be utilized for activities mutually agreed upon by the US and Khmer government. It is our current intention that such counterpart will be used entirely or mostly for budget support'.

points of comparison with Laos and Cambodia will be of interest. As in Laos, the US has propped up its client government in South Vietnam with commodity imports for budget support ever since South Vietnam became a nominally independent state in 1955. The artificial and import-dependent nature of the economy has intensified sharply since the United States committed its military power and national prestige to the defeat of the National Liberation Front. In 1963 Saigon's trade balance was a lopsided $93 million in exports to $238 million imports; by 1967, after massive American intervention, it was exporting only $40 million worth of goods and importing $370 million, not including military imports.[65] As in Laos and Cambodia, this deepening trade deficit was not due to a necessity to import products which the population needed but could not produce itself; it was rather the need of the government to substitute imported commodities for the revenue it was unable to collect via taxation. The trade deficit was merely the direct consequence of the internal budget deficit.[66]

An exchange stabilization programme along the lines of FEOF and ESF has not been tried in South Vietnam, probably because an open-ended commitment to supply foreign exchange would prove exorbitantly expensive in Vietnam. The commodity import programme has been extremely detrimental to the economy, since the market for local manufactures has been usurped by the avalanche of aid-financed imports. In 1966, South Vietnam imported $57·7 million worth of textiles, ten times more than the previous year, while 22,000 looms in the country stood idle and 30 million metres of locally produced fabrics lay unsold in warehouses.[67]

There was little pretence of any effort to limit AID finance to 'essential' imports; in the emergency situation of Vietnam waivers from congressional restrictions can be easily obtained. As the director of AID's Commercial Import Division told a congressional committee, Vietnam's national import requirements are determined by importers.

We have not tried to establish a government control system here of determining by fiat what we should import – in other words, what is good for the Vietnamese to have or what is not good for the Vietnamese to have. The whole system in Vietnam has been based on the freedom of the individual importer to make his own decisions based on his own knowledge of the market and what he feels he can sell.[68]

As in Laos and Cambodia, this aid system has skewed the entire social structure in the direction of external dependency. The cost-reward structure in the private sector works to divert entrepreneurial ambitions away from production to the easy profits which can be made from imports at an overvalued exchange rate. Government economic policies have likewise been adjusted to the artificial system of the import surplus economy.

The IMF has played a less important role in Vietnam than in Laos and Cambodia, though it has been called in on occasion to give rubber-stamp approval and technical advice for changes decided upon by the US. In May 1966 the IMF sent a special team to Saigon to study the economic situation; this was followed by a package of economic reforms which went into effect on 18 June. The package included a devaluation of the piastre. Government employees – a political category whose loyalty was critical for the US – were given a pay increase to compensate for the consequent higher prices, but the rest of the population simply had to take the inflationary consequences without any offsetting income compensation. The import and foreign exchange allocation system, which had been inherited from the French colonial administration, was abolished as a necessary precondition for the influx of aid-financed imports.[69]

The IMF surveyed the South Vietnamese economy again in 1969, this time to legitimize US pressure on Saigon (exercised through a six-week aid cut-off) to take more reform measures. The US resumed aid, as everyone knew it would, before any serious damage was done, but it insisted that the resumption was on condition that the South Vietnamese government either devalue or raise tax levels. Fearing the political consequences of devaluation, which would affect everyone's pocketbook in such an import-dependent society, Saigon reluctantly opted for the latter, but Parliament was hostile to tax increases and nearly a year later no progress had been made in improving tax collection.[70]

114

Two points should be emphasized in conclusion. The first is that the US, and the IMF following its lead, have been encouraging practices in the American client states of Indochina which in theory, and in other real life contexts, they frown upon. The notable example is that of overvalued, multiple exchange rate systems. Overvaluation is tolerated because these régimes, like most governments, shrink from the political consequences of an across-the-board price rise, and their powerful patron likewise fears any measures that might give rise to discontent among the urban population. Overvaluation makes aid programmes more expensive for the US, so periodically devaluations have been forced upon the unwilling governments. In the newest programme in Cambodia, a floating rate has been introduced in an attempt to make the adjustment a continuous one. It is hoped that frequent small devaluations will be less noticeable to the consumer than large adjustments at intervals of several years.

Overvaluation and multiple exchange rates cannot be abolished, however, because the whole system of financing government deficits via commodity imports depends on preferential exchange rates for aid commodities, which would be otherwise too expensive to attract customers. Where the money is provided by untied cash grants in the stabilization funds, it is spent on cheaper imports from Japan, Hong Kong, Formosa, and Thailand, which worsens the US balance of payments and cannot be afforded on a larger scale. Therefore a preferential exchange rate allows US goods to be sold at only 40 per cent of their world market price in Laos and South Vietnam, and about 65 per cent in Cambodia. This is certainly a perversion of the principle of a free and competitive market, but thanks to the double standard of power the US and IMF can permit to some what they forbid to others.

In conclusion, we must emphasize once again the very political role played by the IMF in legitimizing US manipulation of these dependent economies. On the one hand, the IMF lends its prestige to US pressures on Saigon, Vientiane, and Phnom Penh for devaluations and import and exchange liberalization. More importantly, however, the IMF serves US propaganda purposes by assisting in the pretence that the small cliques in the capital cities represent real nations and economies, when in fact they are merely presiding over artificial and externally sustained import programmes.

AID officials have made this function quite clear in explaining their programme to congressional investigators. This excerpt from testimony given in 1971 speaks for itself:

Mr Moorhead: Does the Treasury Department favour the flexible rate for Cambodia?

Mr O'Connor: I think the whole US government basically favours it. Most of these plans will be inter-agency and are not just AID plans, but basically US government plans. That does not mean we haven't attempted to leave the negotiation of this matter primarily to the IMF, for obvious political reasons. We don't want to get into a position where we are the court of last resort for everything. Cambodia felt the need.

We have regarded the presence of the international institution and its permanent resident – of course we keep in close touch with what he is doing back here – we have regarded his presence as being all important to this effort to try to keep us from being totally engaged.

And in the mind of the whole government, I think also totally committed to every aspect of economic policy. We are trying an arm's length sort of operation here. That does not mean we haven't made our views quite clear as to the direction we would like to see things go in the monetary and fiscal field, but it does mean we have tried to have the IMF make the major thrust of the negotiations, and I think they welcome that role.

Mr Moorhead: Presumably our Treasury Department representative on the IMF would be doing what he could to persuade the IMF to act in this direction.

Mr O'Connor: I am sure we would, sir.[71]

6

Yugoslavia: The IMF and Market Socialism

At the same time as it assisted the war effort against communist-led revolutionaries in Indochina, the IMF was cooperating happily with a communist government in Yugoslavia by offering credits to support the cost of an important economic reform. In striking contrast to all other communist-led nations, Yugoslavia has been a member in good standing of the IMF since its founding.

The USSR, although participating in the Bretton Woods negotiations, declined to enter the Fund when it was established. Poland resigned its membership in 1950, charging that the Fund had become a 'submissive instrument of the government of the United States'. Czechoslovakia withdrew in 1955, after a dispute involving its right to withhold sensitive trade information from the Fund. Following the US lead, the Fund recognized Chiang Kai-shek's refugee government on Taiwan as 'China' and ignored the People's Republic. The revolutionary government of Cuba resigned its membership in 1964 after several years of cool relations. A Fund official whom I interviewed was convinced that it was the Czechoslovak reformers' desire to rejoin the Fund that was the cause of the Russian invasion of 1968.

The centrally planned economies – 'communist' in common parlance – are the only significant non-members of the Fund, with the exception of Switzerland. If the Fund, as this work argues, is a key instrument promoting capitalist imperialism, then this incompatibility is perfectly comprehensible. But what about Yugoslavia? Is it the exception that proves the rule? Our first clue is the fact that Yugoslavia, although calling itself communist, is *not* a centrally planned economy.

The admission of Romania to the Fund in early 1973, and indications that other Eastern European states are investigating the possibility of joining, makes an understanding of Yugoslavia's relations with the Fund particularly important.

The Debt Trap

It is remarkable that no one has ever taken a serious look at the relationship between Western economic aid to Yugoslavia and the successive economic reforms in that country. In virtually all scholarly studies, the two phenomena have been treated separately. Western aid, which began flowing within a year or two after the break with the Soviet Union in 1948–9, is usually viewed as a shrewd foreign policy decision (remarkable in view of the hysterical anti-communism in the United States at that time) to encourage the breakaway from the Soviet bloc. It was that, of course, but the assumption that this provided both the necessary and the sufficient motivation for aid to the Tito government, and that therefore no other concessions were asked for or given, is simply not true.

Similarly, the successive liberalization programmes for the Yugoslav economy, notably the decentralization decisions of 1950–2, the foreign exchange reform of 1961, and the major reforms of 1965, are ascribed in Western scholarship to the Yugoslav desire to avoid the mistakes of the Soviet path to development, and to the democratic spirit of the Yugoslav leaders and people. In fact, a close study of the circumstances of each of these reforms shows that in none of the three cases was it a matter of purely free choice. In the early 1950s and in 1965 the country was in a foreign exchange crisis and in drastic need (or so the leadership believed) of foreign aid and foreign debt rescheduling. Though the principal actors have said very little, the circumstantial evidence is that the reforms were adopted under Western pressure, as the price of the desired aid. In 1961 the reforms were explicitly a prerequisite to the maintenance of important trading ties with the West through Yugoslav entry into the General Agreement on Trades and Tariffs (GATT). The cumulative effects of the reform and foreign aid have not been far different from the experience of other countries in this study: externally, debt and dependence, and internally, increased unemployment and worsening distribution of income. Although capitalism, in the sense of private ownership of the means of production, was abolished early in the post-war years, Yugoslavia today is suffering many of the typical ills of the dependent capitalist economies.

At the end of the Second World War the Yugoslav Communist Party headed by Marshal Tito came to power. Because of the leading role which the party had played in the resistance to the Nazis and the liberation of the country, it possessed more popular support and military power than the other East European leaders who were, for the most part, directly dependent on the Soviet Army for their positions. Flattering the USSR by imitation, the Yugoslav leaders prepared an extremely ambitious Five Year Plan calling for the rapid construction of heavy industry. To implement this plan they introduced the Soviet system of centralized control of prices and trade, particularly foreign trade. In so far as foreign trade was necessary, it was to be carried out on a bilateral basis with the Soviet Union and the Eastern European countries.[1]

The Soviet leaders, however, were not pleased at this imitation of their own development strategy, and attempted to persuade the Yugoslavs to develop their economy in a way that would complement the already industrialized USSR. 'Why do you want heavy industry', Stalin reportedly chided them, 'when we have everything you need in the Urals?' Aid from the Soviet Union was not forthcoming in sufficient quantity or on the desired basis, but the Yugoslavs stuck to their plans as far as they could on the basis of their own resources and trading agreements with other socialist governments.

The eventual result of Yugoslav independence, in foreign and bloc affairs as well as in economic policy, was excommunication from the socialist bloc. Economically, this resulted in a total blockade of trade – a major catastrophe since Yugoslav trade had been completely re-oriented towards the bloc. By the fall of 1948 the USSR, Czechoslovakia and Hungary were reneging on deliveries of vitally needed manufactures, industrial goods, and raw materials on which Yugoslavia had already paid substantial deposits. At that time Yugoslavia was dependent on the Eastern bloc for about 50 per cent of its imports. These included all of its coal and coke imports, 80 per cent of its pig iron needs, 60 per cent of its petroleum products, four-fifths of its fertilizer requirements and virtually all specialized machinery, steel tubes, and railway cars and locomotives.[2] On top of this loss of essential trade, fears of an invasion from the Soviet Union meant that additional resources had to be diverted to defence expenditures, which put another strain on the economy.

Convinced, despite this blow, that the independence and economic development of their country depended on the fulfilment of their industrialization plan, the Yugoslav leaders turned west to meet their import needs. Since, in the early stages of the blockade, their staunch communism made foreign aid from the West seem out of the question, they spent all their foreign exchange reserves on imports to keep the plan going. In addition, they appealed to the youth of the country to contribute voluntary labour for the construction of the country. Voluntary labour, however, could not pay for imports; and the reserves were soon exhausted. By 1950 the country was in crisis. Factories and mines were standing idle because machinery required for their operation was not available.[3] Then natural disaster compounded the economic crisis: a severe drought in the summer of 1950 caused a loss of 2,000,000 tons of foodstuffs, which threatened both internal consumption and food exports which were to pay for needed industrial imports.

Yugoslavia had received some small credits from the United States Export–Import Bank and from Great Britain in 1949 and early 1950; it had also received some foreign exchange from the IMF and the IBRD, to which it belonged. The Yugoslavs hoped to get World Bank help to finance the industrial investment in their plan, but they did not succeed in obtaining large-scale assistance and even a modest $25 million loan was mysteriously delayed for two years of the nation's economic crisis. Even these minor tentatives of aid – tokens of the West's interest in keeping the rebel communist régime alive – had their *quid pro quo*. Yugoslavia negotiated agreements with the US, Britain, and France to pay for property which had been nationalized by the revolution. At a time when the country could not pay for their own badly needed imports, it agreed to pay $17 million to the Americans and £4·5 million to Britain in compensation.[4] In addition, the World Bank raised the issue of private debts which had been contracted by earlier Yugoslav governments, and indicated that it would like to see progress towards a settlement before granting a new loan.[5] Further, Yugoslavia agreed to supply the US with strategic materials, notably copper.

On other points, however, the Yugoslavs remained defiantly independent. In early 1950 Marshal Tito asserted by implication that the United States was holding up the World Bank loan in an attempt to force Yugoslavia to change its foreign policy. He said that his government would rather go 'naked' than submit to any form of pressure aimed at making it sacrifice its socialist principles.[6] The Yugoslavs also resisted Western criticism of their 'unrealistic' industrial investment programme, and rebuffed suggestions that they should concentrate on mining, hydro-electric construction, and the promotion of agriculture with the retort that that was just what the Russians had demanded of them – in order to keep the country dependent on imports indefinitely.[7]

The harvest crisis of 1950 seems to have given both Yugoslavia and the West a push towards closer cooperation. For the first time, US President Truman requested the Congress to vote aid to Yugoslavia, saying in his speech that the independence of Yugoslavia was a vital concern of the West. Congress indicated its agreement by approving the request for $69 million in emergency aid. The recipient, for its part, was reminded by the crisis of its perilous situation. By late 1951 the United States had organized a sort of aid-giving consortium with Britain and France as junior partners, with the express intention of financing Yugoslavia's trade deficit. And Yugoslavia was introducing its first series of 'liberalizing' reforms.

It is impossible, until either the IMF or the government of Yugoslavia opens its records to public inspection, to evaluate the contribution of external pressure, exercised through the Yugoslavs' desperate need for foreign aid, to the formulation of Yugoslavia's pioneering new system of market socialism. There were certainly internal and autonomous reasons inclining the Yugoslav government towards such a system. The idea of workers' councils and workers' control had early and honourable precedent in socialist theory and practice. Also the Yugoslav leadership, stung to the quick by the dishonest tirades against them emanating from Moscow, embarked on a searching critique of the Soviet form of development. They had well-grounded suspicions of the excesses of centralized authority, and they were anxious to differentiate their system from that of the Russians.

Yugoslavia's nationalities problem may also have provided compelling arguments for decentralization of the economy. As the immediate post-war euphoria gave way to the difficult struggle to reconstruct the economy, it seemed that decentralization might provide a way to placate separatist sentiments. If so, it was a short-sighted policy, whose effects will be discussed near the end of this chapter. But at the time, there were reasons enough to make decentralization seem an attractive idea to the nation's leaders.

In the light of these considerations, it may seem superfluous to suggest that the IMF also had a hand in designing the Yugoslav system. And yet available evidence suggests that the Fund did exert some powerful leverage on behalf of the Tripartite aid-givers during late 1951 and 1952, the months in which the specific content of Yugoslavia's new style of communism was hammered out. The following account is necessarily hypothesis, but it is firmly consistent with many other cases described in this book.

It is a fact that a delegation from the staff of the International Monetary Fund was in Belgrade conferring with Yugoslav policymakers between 26 September and 12 November 1951, a period of less than seven weeks during which some of the most important of the new liberal reforms were introduced. The three members of the mission subsequently published an account of the reforms they had observed in the *IMF Staff Papers*,[8] which was a revised version of part of the mission's report presented to the Executive Board of the Fund. The mission also gave an interview to the *New York Herald Tribune* upon their return to the United States. The article gives no hint that the mission was responsible in any way for the reforms they describe, although a prefatory note remarks that their visit 'coincided with the beginning of the transition period in Yugoslavia from the old to the new economic system'. In the interview the IMF economists reported that they were in Yugoslavia 'to help that country work out a "realistic" exchange rate', but they also noted 'with satisfaction' the other innovations, such as abolition of the food subsidy, a move to give companies more autonomy, and the use of orthodox (i.e. capitalist) monetary and fiscal policies of taxation and credit controls.[9]

The circumstantial evidence strongly suggests, however, that the IMF mission not only observed the reforms with satisfaction, but had some influence on their adoption in the first place. The fact that the series of liberalizing reforms took place *after* the agreement in principle by the United States, Britain and France, to subsidize Yugoslavia's balance-of-payments deficit, but *before* the conclusion of a formal agreement in the following year suggests that – as in many other countries, and on later occasions in Yugoslavia itself – the badly desired economic aid was made conditional on acceptance of IMF advice. The question as to whether the reforms were freely chosen by the Yugoslavs misses the point, which is that they were choosing from a position of weakness, not strength.

The alternatives were grim enough; if (as the Chinese have charged) Yugoslavia 'sold out' to the West, one must nevertheless appreciate the dilemma the leadership was faced with. The military threat from the Soviet Union was close enough that the survival of Tito's government itself was threatened if protection from the West was not guaranteed, or if the economy were to collapse. In those conditions, aid seemed an absolute necessity. But in addition, the leadership believed that their ambitious development plans could not be fulfilled without aid, from one side or the other, to finance capital imports.

The reforms introduced in late 1951 and early 1952 included a major shift away from the system of federal, republican, and local plans which predetermined most technical and financial decisions, to a system under which individual enterprises had much more freedom to decide what to produce and to set prices for their products, and were permitted to retain, for distribution within their enterprise, a much larger percentage of the profits earned by that enterprise.

This time it was not just a matter of delegating responsibility for detailed planning to lower organs in the administration. Operational planning was scrapped along with its paraphernalia of allocation and production orders, its fastidious inventory checks and its incessant control. Eventually even the all-powerful Planning Commission was deprived of its executive powers and turned into an advisory council of the government for drawing up long-range development plans and analysing current economic conditions.[10]

A major reform that took place while the IMF mission was in the country was the end of consumer rationing in foodstuffs, which usually forms part of the classic IMF stabilization package. The natural effect of this measure was a sharp rise in the price of food; wage rises which had been part of the original plan, with the aim of softening the impact on the consumer, were scrapped at the last minute because they would contribute to inflation. Another part of the package was a planned rise in the administered prices of transportation, electricity, water, postal services, and motion pictures and theatres.[11] The consumer thus suffered the worst effects of inflation – price rises in essential commodities – without the compensation of an increased pay packet. In January 1952 the allocation of foreign exchange to exporters was decentralized by the creation of autonomous pools for different sectors of the economy; in July, exporters were authorized to retain nearly half of their foreign exchange earnings, from which they could draw for their own import needs or sell on an exchange market at higher than official rates.[12] All these reforms are consistent with IMF preferences.

Another decision taken while the IMF team was still in Belgrade was to reduce the annual rate of capital investment from 28 per cent of the national income to 20 per cent. The cut was made, according to a *New York Times* report, 'primarily to convince the Western governments that the modified industrialization programme would be more feasible than the original one and therefore worthy of support'.[13] The feasibility of the Yugoslavs' development plan remained a major issue between the aid-givers and the recipient during the following year. The tension between the parties surfaced in two speeches made in early October 1951. The first was made by Boris Kidric, president of the Yugoslav Economic Council and the leading economic policymaker, who attacked those who criticized the investment programme as too ambitious and maintained that the Yugoslavs were 'going with their heads against the walls' simply for reasons of prestige:

> It is necessary to stress that we already have broken the walls even if we did it with our heads.
> This is not a matter of prestige, but of the most painful necessity for our own people and our country, its independence and freedom.

On the following day Marshal Tito rebuked the West in a speech for 'poisoning' the Yugoslav people with anti-social propaganda. He said that the fact the West had given Yugoslavia economic aid did not entitle it to interfere in the country's internal affairs.[14]

The ostensible focus of the argument was the need for Yugoslavia to reduce its balance of payments deficit as quickly as possible, a goal which was accepted in principle by both parties. The Western powers maintained that Yugoslavia should emphasize those sectors of its economy that could produce more for export markets. Belgrade, however, contended that payments could be balanced only if its capital investment programme were carried out as planned.[15]

In January 1952 the United States and Yugoslavia signed an agreement of economic cooperation in which Yugoslavia promised to develop its industry and agriculture 'on a sound basis', and agreed to furnish the US government with a 'detailed proposal of specific projects' which Belgrade might plan to undertake with the aid.[16] The most significant negotiations took place, however, in the autumn of that year when the United States, Britain, and France negotiated an agreement with Belgrade for continued financing of its trade deficit. The negotiations were stormy and the Yugoslavs rejected the first draft of the agreement which the Tripartite powers presented for their signature. They objected both to the downgrading of their ambitious investment programme – the Western powers showed themselves consistently willing to pay for current imports of raw materials and consumer goods but not capital investments – and to the language of the note, which they regarded as rude and provocative. It took about two months to produce a new version of the agreement, in which some concessions were made to Yugoslav sensibilities but the basic emphasis was not changed. Nature intervened once again, however, with a drought comparable in severity to that of two years before, and the Yugoslavs saw no choice.

The final agreement contained the following points: [17]

(1) Agreement among the four signatories concerning the criteria of government investment priorities in Yugoslavia's economic planning.

(2) Agreement by the Yugoslav government to consult with the three Western governments before contracting any more foreign loans for its investment programme other than loans from the IBRD. This provision reflected Western fears that their aid might serve, even indirectly, to finance the investment plan desired by the Yugoslavs. To prevent this, they refused to allow alternate sources of borrowing.

(3) Consultation with the three Western governments with a view to finding effective means to improve Yugoslavia's foreign debt position.

(4) Consultation with a view to assisting the Yugoslav government to balance its payments as soon as possible.

(5) Recognition by the three Western governments of the importance of the industrial development of Yugoslavia (a clause probably inserted into the second version to pacify the Yugoslavs) and an increase in agricultural production.

(6) Agreement by the three Western powers to further the development of technical assistance to Yugoslavia.

With this agreement, and the necessary relinquishment of at least part of their capital investment plans, the course of Yugoslavia's economic development in the 1950s was set. It may be that the most 'unrealistic' aspect of their ambitious programme was its hopeful dependence on outside finance. After the 1952 Tripartite Aid Agreement assuring Western surveillance over the use of the aid, the money did flow freely: in the next ten years, aid from the West financed a heavy surplus of imports over exports. Throughout the 1950s the proportion of exports as a percentage of imports averaged only 62 per cent.

The system which emerged in 1952 after three years of experimentation on the part of the Yugoslavs and negotiations with Western aid-givers was such a novel hybrid of socialism (in the ownership of the means of production, and in certain aspects of economic planning and social priorities which the government retained control of) and capitalism (in the form of competing enterprises in the context of a market economy) that the proponents of either system could claim the successes for their own ideology and blame the failures and problems on the opposing one. Western newspaper reports typically blamed shortcomings and 'bottlenecks' in production on the remnants of centralized control; this account takes the opposite view. Certainly Yugoslavia enjoyed success of a sort: by the end of the 1950s it had what was probably the fastest growing economy in the world, leaping forward at the average rate of 13 per cent per year from 1957 to 1960. A detailed analysis of this era of development, its causes, strengths, and limitations, is beyond the scope of this work. Certainly foreign aid, including some from the Eastern bloc (with which Yugoslavia mended its quarrel after the death of Stalin) contributed to the growth. For our purposes, however, two points may be made.

The first is that the spectacular spurt of growth was preceded, and no doubt assisted by, some backsliding on the subject of foreign exchange control, which had been so boldly liberalized in early 1952. As early as November of the same year, the percentage of export earnings which exporting firms were allowed to retain for use or sale was lowered from the high figure of 45 per cent introduced in July, back down to 20 per cent.[18] Even this caused serious leakages which contributed to balance of payments difficulties, since the enterprises used or sold the foreign exchange to enhance their own profits, without regard to national priorities – with the result that badly needed hard currencies were utilized for importing non-essential items.[19] The retention percentage was therefore reduced in 1955 to a minimal 2 per cent. This measure was accompanied by other forms of 'backsliding' towards administrative methods of planning and control, and a reassertion of judgements of social priority over the determination of investments by market criteria.[20]

A second point to be made about Yugoslavia's industrial growth is that – not surprisingly, considering the heavy dependence on Western aid financing Western-made imports – much of it was in the form of industries constructed with Western capital, technology, raw materials, and semi-finished components. It was thus similar in many respects to the development which was taking place during the same years in the Philippines and Brazil, which were by no means socialist countries. And the weaknesses of this type of growth were also apparent in Yugoslavia, notably the continued dependence on raw materials and spare parts from the aid suppliers which meant that the gap between imports and exports remained stubbornly wide. Yugoslavia's exports remained, for the most part, the traditional ones of mining and agricultural products: copper, lead, mercury, manganese and chrome ores; wood products, foodstuffs, tobacco, hops, and medicinal plants.[21]

This trade imbalance meant, in its turn, an increasing load of foreign debt. Although aid in the early 1950s had been largely in the form of grant aid which required no repayment, after 1956 the aid continued, but on a loan basis. The total foreign debt had mounted by 1961 to a figure of about $800 million, a sizeable proportion of it in short-term credits whose repayment loomed as an additional burden on the balance of payments. Despite the apparent prosperity of Yugoslavia as it entered the 1960s, externally the economy was in a 'highly strained financial situation which came about in this way with the growth of imports from the preceding period, uncovered by economic assistance, being financed by the contracting of short-term loans'.[22]

Yugoslav planners were also worried by the fact that Europe was forming into two rival economic blocs, the eastern Comecon and the western GATT; whereas Yugoslavia, neither fish nor fowl, belonged to neither. It did enjoy observer status at GATT; and had applied for similar rights on Comecon (without, however, seeking the obligations of membership) but had been rebuffed. By 1960, after the failure of yet another approach to Comecon, Yugoslavia decided to plunge westward, feeling that full membership in GATT was essential if Yugoslavia was to preserve its trading position in Western Europe in the face of the developing economic integration of that area.[23]

In order to become a full member of GATT, Yugoslavia would have to carry out a major foreign exchange reform to bring its trading system in line with those of its trading partners. The ultimate goal was currency convertibility – which had never been attained, nor indeed sought, by any other communist-ruled country, including the Soviet Union. The Yugoslavs spent most of 1960 discussing the details of their reform with missions from the IMF, the World Bank, and countries which might contribute financial assistance. Per Jacobsson, the Managing Director of the IMF, spent four days in Belgrade in July 'to smell out the situation' as he told reporters; he was followed closely by Douglas Dillon, the US Undersecretary of State for Economic Affairs, whom we met in Chapter Two.

The main negotiations were conducted by the IMF. According to one newspaper account:

The Fund representatives argued for as little government interference in the market as possible, while the Yugoslavs, fearing their financial position might not be strong enough to rely on secondary controls, wanted firm supervision. The result, the source said, was a compromise.[25]

Another report said that the Yugoslavs had set three principles to observe in drawing up their programme:

(1) There must be no interference with the nation's high rate of economic growth;

(2) Yugoslavia must remain a 'Socialist' country and the programme must be designed to maintain and strengthen the system;

(3) There must be no reduction of the standard of living.[26]

The main feature of the reform introduced on 1 January 1961, was the unification of the dinar's exchange rate. Yugoslavia had emerged from the first round of negotiations with the IMF, in 1952, with a complex system of 'co-efficients', which amounted to a multiple exchange rate system. It was a compromise between the IMF ideal of a unitary, free exchange rate, and the Soviet system of state trading which virtually disregarded exchange rates in foreign trade. The co-efficients, or multiple rates, had their usual purpose of selectively encouraging or discouraging certain lines of imports and exports by effectively taxing the activities to be discouraged and subsidizing the desired ones. In the Yugoslav case, agricultural exports had been taxed by the application of the rate of 300 dinars to the dollar; while manufacturing had been subsidized by rates ranging as high as 1,250 : 1. The unification of the exchange rate in the 1961 reforms, at the rate of 750 dinars to the dollar, would thus encourage agricultural exports by lifting the exchange 'tax', but handicap industries by the sudden withdrawal of their exchange rate subsidies. Because the new rate lay between the two extremes, it could not be described as a simple devaluation or revaluation, but had aspects of both.

The reform was on balance a boost to agricultural producers and to agricultural exports, but a blow to the recently developed industrial sector, which would have henceforth much more difficulty in competing in both home and export markets. As usual, the blow was administered in the name of more efficient production; only those firms which were 'fittest', in the sense of streamlining operating costs, would survive the chill wind of competition.

As is also usual in the IMF reform syndrome, a good part of the competition would be financed by the competitors in the name of aid. The IMF and the United States marshalled an informal aid consortium consisting of themselves and Yugoslavia's main Western European trading partners (Austria, Italy, France, Netherlands, Switzerland, Britain, and West Germany) which provided credits of $275 million to support the reform. The participation of West Germany raised an interesting problem, since although it was Yugoslavia's major European trading partner, Yugoslavia had diplomatic relations only with its eastern rival, the German Democratic Republic. The dilemma was solved by arranging for the participation of some private West German banks in the consortium, to which the West German government raised no objection.[27] The aid money was to be used to finance the conversion of export industries which would not survive the new competitive conditions, and to pay for increased imports.

The exchange rate unification was accompanied by the introduction of partial currency convertibility, the liberalization of import restrictions, and their replacement by customs tariffs. The list of liberalized imports was not limited to essentials; it contained, aside from industrial raw materials, exotic fruits, tea, herbs, fruit and vegetable juices, strong alcoholic drinks, fine and aromatic wines, sparkling wine, beer, tobacco products, tobacco extract and essences, unexposed film and paper for colour photography, and paints for artists.[28] The young industrial sector was to be exposed to a triple dose of intensified competition: from revaluation of the exchange rate, from aid-financed imports, and from the liberalization of import restrictions.

The reform's effects could not, and did not, fulfil the three criteria the Yugoslavs had laid down in negotiations. The effect of the competition from abroad on the economy was immediately reflected in a sharply falling rate of growth: from an annual rate of 15 per cent in 1960, to 7 per cent in 1961, to less than 5 per cent in the first half of 1962.[29] The standard of living of the population was attacked by inflation in the prices of farm products, diverted by the attractive exchange rate from domestic consumption to export. The credits marshalled by the IMF-led consortium were not effective in cushioning this inflation, and the Yugoslav government had to request the US to send 500,000 tons of surplus wheat as higher food prices diverted consumption to the cheapest food, bread.[30] And, as to the stipulation that the reform must maintain and strengthen Yugoslavia's 'socialist' system – this was hardly compatible with a programme designed to bring price relationships more in line with those in Western European countries!

The loosening of foreign exchange restrictions and the effective revaluation of the exchange rate for industrial products not surprisingly worsened the balance of payments rather than improving it. The rise in agricultural exports was more than offset by the flood of manufactured imports, and the overall trade deficit rose by 32 per cent in 1961 over that of the previous year. In the face of this continuing deficit and the aid which financed some of it, the external debt naturally continued to rise, despite the growing importance of tourism as an 'invisible' export which offset part of the visible trade deficit.

The reforms of 1965, greeted in the West as the biggest step yet in Yugoslavia's liberalization process, were even more obviously a choice made from weakness, rather than strength, and under pressure from the West. Repayments due on Yugoslavia's foreign debt for that year alone amounted to $290 million. Internally, production suffered because the country could not afford the imported inputs necessary to keep factories running.[31]

The 1965 reform, like previous liberalization programmes, was decided upon in consultation with the IMF and the major Western creditor countries and bore a close connection with Yugoslavia's need for debt rescheduling and new credits. The main features of the new programme were:

(1) Devaluation of the dinar from 750 per dollar to 1,250:1, a change of 67 per cent downward from the old parity;

(2) Liberalization of imports of raw materials;

(3) An end to subsidies for inefficient enterprises;

(4) A rise in the percentage of net earnings which enterprises could keep for their own use, from 51 per cent to 71 per cent.

The 1965 reforms were in some respects a repetition of the 1961 package, for the government had found the social consequences of the earlier reform (unemployment, stagnation of production, and widening income disparity) so unacceptable that it had reversed several of the reform measures. In other respects the new measures were the logical extension of the earlier package, with the decentralization of investment decisions profoundly influencing the structure of domestic production. As a Yugoslav economist pointed out, if the country changes its exchange rate structure in an effort to encourage exports to Western markets, then the mechanism of internal investment must also be decontrolled to permit enterprises to adjust their production according to the incentives and pressures of foreign supply and demand.[32]

The IMF negotiators reportedly achieved a 'full identity of views' with the Yugoslav authorities on the liberalization programme,[33] but opinion within the country was not so harmonious.

There is no doubt that resistance and opposition to reform is considerable. It comes from government circles in the less developed republics, which are bound to feel the unpleasant consequences more than the better developed regions which have been pressing for reforms. It comes also from the trade unions, as unemployment, already high, is expected to increase with factories, now left to themselves, having to operate as independent economic units like any capitalist enterprise.[34]

The Yugoslav consumers showed their opinion of the reforms by withdrawing savings deposits and engaging in a spree of purchases for hoarding; an understandable reaction in light of the official (and conservative) estimate that the cost of living would rise by 24 per cent as a result of the reforms.[35] A few months after the reform, the *New York Times* printed the following vignettes on its effects:

A hotel barber who had been scraping along on a wage of $20 a month and tips quit his job and emigrated to West Germany.

An engineer who found himself paying $4 a month for his son's school supplies took the child out of kindergarten.

Housewives ... began to buy dark bread instead of the preferred white bread. Meatless meals increased by 50 per cent.

... Taverns and cafés are half empty as a result of price increases for coffee and beer. A recent cartoon in *Borba*, the party newspaper, showed four Montenegrins in a restaurant ordering 'one Turkish coffee and four cups'.[36]

As in 1961, industrial stagnation was another effect of the reforms. The rate of growth of industrial production, which had revived to a vigorous annual rate of 11 per cent after the brakes to investment were taken off in 1963, fell to 4·3 per cent in 1966, and production actually declined during the first nine months of 1967.[37] The slowdown in production and the shutdown of inefficient enterprises meant a sharp and massive rise in unemployment, but this time the authorities found a partial solution in the encouragement of labour emigration. The number of Yugoslav workers employed in the more prosperous countries of Western Europe, chiefly Germany, rose until it is now estimated to be close to one million. Yugoslavia's total population is about twenty million.

This emigrant labour made a welcome contribution to the stumbling Yugoslav economy in the form of remittances home of the strong currencies earned abroad, and this category of 'invisible' earning joined tourism as an important counterweight to the stubbornly persistent trade deficit. Sixteen years after the Yugoslavs and the Tripartite aid-givers had differed over the best way to improve the balance of trade, no solution had been found. Despite the drastic devaluation of 1965, which did increase exports, imports grew even more rapidly under the liberalized régime and the trade deficit gap increased by 25·5 per cent in 1967 over the previous year. This trade gap reflected the fact that the liberalization had made the Yugoslavs good customers for the factories of Western Europe: in the two years after the great reform, imports from Western Europe grew from 6 to 10 billion new dinars, and Western Europe's share in total Yugoslav imports grew from 30 to 50 per cent.[38] Yugoslavia had indeed become integrated into the capitalist world economy, as her technocrats had wished when they set out to join GATT, but the advantages of this integration to Yugoslavia are questionable.

By 1967, however, the process had advanced so far that none of their economists or policymakers could think of any solution except that of pushing the integration process still further. The step that was taken that year, the decision to allow the investment of foreign private capital in Yugoslav enterprises, was sensational because Yugoslavia still called itself a communist state, but it was merely symptomatic of the direction in which the country had been moving intermittently since 1950. It was less significant in its immediate effects than the previous liberalization measures.

The decision was preceded by heated debate since the leadership was by no means unanimous about the desirability of foreign investment, but the opposition was scarcely radical. Rather, the opponents of foreign private capital simply felt that Yugoslavia ought to continue to obtain the foreign exchange it needed via government loans from other governments and from the World Bank. These opponents, who were labelled 'dogmatists' by the proponents of private foreign investment, did make some thoughtful points. They argued:

(1) Western capitalism would invest only where it suited its own interests, rather than Yugoslavia's;

(2) Foreign private capital would exploit the weaknesses and imperfections of Yugoslavia's self-management system, including its regionalism and localism;

(3) The necessary distribution of income to investors which the new system implied was contrary to Marxist doctrine that labour is the source of all value;

(4) Units which received outside financing would create a privileged stratum of workers, earning perhaps several times the salaries which could be paid by native enterprises.

The 'dogmatists', criticisms were brushed aside, however, by the advocates of the new investment law, who accused them of trying to strengthen the state and take away from the producer control over the entire product of his labour! They produced the ingenious argument, derived from a reading of Marx, that Yugoslavia should take its place in the international division of labour because 'without division of labour on a world scale, the socialization of production on a world scale – which is the prerequisite for the transition from capitalism to communism – is not attainable'.[39] They pointed out that massive public loans had had little effect other than making Yugoslavia one of the seven most indebted developing countries in the world, and hoped that foreign private investment might prove a cheaper way of getting capital.[40]

When the law was passed on 25 July 1967, permitting Yugoslavian enterprises to contract with foreign partners whose participation might reach 49 per cent, the limitations on the freedom of the foreign firm made investment a not immediately attractive proposition. The most serious restriction, from a foreign investor's viewpoint, was the fact that Yugoslav firms could retain (at that time) only 7 per cent of their foreign exchange earnings; and the convertibility and repatriation of dinar earnings was likewise subject to Yugoslavian law. There was no great rush on the part of foreign investors to get in on the bonanza, perhaps in part because the economy was not at all healthy enough to be attractive. Once the principle of allowing foreign investment was admitted, however, restrictions were expected to be loosened eventually. The Western powers had learned that it paid well to get one foot in Yugoslavia's door and then wait patiently until the inherent difficulties of the situation opened the door wider. One week after the foreign investment law was adopted by the Yugoslav parliament, the World Bank approved a $10·5 million loan to that country to cover the foreign exchange cost of investments to modernize several industrial enterprises. The *Financial Times* of London remarked that, although the World Bank had lent a total of $210 million to Yugoslavia before, 'The loans up to now have been for infrastructure projects – dams, power stations, roads, railways, etc. A loan for manufacturing industry represents a definite change of policy either on the part of Yugoslavia or of the World Bank'.[41] The question may be raised: Was there a *quid pro quo*?

Nothing sufficed to stop the cycle of deficit and debt, however, and in 1971 yet another 'stabilization' programme, supported with credits from the IMF and from Yugoslavia's Western trading partners, was necessary. This programme contained most of the features that had become depressingly familiar from previous ones: increases in the administered prices of oil, electricity, and railway, postal, and telephone services; credit restrictions so stringent that tens of thousands of workers could not be paid because the banks would not cover their company payrolls; and another devaluation. This last step, establishing the new rate of 15 new dinars to the dollar (a new dinar was worth 100 of the old), meant that the dinar was now worth, in dollars, only 20 per cent of what it had been when the IMF first helped the Yugoslavs select a 'realistic' rate in

January 1952. Despite or because of these measures, in 1971
the cost of living rose by 17 per cent and the trade deficit
reached the astronomical figure of $1,500 million for that one
year. Tourism and remittances from Yugoslav workers in
Western Europe – 'invisible' exports of the type supplied by
poor countries to rich ones – made up most of the trade deficit,
but a balance of payments gap of $318 million remained even
then.[42]

More than twenty years after Western aid to Yugoslavia began, the country is more dependent on external financing than
ever. With a total external debt which was estimated at $2·5
billion in early 1972, Yugoslavia had to contract more loans for
the specific purpose of debt service.[43] Only a small proportion
of this massive borrowing has been used for investment; most
has gone to finance consumption and operating capital imports,
as the original aid agreement of 1952 had intended.

The internal consequences for Yugoslavian society of this
external dependence have been profound. The leadership's decision (if it was entirely their own decision) to create a new sort
of communism based on enterprise autonomy and regional decentralization has resulted in a type of development that
resembles capitalism in every respect except in the existence of
a frankly capitalist class owning the largest enterprises. The fact
that enterprises are permitted to retain a portion of their accounting 'profit' for distribution to employees as a supplement
to wages permitted the growth of profound inequalities of income between individuals, enterprises, and regions of the country. This has been deliberate policy. The IMF team which visited
Yugoslavia in 1951 said in its report: 'The authors of the new
system consider that, in order to create work incentives, and
incentives for improving the standard of education, there has to
be a considerably greater differentiation of individual earnings.'[44] It is unlikely, however, that the Yugoslav leadership
would have approved this principle in 1951 if they could have
foreseen how far away from equality it was eventually to lead
them, for they have shown the vestiges of socialist conscious-
ness in an intermittent reluctance to permit the social consequences of liberalism to take their course. The IMF, on the

other hand, has used every opportunity to encourage extension of the principle of self-management, particularly in decision-making about prices and investment, and has consistently pressed the Yugoslavs to let enterprises keep a large proportion of their earnings, both in dinars and foreign exchange. In its enthusiasm for workers' control (or more accurately, for decentralization, which is not the same thing) the IMF has been more enthusiastic than the Yugoslavs themselves.

There are some genuine capitalists in Yugoslavia, although they are not permitted to employ more than a few workers, but the system has fostered the growth of a much more significant 'new' class which does have a personal pecuniary interest in Western-style liberalization of the economy. This class consists of the managers and skilled employees and, to a lesser extent, the entire working force of enterprises which are relatively efficient and thus are the beneficiaries of uneven development. The Yugoslav League of Communists has itself become a spokesman for this class, particularly in the wealthier republics, whose administrations likewise benefit from decentralization measures.

There is, of course, necessarily a disadvantaged counterpart to this privileged class: the unskilled workers, the less efficient enterprises, the backward regions of the nation. The unemployment problem, only partially resolved by the export of Yugoslav labour, has already been mentioned. It has been estimated that one-third of all workers receive salaries which are below the subsistence minimum, and one can read in a Western newspaper that 'the stark contrasts between conspicuous consumption and the low living standard of large segments of the working class inflames social tensions, particularly in the large cities'.[45]

In other respects Yugoslavia resembles a capitalist society. Advertising and a rudimentary stock exchange have made their appearance. Banks and export finance companies, insurance and foreign trade firms are the major centres of economic power.[46] Western tourists provide more examples of conspicuous consumption out of the reach of most Yugoslavs.

The disparity in income among the different republics, as

the constituent states of Yugoslavia are called – deserves special attention because of the critical political problem that Croatian separatism has become in recent years. The nationhood of Yugoslavia has always been more of a hopeful aspiration than a reality, as regional loyalties have remained strong. The northeastern states of Croatia and Slovenia, closest to Western Europe in every sense, are the efficient and prosperous ones, while Montenegro, Bosnia-Herzegovina, and the Province of Kosovo are notably poor and undeveloped. Macedonia and Serbia occupy an intermediate position, but the latter has a special status since natives of that area have, in the past as in the present, tended to dominate politics and administration.

When the Communist Party took power, one of the purposes of the planned economy which it set up initially was to narrow the economic differentiation among regions which prevented the emergence of a genuine national loyalty. The centrally planned economy, as orignally erected, could work to counteract inequalities by directing investment to underdeveloped regions and diverting resources from surplus areas to poor ones. The inevitable effect of decentralization, however, was to reverse this process by letting the more prosperous and efficient enterprises, and regions, keep a larger part of their earnings. The IMF encouraged this trend by frowning on investments which were determined by any other than market criteria, and possibly had a direct hand in abolishing the first agency set up for promoting development in poorer regions. The Yugoslav government has never disavowed the principle that the poor provinces must be aided, but the logic of decentralized planning and control over resources means in practice that the funds available for redistribution have dwindled to a pittance in recent years. As a result, the income differential between regions has widened, rather than narrowed, over time. In 1971 Slovenia, the richest republic, had a per capita income of S1,000 while the poorest unit, Kosovo, had only $240.[47]

It is, however, not the poorest regions that are currently making trouble, but Croatia, which has become one of the richest because it has profited from the tourist boom. The demand to

139

retain most or all of the foreign exchange within the republic has been one of the fundamental planks of Croatian separatism. The federal government has made important concessions to this demand, notably in the form of separate regulations for the tourism industry which allow firms in that field to keep a much higher percentage of their foreign exchange earnings than other enterprises; and in a new constitution introduced in 1971, which allows the republics to keep and spend for themselves almost all their foreign exchange earnings.

Such concessions, however, seem only to embolden the Croatians to more extreme demands, including total independence (which would allow them to keep *all* their foreign exchange earnings). This arrogance is resented by the other republics, who point out that Croatia is dependent upon supplies from other parts of the nation. A Macedonian businessman retorted to the Croats, 'We demand foreign exchange for our tomatoes, salad greens, and fruits!' Enterprises in other republics announced that they might demand foreign exchange for supplying Croatia with furniture, copper, charcoal, lead, maize, etc. The Bosnians even asked why they should not be paid in foreign exchange for damage to their roads caused by tourists driving through.[48] This irony has not amused the Croatian nationalists, who continue to press their demands at home and abroad, sometimes by terrorist means and reportedly even through the resuscitation of the wartime fascist organization, the Ustase.

Yugoslavia is presently in a serious crisis which can be traced both directly and indirectly to the economic decisions we have discussed. The stabilization programme for 1971 has been succeeded by those for 1972 and 1973, and in June 1973, in the face of a rapidly deteriorating economic situation, there was an open admission from the highest body of the Yugoslavian Communist League that the stabilization programme had failed.

In September 1972 Tito published a warning against what he perceived to be three enemies of Yugoslav society: the nationalists, the technocrats, and the liberals. It was a strange group of bedfellows, particularly since one group, the liberals, would seem from their published declarations to be sincere critics of the excesses of the other two categories, the nationalists and technocrats, both of which have been strengthened by the 'liberal' economic reforms.

The double use of the term 'liberal' in both its economic and political meanings, is particularly poignant at this time in Yugoslavia, where for two decades the two senses of the word did seem to bear an intrinsic relationship as political and cultural liberalism advanced in step with, and seemingly in a necessary relationship with, economic liberalization.

In the present troubles, however, Tito has sundered the relationship and inverted it. Faced with internal dissension, he has chosen to press ahead with economic liberalization while condemning political liberalization as the source of his troubles. Although he has also blamed the inequality of incomes and the persistence of social injustice, he has taken no concrete steps to correct those ills. Until he does, his pronouncements on that theme need to be taken no more seriously than the similar warnings of Robert S. McNamara, president of the World Bank, with respect to Brazil and India.* At the moment of writing, political repression seemed to be Tito's sole answer to the crisis of Yugoslavian society.

This account has made it easier to understand why the IMF has been able to cooperate so long and so cordially with a communist state. Through the adoption of 'market socialism' the Yugoslavs have gradually reproduced many of the features of a capitalistic society, and the development they have achieved has been as dependent on foreign capital as that of most Third World countries. The outcome of events suggests that the IMF was more prescient, in the formative years of the Yugoslav system in 1951–2, than the Yugoslav communists themselves.

The initial decision to substitute production for profit for central planning and socialist incentives as the driving force of the economy produced its own vested interests, which subsequently joined in alliance with Western creditors and the IMF to enlarge the scope of the market in later reforms. It seems likely that the Western aid-givers applauded enterprise decen-

*See chapters 7 and 8.

tralization because it provided an opening wedge for movement away from a planned economy and towards a market economy of the type they understood and could more easily penetrate. While the Western powers have consistently pressed for *more* enterprise autonomy, the Yugoslav authorities seem to have had occasional, though ultimately futile, second thoughts about the wisdom of relinquishing central control.

To what extent was the original decision the result of outside pressure, or of their own inclinations, or a combination of both? Present evidence does not allow us to give definite answers to these questions, or to separate the real reason for the adoption of the system from the rationalizations and the incidental effects. It can hardly be denied, however, that the initial step had profound and probably not foreseen consequences.

'I have also been struck,' writes a student of Yugoslav economic thought, 'by the extent to which a single change can have broad consequences ...'

As more socialist countries attain levels of development at which Soviet-type planning of the classic form no longer seems appropriate, they are likely to experiment with economic reforms. The ultimate consequences of these reforms are not yet known but the Yugoslav experience suggests that the results may be more far-reaching than the reformers either intended or anticipated.[49]

The socialist writer Paul Sweezy came to similar conclusions from his study of Yugoslavia:

Beware of the market: it is capitalism's secret weapon! Comprehensive planning is the heart and core of genuine socialism! ... [M]arket relations must be strictly supervised and controlled lest, like a metastasizing cancer, they get out of hand and fatally undermine the health of the socialist body politic.[50]

As the IMF mission reported, approvingly, in 1952, 'It is difficult to imagine that the development of the new system could be stopped.'[51]

7

The Destruction of Democracy in Brazil

Brazil, like Indonesia, is one of the few 'success stories' claimed by the IMF. After a strong and bitter dose of stabilization policies applied by the military government in the mid-1960s, Brazil has in recent years experienced a remarkable economic boom and claimed in 1971 the distinction of being the fastest growing economy in the world. In contrast to most other Third World countries, its exports are leaping ahead, with manufactures as an ever-growing proportion of the expanding total, about 30 per cent in 1972. Could Brazil then be considered as a model of how poor countries can develop within the framework of international capitalism? This chapter will suggest some answers to that question.

The first point which should be made is that it is Brazil's stagnation and the fact that its per capita income is still very low which has to be explained – not its growth. Brazil dominates the South American continent in area. Its rapidly growing population of 100,000,000 makes it the second most important market in the Western hemisphere even though, due to the maldistribution of income, only a minority of that population can be considered in the market for consumer goods. Its natural wealth is breathtaking. Its agricultural potential has never been fully developed because of its inequitable and uneconomic land distribution system, but it encompasses grain and livestock farming as well as the plantation crops of coffee, cocoa, sugar, cotton, and tobacco which still dominate its export structure.

Its mineral wealth is still more astonishing. It is known to have the largest deposits of high-grade iron ore in the world; the world's largest deposits of antimony and quartz crystals (used in electronic and optical equipment); possibly the biggest tin reserves in the world; huge quantities of manganese, bauxite, and uranium ores.[1]

In terms of natural wealth, it is surely Brazil which is the 'have' and Japan the 'have-not'. This is the significant factor behind the loans and investments which Japan (and other developed countries) send to Brazil – not, certainly, disinterested charity nor an impulse to share technology. Further, the past forty years have shown that Brazilian entrepreneurs are agile, aggressive, and quick to seize on any opportunities which are offered for profitable investment. If Brazil's *per capita* GNP is still one of the lowest in Latin America, one must seek the causes elsewhere.

Like the rest of Latin America, Brazil has been subjected for centuries to the commercial needs of foreign powers – first Portugal as the colonizing power, then England in the nineteenth century and the Yankee colossus in the twentieth. Up to the 1930s, most educated and influential Brazilians accepted Brazil's situation as exporter of raw materials and importer of consumer goods as the natural order of things. The Depression, however, was a bitter shock as Brazil's export markets and earnings collapsed and also, therefore, its ability to import the consumer goods desired by the upper classes. Spontaneous 'import substitution' industries grew up to fill the gap. Equally important, many Brazilians began to question the wisdom of depending so completely on the external market, and to adopt a new ideology of economic development.[2]

The Second World War followed the Depression. The market for Brazil's exports revived but imports were unobtainable because the rich countries were diverting all their production to war needs. The 'import substitution' industrialization continued, and Brazil's export earnings accumulated in its holdings of reserves.

Yet after the war these reserves were dissipated without any lasting benefit to the nation. A new government devoted to economic liberalization abolished exchange and import controls in 1946; the result was a flood of consumer goods imports which emptied the treasury within a year and a half. When the reserves were exhausted the government met the crisis by licensing imports rather than by devaluation. Although import licensing was, at first, merely a reaction to the exchange crisis,

Brazilian policymakers soon realized they had stumbled upon a powerful incentive for a new wave of import substitution and began to apply exchange controls as a conscious form of protection for Brazilian industry. The 'law of similars' protected existing industries by discriminating against the import of products 'similar' to those that were being produced, or could be produced, in Brazil.[3] Exporters, at that time mainly the coffee-planting élite, were subjected through the overvalued exchange rate to a high tax on their dollar earnings.

However, even then no real effort was made to order priorities so that resources – particularly scarce foreign exchange – could be channelled to the highest priority sectors. As in most 'import substitution' situations, industries grew up indiscriminately, without regard to Brazil's potential comparative advantage or the real needs of its people. These industries produced chiefly those consumer goods which had previously been imported but it was not asked whether the country would actually save foreign exchange in the long run – or whether the nation should be consuming such goods at all.[4]

The import licensing system also displayed its characteristic vulnerability to corruption. The favourable exchange rate, justified as a 'subsidy to industry', gave the licences a market value which was two to three times their official price, and soon a black market in licences developed. This meant that a substantial proportion of the 'subsidy' was diverted to high profit consumer imports, and to the pockets of exchange officials who might be bribed to issue licences contrary to the rules.[5] These defects of the system, and particularly the fact that more imports were licensed than Brazil had the exchange to pay for, created another crisis in 1952, and the system was changed to one of 'exchange auctions'. Under this system, which lasted for eight years, the government allotted a fixed sum of foreign exchange to each of several different categories of imports, from those considered most essential to luxury goods. This exchange was auctioned off to the importers willing to pay the highest price for it. Through this system the traders were forced to pay a higher price for the privilege to import, thus reducing their windfall profits and diverting the extra cruzeiros into the government treasury. The effect was a multiple exchange rate system, with the rate within each category determined by supply and demand.

Also in 1953, limitations on the remittance of profits and dividends by foreign companies were removed, which gladdened foreign investors considerably even though the exchange rate for such remittances became much less favourable. The exchange controls, which limited profit remittances to a percentage of capital invested, irritated foreign investors who would have liked unlimited freedom to take their profits out of the country. Having no hope of achieving that from the Brazilian government, however, they concentrated instead on insisting that *reinvested* profit should be added on to the amount of capital which had been originally brought in, so that future remittances would be higher when figured as a percentage of a higher total investment.

Despite the irritations caused to foreign investors by exchange restrictions and by inflation which became a chronic problem in the 1950s, the size of Brazil's population and its booming economy made the country too attractive to resist. Most of the foreign investment was, in fact, made by companies which had previously supplied imports to Brazil and, in the face of import restrictions, had to build factories within the country in order to hang on to their market. When Brazilian laws made trade more difficult, these companies established 'tariff-jumping' industries and took advantage of the new incentives offered to import substitution industries.[6]

The economy was certainly booming: for the decade of the 1950s Brazil's per capita growth was three times that of the rest of Latin America.[7] And yet this growth had flaws and limitations which made both the economy and the political system inherently unstable. Brazil provides one of the clearest examples of how a democratic political system may prove unequal to the difficult challenge posed by the foreign exchange constraint. For more than a decade – from the exchange crisis and reform of 1952–3 until the assumption of power by the military in April 1964 – Brazilian presidents ricochetted helplessly back and forth trying to reconcile conflicting imperatives which were in

146

fact insoluble within the limits of that political system. No president was able to solve it: Vargas committed suicide, Kubitschek completed his term with apparent success but bequeathed the crisis to his successors; Quadros resigned after eight months; Goulart was deposed. It is important to understand the nature of the dilemma which defeated them all.

The boom of the 1950s rested on two economic conditions which made it untenable over the long run. The first was that of a chronic trade deficit: the sum of the balance of payments deficits for the decade amounted to $2·5 billion. The deficit was financed by direct foreign investment and by borrowing, both of which eventually required a reverse flow of exchange.

The second condition was inflation. Brazilian 'structuralist' economists have argued that inflation is unavoidable in the process of development, which as a general proposition is dubious. It does seem, however, that in the particular Brazilian conditions any anti-inflationary programme has severely depressive effects on production. Equally important, inflation played an important political role. In a situation where capitalists, coffee planters, the middle class, and the urban working class were mobilized voting components of the political system, inflation allowed politicians to evade choices about the real distribution of resources by giving everyone a larger supply of money. The fault, it must be noted, does not lie only with the presidents who draw most of the attention. Congress had the habit of voting for subsidies to coffee growers, for a higher minimum wage, etc., without worrying whether these statutory expenditures could be covered by new revenue; the presidents were left to cope with the resulting financial dilemmas, and to draw the political fire if they attempted to reduce anyone's share of the (depreciating) money. Since nearly every president was elected by a 'populist' coalition of voters spanning class lines, the party system itself discouraged strategies that might put any significant group at a disadvantage. And when inflation seemed to be fuelling an economic growth rate that was one of the highest in the world, the only constraint was the external one: balance of payments pressures and the disapproval of the nation's creditors.

Each of several abortive stabilization efforts of the 1950s was frustrated by the internal political situation and the fear of a depression. The first efforts were made by President Getulio Vargas' government, simultaneously with the exchange reforms of 1953. The tight credit policies were unpopular with business-men, however, and Vargas complained by the end of the year that the 'free exchange market has proved itself an inadequate instrument' to improve Brazil's balance of payments. Finally Vargas torpedoed his own stabilization programme by decree-ing a 100 per cent increase in the minimum wage. Four months later, on the point of his ouster by the military, Vargas com-mitted suicide, leaving a message to the country which accused the international cartels of allying with anti-worker Brazilian groups to cause his downfall.

The 'caretaker' government of Café Filho made another at-tempt to cope with the inflation problem and to satisfy Brazil's foreign creditors. His first effort resulted in a drastic constric-tion of credit which closed several banks and sent industrialists into a panic. The Finance Minister resigned (the position of Finance Minister was even more perilous than that of Presi-dent). He was replaced by another who relaxed the credit re-strictions and planned another exchange reform, in close consultation with the IMF, which would have given coffee growers the full amount in cruzeiros of their export earnings. Café Filho, however, hesitated to sacrifice the government's leverage over the distribution of foreign exchange, and decided not to bind his successor government to so drastic a change.[8]

His successor was Juscelino Kubitschek, who accelerated Brazil's growth but indebted the country further in the process. The Kubitschek government did make an effort to plan Brazil's further industrialization, rather than leaving it to the hap-hazard process of spontaneous import substitution. Like the presidents before him, however, he made no serious effort to reduce Brazil's overall dependence on a high level of imports, or to devise an export policy to counteract the stagnation in that sector. Rather, he embarked on a policy of 'determined external indebtedness' to fill the foreign exchange gap in his plans.

In 1958 it became necessary, in order to secure a $300 million loan from the United States, to come to an agreement with the International Monetary Fund on stabilization measures. Kubitschek was at first confident that this could be achieved, and a stabilization plan was drafted by his Finance Minister, Lucas Lopes, and the director of the National Bank for Economic Planning, Roberto Campos. But Kubitschek soon ran into the same political difficulties which had frustrated previous administrations. The President of the Bank of Brazil refused to go along with the credit squeeze which threatened to cause a depression in the private sector. The coffee growers protested when the coffee purchase programme was cut back. Kubitschek's own plan targets and his goal of eliminating structural bottlenecks in the economy would have been threatened if public expenditures were cut back significantly enough to make a dent in the inflation. Radical nationalists accused him of selling the country to the US and the IMF.

After floundering around for several months with half-way measures that never went far enough to satisfy the IMF, Kubitschek broke off negotiations and gave up hope of the American loan. This gesture of defiance won him great admiration both inside and outside Brazil, and he completed his term of office in triumph. He managed to obtain the necessary foreign financing by means of short-term high-cost borrowing from private sources abroad.[9] His successor, Jânio Quadros, inherited the bitter fruit of Kubitschek's economic boom and his resistance to the IMF: a full-scale debt repayment crisis that could no longer be postponed.

Quadros immediately came to terms with the IMF and the foreign creditors. He saw no choice. 'We have spent,' he told the nation in his inaugural speech, 'drawing on our future to a greater extent than the imagination dares to contemplate.' Two billion dollars of Brazil's foreign debt was due for repayment during his term of office, $600 million in the first year alone.

Quadros reformed the exchange system, abolishing the exchange auctions and substituting for them a simpler dual exchange rate. 'Necessary' imports and invisible transactions would take place at a preferred rate which represented an effective devaluation of the cruzeiro by 50 per cent; all other transactions would be handled on the free market. It was a long step towards the ideal of the IMF, which announced its approval of the reform 'on the understanding that they are not final and that further efforts will be made to simplify Brazil's multiple exchange system'.[10] The Vice-President, João Goulart (who had been independently elected on another party's ticket) condemned the reform as 'bowing to' the IMF.[11] In July the preferential rate was abolished and all exchange transactions were to take place at the free market rate.

On the strength of this performance, the Quadros government succeeded in negotiating new credits and rescheduling payments on the old ones in negotiations with the US and its European creditors. Inflation still raged, however, and although Quadros limited credit once again, he too began to feel the political counterpressures which had weakened the resolve of past Brazilian presidents. His term of office was cut short after only eight months by his sudden resignation. There seemed to be no compelling reason for the resignation; it is likely that this was a gesture intended to strengthen his hand against opponents, which he did not seriously expect the legislature to accept. They did, however; and after some hesitation Goulart was installed as President.

Jânio Quadros had attracted international attention because of his efforts to chart a foreign policy for Brazil which was moderately independent from that of the United States. He refused to support US hostility towards Fidel Castro's Cuba (which he visited in 1960, before his election); he sent trade missions to communist countries and showed considerable affinity for 'neutralist' Third World nations such as India, Egypt, and Yugoslavia. To a public accustomed to cold war rhetoric, he seemed to be defying the colossus to the north. As a result, when he resigned leaving an ambiguous accusation against his enemies (reminiscent of Vargas' suicide note), leftists within and outside the country were quick to blame the CIA for his departure. The Soviet press agency *Tass* charged that he had been compelled to quit by US economic pressure (which was perhaps true in an oblique sense, though not in the usual one); and Fidel Castro blamed 'imperialism's paw' for the resignation.[12]

It should be apparent from our survey of economic policy that this was highly unlikely. Quadros had, in fact, been the American government's last hope of bringing the desired monetary stability to Brazil within a democratic framework. He had been invited to visit Washington later that year, before his resignation made the invitation irrelevant. As a London newspaper remarked with some bemusement, 'Senhor Quadros so far has had remarkably tolerant acceptance from American officials and newspapers normally hypersensitive to any increase in Communist bloc influence in the hemisphere.'[13] There was really no reason to doubt the *New York Times'* assessment of the mood of the US State Department upon his resignation as 'one of fear that the departure of President Quadros from Brazil's political scene, if it is not reversed, would plunge the country into serious political difficulties threatening its stability and interfering with the financial and economic stabilization programme'.[14] Goulart, whose political strength came from his close ties with the unions he had fostered as Minister of Labour under Vargas, was to the left of the spectrum of Brazilian politics. If Quadros could not carry through his stabilization programme, there seemed even less to hope for from Goulart in that respect.

During the Goulart presidency the contradictions inherent in Brazil's post-war development strategy reached the breaking point. To make matters worse, the high growth rate of the 1950s, which had helped to moderate social tensions, had levelled off by 1962. Explanations were sought for this economic stagnation. A crude one offered by the US Government and superficial journalism blamed Goulart's leftist tendencies, but he had inherited the accumulated problems of fifteen years of inflation and foreign borrowing which none of his predecessors had tackled successfully. A sophisticated explanation was offered by the 'structuralist' economists on the United Nations Economic Commission for Latin America (ECLA). They reasoned that Brazil had reached the natural limits of its import substitution policy, and that the bottleneck could be

151

broken only by widening the market by improving the income of poorer sectors of the population through structural reforms such as land redistribution. Another hypothesis held that over-investment by both foreign and domestic capitalists in the euphoria of the Kubitschek boom years had resulted in excess capacity and a cyclical depression.

Less attention has been given to the effects of foreign trade and exchange policies, although the continued high import dependence of the Brazilian economy (despite its successful 'import substitution' growth) suggests that attention is needed. To my knowledge, no study has been published of the effects of the important 1961 exchange reform on the speed and direction of economic growth, although common sense, and the experience of other countries, would indicate that there must have been some effect.

The last serious attempt at stabilization under the democratic system was made in 1963: the Three Year Plan of Minister for Economic Planning, Celso Furtado and Minister of Finance, San Thiago Dantas. This plan emphasized the importance of resuming a high rate of growth and of carrying out tax and agrarian reforms while simultaneously curbing inflation. It, like all previous stabilization plans, was designed with one eye on Washington in the hope of securing the approval of the IMF, a condition for new credits and/or deferral of the crushing foreign debt repayment burden, which if not deferred or repudiated would eat up 45 per cent of Brazil's export earnings. An exchange reform and devaluation in January 1963 repeated Quadros' 1961 reform, since exchange subsidies on the import of wheat and petroleum (both basic items in the cost of living) had been reintroduced and had to be abolished once again to satisfy the IMF. Restrictions on the budget deficit, on the expansion of credit, and on wage increases completed the standard list of items for an inflation control programme.

Dantas travelled to Washington in the hope of securing new aid, where he and Brazilian Ambassador Roberto Campos engaged in hard bargaining with a sceptical US government. At one point the two Brazilians, disappointed by the hard conditions and meagre support they encountered from the US and the IMF, considered breaking off the negotiations and mobilizing Brazilians for an austerity programme which would enable the country to survive without foreign aid. Their reasons for rejecting this course of action were significant:

> Dantas and Campos concluded that Brazil could not risk relying on her own resources alone because the government lacked 'sufficient cohesion', and because Brazilian nationalism was too shallow to generate the necessary political support for the resulting austerity. In effect, they were admitting to themselves the severe political limitations that Brazilian democracy placed on the mobilization of *domestic* resources for economic development.[15]

Dantas finally signed an agreement with AID director David Bell for a total of $398·5 million, but its release was dependent on Brazil's sticking to the agreed stabilization programme.

The Dantas-Furtado programme ran into problems back home that were similar to those besetting every such attempt in the past. This time the failure of the programme was signalled by the Goulart government's inability to hold the line on wages. A 70 per cent pay rise for government employees, including the military, was under consideration. The government was caught in a squeeze between, on the one hand, the two groups – civil servants and the military – whose loyalty was instrumental to its own exercise of power, and, on the other hand, the need to continue the stabilization programme so foreign credits would continue flowing in. It was the stabilization programme which gave way. The US suspended its aid disbursements.

American officials thereafter did not try to hide their hostility towards Goulart. This was not due solely to the inflation which was now raging unchecked at the rate of 100 per cent a year, but also to some defiantly nationalistic actions taken by the Goulart government against American-owned corporations in Brazil, and specifically to the Profit Remittance Law. In 1962 Goulart signed a law sent to him by Congress which infuriated foreign investors, and the American ambassador, by providing that profit remittances could be calculated only on the amount of capital originally brought into the country, and not on the

153

(much larger) unremitted past profits which had been reinvested in Brazil. The conservative Octavio Gouvêa de Bulhões resigned his post as Director of the Superintendency of Currency and Credit to emphasize his disagreement with this slap against foreign investment. Foreign companies with large profits in cruzeiros found themselves unable to send most of their profits abroad.[16]

The US indicated its distaste for Goulart in numerous ways, but primarily through its aid policy. It did not merely cut off aid to the central government, refusing all budgetary and balance-of-payments support that would benefit Goulart directly. It continued giving aid to certain conservative state governors with whom it thought it could do business – the so-called 'islands of sanity' strategy. This ploy was aimed at keeping a foothold in Brazilian politics despite Goulart, and most probably also intended to encourage the subversion of the Goulart government. (Testimony of US officials to Congressional committees on this subject is laced with security deletions.)[17]

Goulart had the worst of all worlds as a result of his ambivalence about aid and stabilization. He earned the criticism of nationalists for bowing to the will of international agencies, and the enmity of pressure groups who resented being asked to bear the costs of stabilization; but he was so irresolute in the face of these domestic pressures that his foreign creditors gave up on him and more or less overtly opposed his government. In early 1964, with inflation soaring even higher, he made a desperate last-ditch attempt to placate his creditors. A three-man IMF team spent two weeks in Brazil discussing still another exchange reform – this one again scarcely regaining the ground lost (in terms of IMF desires) since the last one a year before – and the rescheduling of the foreign debt. This time the US indicated that Goulart would have to come to terms with his European creditors first, so negotiations were begun to that end in March. They had little hope of success, however, since in mid-March Goulart shifted his ground in an attempt to meet the demands of the Brazilian left. He announced that in response to the growing waves of rural agitation by peasant leagues, large tracts of private land would be subject to expro-

priation and redistribution. He announced also the nationalization of all private oil refineries in Brazil, and indicated that
more radical measures would follow.

Given the situation which already existed of both domestic
and international hostility to Goulart, this adoption of a leftist
strategy was more effective in mobilizing his rightist enemies
than in inspiring potential left supporters. The military acted
quickly to depose Goulart, and the generals decided to form
their own caretaker government. Although they announced
their intention of restoring civilian government within a reasonable period, subsequent events have shown that the overthrow
of João Goulart put an end to the democratic constitution of
Brazil which had been in effect since 1946.

The destruction of democracy in Brazil was not the result of
voter ignorance or apathy. Rather, it was evidence of the im-
possibility of serving two masters: of reconciling voter and
pressure group demands – theoretically the lifeblood of a democratic system – with the external economic constraint, expressed in the form of pressure from Brazil's creditors. But, as
the final act showed, failure to conform to those pressures,
which resulted in a cut-off of aid and curtailment of imports,
was equally unacceptable to non-democratic pressure groups,
including the military. The solution of the economic question,
which to them meant primarily the resumption of foreign aid,
was the chief objective of the military government as their first
actions and appointments demonstrate.

The haste with which the United States moved to con-
gratulate, recognize, and send aid to the new military leaders of
Brazil was embarrassing even to their sympathizers. Goulart
was overthrown on 1 April 1964, the recognition and con-
gratulations followed the next day, and by 5 April the *New
York Times* reported that 'the ouster of the Goulart régime
has made a financial rescue operation possible for Brazil',
since Goulart had become 'an obstacle to negotiation and extension of Brazil's towering debt'.[18] According to the later
testimony of the deputy US coordinator of the Alliance for
Progress, Brazil's need was urgent:

... [I]n 1964, the Brazilian government foreign exchange reserves were depleted. In fact they had $300 million of current bills, not loans, not credit but current bills unpaid, mainly to US companies. So without this US aid, without these programme loans, there would have had to have been extreme belt-tightening on important imports. I am not talking about consumer goods, perfumes and racehorses and the like, I am talking about basic industrial raw materials which would have resulted in a severe recession. They would have had no option; otherwise their international credit rating would have been ruined.[19]

The new military government headed by General Castello Branco did its best to meet the expectations of the United States. The key ministries of Finance and Planning went to Octavio Bulhões (who had resigned in protest over the nationalistic profit remittance law of Goulart's government) and Roberto Campos (who had designed several of the abortive stabilization programmes of the past). In May these two simplified the exchange system once again, abolishing the import subsidies on wheat and petroleum. The policy was introduced against the wishes of Castello Branco's political advisers, who warned that the resulting price rises for bread and transport would make the new government unpopular. United States and IMF officials, however, approvingly called the action 'an indispensable step towards slowing down Brazil's violent inflation'.[20] Equally significant, by August the restrictive profit remittance law (which although passed in 1962 had only begun to be implemented that year) was revoked before it could do any serious harm to foreign capitalists. With the change, reinvested profits could once again be calculated in the 'capital base' figure on which allowable profit remittance was figured.

This compliance on the part of the Brazilian rulers was met by immediate and substantial aid from the World Bank, which had had nothing to do with Brazil since the early Kubitschek years; the IMF, which in January 1965 concluded its first standby agreement with Brazil since the one with Quadros in 1961; and new credits and debt rescheduling from US, European, and Japanese creditors. Between 1964 and 1968 US aid to Brazil totalled about $1·6 billion, an amount which USAID officials judged 'has allowed Brazil to avoid a very hard choice between higher growth rates and inflation'.

I think it is clear that if they had not had this enormous amount of outside assistance, largely from the United States, they would have been faced with a very difficult dilemma of tightening up the economy, tightening up credit, government expenditures, imports, which would have resulted in a serious recession in Brazil; or, on the other hand, attempting to maintain a higher growth but incurring a continued high rate of inflation ...[21]

Brazilians would probably be surprised at this statement, since most of them thought that they did experience a serious recession during the three Castello Branco years (1964–7). The number of bankruptcies and receiverships in São Paulo, Brazil's leading industrial city, in the two years 1966 and 1967 totalled 1,500 or about four times the number in 1962 and 1963; many of these companies, defeated by tight credit and reduced protection from imports, were forced to sell out to foreign competitors. The latter, for their part, showed little inclination to establish new enterprises in conditions of recession.[22] Industrial production fell by 7 per cent in 1965.

Success in controlling inflation was relative rather than absolute. Although the runaway acceleration in the rate of inflation of the Goulart years was halted, living costs increased in 1965 by 45 per cent (according to the Getúlio Vargas Foundation) or 60 per cent (according to the Ministry of Labour), and the following year the consumer price index rose by another 40 per cent.[23]

This relative success was made possible not only by a credit policy which squeezed the life out of many Brazilian companies, but also by a deliberate policy of repressing workers. The voting power of the working class was, of course, rendered irrelevant by the suspension of electoral politics. Beyond that, the most powerful unions were dissolved. If this could be partially justified by reference to past abuses (it was reported, for example, that members of the highly paid stevedores' union auctioned off their actual work responsibilities to other, less fortunate workers at a much lower rate of pay) the régime

157

demonstrated that it was not about to tolerate pressure from any group of workers. As a future American ambassador admitted, 'The right to bargain collectively is so restricted as to be of negligible importance. The right to strike legally virtually does not exist.'[24] Leaders of trade unions, and of the rural peasant leagues, were imprisoned, and many suffered the torture which has been well documented as a feature of Brazilian prisons under military rule. Although the continuing inflation made some sort of wage adjustment necessary, the new policy of the military government deliberately kept wage increases *below* the rise in the cost of living, so that real wages declined steadily.

It is interesting that despite the suspension of the democratic political process, and despite the warm *rapprochement* with the United States and other creditors, the same struggles continued in a muted form after 1964 as before. Within Brazil, the stabilization measures were so unpopular that the military's initial seizure of power had to be followed by progressively more blatant attacks on any semblance of democratic politics. Although state elections were permitted in 1965, the results showed such dissatisfaction with the military government that a Second Institutional Act (the first was that by which the military had initially seized power) re-organized the political parties and decreed that the election of Castello Branco's successor in 1966 would be indirect, by Congress, rather than direct, by the voters. In that election Congress docilely approved the choice of the military, General Costa e Silva, as President; Skidmore reports that continuation of the stabilization programme was 'the one issue on which Castello Branco demanded a commitment' from his successor.[25]

If Costa e Silva actually gave such a commitment, he did not honour it. There continued to be strong disagreement over the desirability of a drastic stabilization programme, both between the US and its new Brazilian allies and within the Brazilian ruling class itself. In the first months of the military government the IMF had reportedly criticized Brazilian efforts as 'weak', and urged more drastic action; while Campos and Bulhões argued for a 'gradual' attack on inflation, fearing that full-scale conformity with IMF wishes would wreck the economy completely. They put the blame for their failure to effect social reforms on IMF pressure for a tight credit policy.[26]

The United States used its large programme loans to the central government as the instrument for dictating Brazilian policies on exchange rates, taxes, the budget and monetary credit, using the multilateral Inter-American Committee of the Alliance for Progress as a facade to give the bargaining the appearance of an agreement made between equals. The US released its aid money subject to quarterly reviews of Brazilian performance on the major economic guidelines, and a half-year suspension of aid in 1967 proved that these reviews were no mere formality.[27]

The suspension of aid in 1967 was connected to disagreements within the Brazilian élite about the virtues of the stabilization programme. While Campos and Bulhões were pressured by the US and IMF to take stronger measures, they were being criticized by the Brazilian bourgeoisie for the depression caused by the steps they *had* taken. The new President, (General) Costa e Silva, ignoring his pledge to Castello Branco to continue the stabilization efforts, appointed as Minister of Finance Antonio Delfim Neto, who had publicly criticized the Campos policies and stressed the need to revive economic production. He was a spokesman of the São Paulo industrialists and met their demands for easier credit, against the advice of the US and IMF. Because of this departure from the more 'orthodox' stabilization programme of Roberto Campos, aid was suspended but the economy revived.[28]

AID payments were resumed in 1968, only to be halted again pending a review at the end of the year. The occasion for this review was provided by yet another repressive 'Institutional Act', this one dissolving Brazil's Congress. The testimony of AID officials before the US Congress on the events of December 1968 are studded with so many 'security deletions' it seems impossible, with present evidence, to judge accurately the attitude or the role of US officials in this matter. Given their past record in Brazil, it is unlikely that they were horrified by this assault on democratic government and personal liberties. In fact, one sentence of testimony revealed that the US approved the free hand now allowed to policymaking by fiat.

> In terms of general economic policies, I would say if anything there has been a net improvement; the Finance Minister can now do by decree things that before had to go through Congress; they have been passing out decrees left and right, and most of them are to the good. Most of them are very much oriented to strengthening the private sector.
> [Security deletion].[29]

It is possible that the US was displeased with the signs of independence which the Brazilian government was showing in matters other than foreign investment. Washington reportedly justified a 50 per cent cut in programme aid for the fiscal year 1970–71 on the grounds of high world coffee prices, an issue on which the Brazilian and US government had been at loggerheads for several years.

Finance Minister Delfim Neto is arguably the most important member of the Brazilian government at present. He has remained at his post since 1967 even through a change of Presidents and is internationally famous as the wizard of Brazil's economic miracle. That miracle is the subject of euphoric self-congratulation within Brazilian and international business circles. Brazilian GNP has grown by nearly 10 per cent annually since 1968. Exports are booming, with coffee forming a declining, and manufactures a growing, proportion of the total. There is excited talk of Brazil becoming another Japan, of it joining the Group of 10, the rich nations' financial 'club'. Before closing, therefore, we should look more closely at the causes and the nature of this miracle in order to see whether it in fact provides an example for other Third World countries to emulate.

It has become a fashionable cliché to criticize the unequal distribution of income within Brazil. When even Robert S. McNamara, president of the World Bank which has lent Brazil $1 billion since 1968, lashes out at social injustice, one knows the situation must be pretty bad. The rich have certainly profited from Brazil's boom: the top 5 per cent of the urban population, who received 27·7 per cent of total urban income in 1960, had raised their share to 34·9 per cent in 1970. The richest 20 per cent of the population received 62·2 per cent of the national income in 1972.[30] When confronted with figures such as these, Delfim Neto has retorted, 'We know 100 per cent of the population are getting 100 per cent of the national income: the distribution is not important.'[31] Except, perhaps, to the population. Real wages have declined, by some estimates as much as one half, since the military government took power. At the legal minimum wage it took a worker 264 minutes to earn enough to pay for a kilo of meat in 1965; by mid-1972 he had to work 354 minutes. 'In socialist Chile meat must be strictly rationed,' a journalist writes ironically; 'in Brazil that's not necessary.'[32]

Delfim Neto seems at least to lack Mr McNamara's hypocrisy. His candour with the press shows he is quite aware of what is going on. He has denied that the World Bank is putting any real, as opposed to moral, pressure on Brazil (withholding funds, for example) to redistribute income. 'They have never asked us to change anything and I am sure that they will continue to loan in the same way.'[33] To *Le Monde* he was even franker: 'Of course we have a neo-capitalist economy – no denying it – with all of its errors and all its faults. It's an unstable economy and, what is more serious, no mechanism is provided for redistribution of national income. But I would like to know in which capitalist country things are any different.'[34]

Delfim Neto surely knows better than most of his critics that Brazil's present income distribution is not separable from other key facts about the economy which are widely applauded. It is, for example, directly attributable to the IMF–World Bank sponsored stabilization efforts, since breaking the unions and letting wages lag behind price rises has been the Brazilian prescription for braking inflation.

Very low wages have also contributed to the much-heralded boom in manufactured exports, which rose from $255 million in 1969 to $620 million only two years later. Shoes are one of the major manufactured exports. Brazilian shoe workers work a 48 hour week for $0·40 an hour. Their union is under strict government control and strikes are illegal.[35]

More important than low wages, however, are the aggressive export subsidies introduced by Delfim Neto. These subsidies make it more profitable to produce for export than for the home market, because the government exempts export production from taxes to the extent that goods may be exported at prices 40 per cent below what would be charged within Brazil. A variety of other formal and informal pressures are exerted on businessmen to export. 'We have to export, even when our [Brazilian] customers are waiting on goods', they are quoted as saying.[36] Export subsidies are anathema to the free trade doctrine on which the IMF was founded, since they represent another 'distortion' of free market forces; but where, as in Brazil, foreign corporations are the major beneficiaries of the subsidies, this part of the dogma may be conveniently overlooked.

A list of commodities leading this boom in manufactured exports, given by *The Times* (London) in 1972, included instant coffee, steel, processed meat, fruit juices, and shoes. All of these represented rather primitive processing of raw materials that are plentiful in Brazil. The article predicts that 'attempts to break into established sectors such as electronics and textiles will be countered by those producer-countries already in the field'.[37] (An example of this opposition was the instant coffee dispute with the United States in 1968, in which the US successfully put pressure on Brazil to impose a tax on its own exports by threatening to withdraw its support from the International Coffee Agreement.)[38]

Multinational corporations themselves put significant limits on Brazil's export potential by prohibiting exports that would compete in other markets with products of their other branches and subsidiaries. Brazil is still very far away from repeating Japan's performance in exports. The manufactured exports, too, are not sold in the main to the rich but protected markets of the United States and Europe, but to countries even poorer than Brazil in Latin America, Africa, and the Middle East. The implications of this for the balance of payments are analysed below; it also suggests that Brazil's pattern cannot be copied by every country, based as it is on a sub-imperialism which is already provoking defensive measures in Latin America.

In order to keep its exchange rate at a 'realistic' level, Brazil has adopted a device which has only recently gained respectability in the world of international finance: the 'crawling peg'. This means simply that every month or two the exchange rate is devalued by a few percentage points, which avoids the speculation and shocks to trade that happen when a much larger devaluation takes place at less frequent intervals. By this means Brazil has devalued by about 13 per cent per year in recent years. This device is, in fact (though it is seldom mentioned by the press agents of the Brazilian miracle) an admission that inflation has not been fully conquered in Brazil, though it has been reduced drastically from the runaway rates of the Goulart era. Brazilians have long known how to use compensating mechanisms to enable them to live with inflation; the exchange rate is simply one of the most recent of these.

A look at Brazil's balance of payments in recent years will tell more about the real sources of the boom than most newspaper articles. The most striking fact is that despite the 'export boom', imports have soared even higher. In 1971, the 'best year in history' with a growth in GNP of 11·3 per cent, there was a trade deficit of $800 million. Since the services account is traditionally in deficit, due to interest payments and profit remittances, the total current account deficit amounted to $1,287 million. How was this financed, when US government aid had dropped to a miniscule figure of $10 million? Partly by aid from institutions like the World Bank, partly from the inrush of private investment eager to cash in on the bonanza. Mainly, however, the money comes via short and middle term debts of the private sector. At the end of 1972 the total foreign debt was $10 billion and still growing. Almost half of that represented private debts, which have more than doubled since the end of 1969.

This appears to be deliberate government policy. In August 1968 the government permitted commercial banks and industrial and commercial borrowers more liberal access to foreign credit. The coincidence of this measure with the introduction of the 'crawling peg' exchange system even suggests that the government may be encouraging a type of speculation against the exchange rate which brings in a flow of capital. In any event, the Planning Minister has remarked that the growth of the foreign debt was 'an integral component of our development strategy'.[39]

But what happens when the debts fall due? Will the export boom be sufficient to pay them off and pay for the high level of imports as well? The outlook is dubious. According to the conclusions of one study of Brazil's accumulation of debts and ability to pay them,

... [M]ost of the increased manufacturing exports – nearly 70 per cent – went to other developing countries making payments in non-convertible currencies ... Brazil's export trade has been gradually moving away from convertible currency areas ... Yet the expansion of Brazilian exports to non-convertible currency countries does not by itself contribute to Brazil's capacity to service its external debt obligations.[40]

But, except for exports, in the long run a country like Brazil has no other way of paying for its imports of goods and interest and amortization on its large foreign debt. Charges for the latter amounted in 1971 to 28 per cent of all foreign exchange earnings.

All this is ominously reminiscent of the Kubitschek era. Then, too, government officials lightheartedly considered a large import surplus and external indebtedness part of their development strategy. Then, too, Brazil enjoyed a superficially attractive boom but floated on short-term credits. It is an intrinsically perilous situation, and its eventual collapse is a more imminent danger to Brazil's ruling class than the internal revolution which is so badly needed. A revolutionary government would, of course, precipitate the collapse and suffer from it, as Allende's government in Chile bore the onus of debts contracted by the previous government. But even less revolutionary changes as for example the ouster of Delfim Neto by his enemies within the Brazilian government, could shatter the structure of confidence upon which the continued inflow of capital depends.

What is the IMF's opinion of the Brazilian policies? We may not discover that until the capital inflow reverses, or simply becomes insufficient to cover both the trade and the invisibles deficits. In any case, it should be clear that Brazil is no advertisement for IMF policies. The only period in which it followed instructions very faithfully, 1964 to 1967, was also the period of the worst business depression and a rash of take-overs by foreign companies. The stabilization programme worsened income distribution but could not restore production or put the balance of payments on a stable footing.

The stunning growth record of the recent past had its foundation in the industries built in the Kubitschek era. What growth Brazil has experienced has been due more to a defiance of Fund policies than to obedience. But then, considered carefully, Brazil is no advertisement for Delfim Neto's policies either.* The IMF may soon have another chance to try its hand.

* Delfim Neto was succeeded as Finance Minister by Mário Simonsen when General Ernesto Geisel became President in February 1974. There have been no apparent changes in Delfim Neto's policies. Brazil is expected to have a current account deficit of $3,500 million in 1974 (up from $1,300 million in 1973) but Simonsen predicts this will be covered by a capital inflow of $4,000 million.

8

The Transformation of 'Socialist' India

India is the country which has come to symbolize the problems, hopes, and frustrations of development aid, for a number of reasons: its huge population, the extreme poverty of most of its people, its democratic form of government, its self-styled socialism and attempts at development planning, and its stance of independence and non-alignment in world politics.

India is also, in gross terms, the largest user of IMF facilities among Third World countries. Up to July 1967 India had purchased a total of $1 billion in foreign exchange from the IMF, a sum almost twice as large as that for Brazil, in second place.[1] For all these reasons India merits a place in this work.

Not surprisingly, India's history since independence shows many of the same trends we have already seen in other countries: the rapid depletion of once-large foreign exchange reserves, the subsequent accumulation of massive foreign debts, and along with this the abandonment or modification of independent policies affecting the entire strategy of development, for the purpose of winning foreign loans or investment. All this in the name of economic development, which in the more than a quarter century since independence has produced no real effect in eradicating the poverty which afflicts all but a small minority of its people.

Despite the large drawings which India has made on the IMF, it has not been that institution but its 'twin', the World Bank (where India is also the largest client)* which has been the instrument of Western capitalist pressure on India. Since it is not the IMF as an institution, but the total system of import and aid dependence which we are examining, it will be of particular interest to see how the two institutions – despite their division of labour and considerable efforts at 'product differ-

* In recent years Brazil has received more World Bank loans than India.

entiation'* – can when necessary perform interchangeably the key role in this system.

When India gained its independence in 1947, its foreign exchange reserves were substantial. These were held chiefly in the form of sterling securities, an IOU from Great Britain to the government of its colony for unrequited exports which India had supplied to England during the war, which in 1948 amounted to £1,200 million.

With these large reserves behind them, the Indian government approached the task of planning its economic development with confidence and even – it is possible to say with hindsight – extraordinary complacency. Economic development would require, under their assumptions, a large import surplus which would allow capital investment without requiring curtailment of current consumption. This assumption revealed their aversion to soaking the Indian rich by taxation to pay for development; the philosophy was rather to equalize incomes in India by raising the lowest rather than by cutting down the highest. The import surplus would be financed by a reduction in reserve holdings, supplemented by modest amounts of foreign aid which (influenced by the rhetoric of Point Four) the Indians felt they were eminently entitled to enjoy. Spending rather than saving foreign exchange was considered the high road to development. In the words of an Indian scholar:

This transformation in India's international position – from being one of the important creditors of Great Britain to being the biggest debtor country in the developing world – was the result of deliberate policy. The rise in the foreign debt was not the result of either absent-mindedness or financial irresponsibility. It was a calculated by-product of the strategy for economic development conceived and implemented by Indian planners with the full knowledge and blessing of the Lok Sabha [lower house of the Indian parliament].[2]

It is unlikely that the Indian planners dreamed that the debt would grow so large, or that so many concessions would have to be made along the way to keep aid flowing, when they embarked on their strategy of development via trade deficit.

* These are discussed briefly in appendix I.

India's first Five-Year Plan was only a modest warm-up for the real effort of planning. The nation's economy was still recovering from the effects of 'Partition' (the secession of Pakistan) and the ensuing warfare between Hindus and Muslims. Targets for the first Plan were set at modest levels; the emphasis was on infrastructure investment, on agriculture, and on rehabilitation. Only a modest industrialization programme was attempted.[3] Some reduction in foreign exchange holdings was 'planned', and foreign aid, though included in the Plan, was not a crucial element.

The first Plan proved a great success in terms of gross targets. National income, which was expected to rise by 11 or 12 per cent during the five-year period, in fact rose by 18·4 per cent; the decline in foreign reserves was smaller than planned, and foreign aid was not utilized to the maximum possible extent. Although critics pointed out that this success was probably not the result of planning at all, but of a series of good harvests and other factors external to the planning process, the success gave the impetus to set far more ambitious goals for the Second Five-Year Plan. Planned public expenditure was more than twice as great as for the first Plan, and a much heavier emphasis was put on industrialization and on expansion of the public sector.[4] These ambitious efforts would increase demands for imports and require large expenditure of foreign exchange, but it was hoped that the money could be obtained from increased exports, reduction of non-essential imports, and some further drawing down of reserves.[5] Foreign aid was not yet considered a critical item when the Second Plan was drawn up.

Until the exchange crisis of 1957, India paid very little attention to the need to conserve foreign exchange. There were few import controls and there was practically no short-term foreign exchange budgeting as the country embarked on the Second Plan.[6] The major constraint placed on Indian spending in the first decade after Independence was imposed by Great Britain, whose own economy might have been bankrupted if India had tried to cash in her sterling securities all at once. India reached agreement with Britain in 1948 to hold sterling balances in two accounts, one frozen, one current, with regulated annual transfers of about £40 million a year from the frozen to the current account. This set the ceiling on India's imports from Britain as repayment of the war debt each year.

So India entered upon the ambitious Second Five-Year Plan with scarcely any acknowledgement of the need to budget foreign exchange resources.

As for the foreign exchange gap of Rs 1,100 crores, the planners admitted that it was 'sizeable, both absolutely and in relation to the funds that have so far been forthcoming'. In the nature of things, they could not guarantee that it would be covered; but there was hardly any excuse for their complacent assertion that 'any shortfall in resources to be raised externally' might be 'made good by a greater effort at augmenting domestic resources' ... The alarming irresponsibility of the Second Five-Year Plan's chapter on 'Finance and Foreign Exchange' represents the lowest point ever reached by Indian planning during the whole decade.[8]

The government was soon to be caught up short in the consequences of its irresponsibility, but not before its reserves were virtually wiped out. The heavy import requirements of the private sector and the government's liberal policy in granting it licences resulted in a heavy trade deficit; and the decline in reserves during the first year alone of the Second Plan amounted to more than the total which had been planned for the entire period.

By early 1957 the danger had been recognized and belatedly steps were taken to meet it. New and much more stringent exchange regulations were issued.[9] However, no existing commitments were cancelled, so that the immediate effect of these measures was slight. A stand-by arrangement made with the IMF in February was exhausted by June (this drawing did not dip into the third credit tranche and so was not as severe in its conditions as the stand-by arrangements discussed in other chapters). The crisis persisted.

Its effect was far-reaching. Unwilling to abandon the Plan, the Indians were forced to face the fact that, once their reserves were gone, the import surplus upon which they had counted would have to be supplied by fresh foreign credits or investment. But when they turned to the United States and the World Bank, from whom the bulk of the aid would have to come, they discovered that the aid sources were critical of their development programme as over-ambitious and unrealistic. This was, of course, a self-fulfilling prophecy which meant simply that they were unwilling to finance the type of public sector heavy industry projects which were the heart of India's cherished Plan.

In September 1957 Prime Minister Jawaharlal Nehru said that India would welcome a United States loan of $500 to $600 million to help solve its exchange difficulties. It was the most pointed public appeal that had been made by the Indian leader, and was underlined by the news that he was sending his Finance Minister T. T. Krishnamachari, a declared opponent of dependence on foreign aid, to the United States to explore the prospects for such a loan.[10]

Ten days later, a policy directive signed by the director of the US foreign aid agency announced that no economic aid would be available for state-owned industrial and mining enterprises except in rare cases. This was considered a direct rebuff to India, where state-operated industrial production was precisely what aid was desired for.[11]

The World Bank echoed American criticism that the Plan was 'over-ambitious'. A World Bank mission to India in 1956, the 'McKittrick mission', had condemned the Plan on this ground, and Bank President Eugene Black addressed a letter to the Indian Finance Minister urging the Indian planners to give more scope to private enterprise and more incentives to foreign private investment. The Finance Minister replied to Black, re-iterating India's belief in the importance of public enterprises, and published both letters to dramatize his repudiation of Bank 'advice'.

But when another Bank mission repeated the criticism in 1958, after the recognition of the exchange crisis, the Indians were forced to pay more attention. The 1958 mission urged that future plans should be based on a more realistic assessment of resources, that higher priority should be given to agriculture rather than industry, and that the State should limit its industrial responsibilities.[12] The Vice-President of the Bank, Burke Knapp, toured India and emphasized its position in a speech to the Southern India Chamber of Commerce in Madras:

We are great believers in the private sector and in the economy of every country where we are working, we do everything we can for the climate to be created in which private enterprise can make the maximum contribution to the development of the country.[13]

The pressure of necessity achieved what mere advice could not. The Indian government hastened to assure Western governments and capitalists that it was not at all hostile to private enterprise, domestic or foreign. A convertibility agreement providing for the remittance of profits in dollars was concluded with the United States in late 1957, and by means of new tax concessions and formal invitations the Indian government made clear that foreign majority ownership of joint ventures was acceptable and that foreign capital was welcome in several industries which originally were to have been reserved for the state.[14]

Temporary salvation for the Indian Plan arrived in the summer of 1958 when the World Bank took the initiative in organizing an Aid-India Consortium to provide foreign assistance to India on a continuing basis. The original members of the consortium, apart from the Bank, were the five countries in which India had placed most of its orders for Second Plan projects: Canada, Japan, Britain, West Germany, and the US.[15] This fact, which is usually glossed over, is important in understanding the workings of aid consortiums. The members are not altruistic aid-givers, but governments interested in seeing that the nations which provide markets for their products do not collapse completely, renege on existing debts, or withdraw from the capitalist trade system. But concerted action is necessary so that one creditor does not extend aid which will be used to repay debts to another. According to a Madras newspaper:

All five of India's creditor countries had been desirous of helping her tide over her financial crisis, but each of them had been waiting to see what the others were going to do before committing herself. The Bank, therefore, decided to bring them all together

171

round a table for face to face discussion and thus came about this week's Washington conference.[16]

The IMF was not a party to the original Aid India agreement, for a significant reason. India had already drawn to the limit of its second credit tranche in the IMF, and any borrowings over that level would have involved major commitments to the Fund in return, including a commitment to solve balance of payments deficits. India had decided she could make no such commitment because her whole development plan was based on running a substantial deficit.[17] The Managing Director of the IMF, at that time Per Jacobsson, had said something similar six months previously at the end of a two-week stay, when he told reporters it was not the intention of the Indian government to enter into any kind of short-term borrowing.[18] It was remarkable, nevertheless, that the Fund's highest official had spent two weeks conferring with a government that had no intention of borrowing further from it; and suggests the possibility that negotiations along that line had failed.

Several important changes in the direction of Indian economic policy resulted from this foreign exchange crisis and the eventual 'bailing-out' operation of the Aid-India Consortium. The government intensified its strategy of import substitution, giving incentives, both by design and as a by-product of tight import controls, to the domestic manufacture of items previously imported. This policy was unfortunately applied indiscriminately and across the board, with insufficient calculation of compelling economic needs, and it had the same adverse effects as in other countries which have followed the same strategy (Philippines, Brazil): non-basic consumption goods such as refrigerators were now produced in India, so that instead of importing refrigerators, India imported machines and components for assembling refrigerators. The type of imports changed, but the overall dependence on imports, if anything, increased, simply because it is politically and economically more feasible to ban imports of consumption goods than to ban capital goods and raw materials for factories, even if the factories are producing non-essentials.[19] This situation was to figure directly in the next big foreign exchange crisis.

Further, the Indian government pursued its new policy of incentives for foreign investment, not merely because they knew this was the condition for aid, but because this was viewed as another means of securing the foreign exchange needed for new projects. Total outstanding foreign investment in India more than doubled from December 1956 (the eve of the first crisis) to March 1965 (the eve of the second), from $1,007 million to $2,104 million.[20] As a result, the priorities set by the government's Plan were systematically distorted in the direction of industries which foreign companies were willing to finance. Naturally the foreign companies expected to earn a return on their investment, and payments in foreign currencies on account of remittance of dividends by foreign companies rose steadily in the early 1960s.[21] Government decisions seemed governed by a 'foreign exchange fetishism' which took little account of the long range repayment burden or genuine comparative advantage.[22]

Finally, the Indian government had become wholeheartedly dependent on large amounts of external assistance from the Aid-India Consortium to finance its import-surplus strategy of development; no bones were made about this in the formulation of the Third Five-Year Plan (1961–6) which was explicitly dependent on huge inflows of fresh aid. Total foreign aid utilized during the period of the Third Plan amounted to over $6 billion.[23]

All of these strands – the increased dependence on imports to keep industry running, the growing burden of remittance of profits of foreign companies, and the heavy dependence on external aid – came together in the next great foreign aid crisis, which happened to coincide with the succession crisis caused by Nehru's death. A World Bank mission headed by Bernard Bell visited India in 1964, and issued a report calling for the devaluation of the rupee and abolition of many of the foreign trade controls then in effect.

India's first answer was defiance. T. T. Krishnamachari, who had sparred with Eugene Black in 1956, was again Minister of Finance and again picked up the gauntlet thrown down by the Bank by insisting that devaluation was not the answer. He was supported by the Ministry of Commerce, which issued an official report analysing the structure of India's imports and exports that concluded that devaluation might actually worsen the foreign trade situation. India's largest money-earning exports, jute and tea, were competitive on the world market at the existing exchange rate, and other export industries were being supported in any case by subsidies (which the World Bank wished to see abolished). India's imports, argued the Ministry, were all essential ones and changing the exchange rate would only increase the burden on those who were importing needed raw materials, spare parts, and food grains. (The necessity of all imports was certainly questionable, but the World Bank, which favoured liberalization rather than restriction of imports, could not be expected to raise the right questions.)

By early 1965 it was recognized that India was in its most severe foreign exchange crisis since independence. India negotiated with the IMF for a stand-by arrangement to help it meet its most urgent obligations, and received the promise of $200 million.* The apparent conditions for the drawing were the announcement of a new customs duty of 10 per cent on all except a few import items, and a rise in the Reserve Bank interest rate. Financial commentators predicted that both measures would have a very limited effect in stemming the demand for imports. In any case, the entire $200 million offered under the stand-by had been exhausted before the year was over.

The end of the year found American aid to India abruptly suspended as a result of the Indo-Pakistan war in October. The Indians were furious; was not this arbitrary suspension of aid, for political reasons, exactly why the US had warned India against accepting Russian aid? Defiant Indians began to talk once again about self-reliance, a word that had been almost forgotten during the Third Plan.

That winter, however, the worst drought in history struck India, adding the disaster of a bad harvest to all its other problems. Then Prime Minister Shastri, Nehru's successor, died

*The large amounts which India could borrow were due to the size of its quota, by far the largest of any Third World country.

suddenly. The new Prime Minister, chosen by Congress Party bosses, was Nehru's daughter Indira Gandhi. The new head of government immediately softened the defiant line towards Western creditors and replaced the Finance Minister who had been so rude in his opposition to World Bank advice. The Planning Minister, Asoka Mehta, attacked instead the critics of the World Bank and foreign aid, receiving cautious support from Mrs Gandhi herself. Furthermore, 'controls are now being criticized and pledges of support for foreign private participation are being given more openly than before. Criticism of US policy in Vietnam is muted and nominal.'[24] The Prime Minister, the Planning Minister, and the new Finance Minister all made visits to Washington that spring, a sure sign that aid negotiations were under way.

When Mrs Gandhi went to Washington she was informed that resumption of aid – which had been cut off as a result of the war with Pakistan – was dependent on India coming to terms with the World Bank. The United States had decided to make the Bank its intermediary and arbiter with respect to aid to both India and Pakistan. From its past role as fund-raising organizer and chairman of the aid consortium, the Bank was to move into a more active, critical role in assessing Indian and Pakistani economic plans, in judging their performance under the economic plans, and in determining the amount of aid that should be supplied by consortium members.

The Bank's interest coincided with that of the United States, which already was having critical second thoughts about India's economic progress ... As a result, the Administration found that it could turn to the Bank as an advocate of economic reforms already being urged by the United States.[25]

The Bank's recommendations, echoing the report of the Bell Mission, were for a devaluation of the par value of the rupee, accompanied by the dismantling of the complex machinery of import controls and export subsidies. The report focused on the critical difficulties which import substitution and other industries were experiencing in obtaining foreign exchange for the imports they needed to keep running. It suggested that liberalization of the import of a wide range of materials would damp down domestic inflation and permit fuller utilization of plant and equipment now lying idle or working below capacity for lack of 'maintenance' imports.

It was recognized that India would need massive external financing to pay for the liberalized imports. The incentive offered by the Bank as a prize for acceptance of its advice was a promise that non-project, or balance of payments, aid to the amount of $900 million a year over a period of several years would be made available to India for maintenance imports, above and beyond the aid which would be pledged for specific projects.

For the long run, the Bank report was emphatic in its prediction that prosperity lay down the road it suggested, but ruin awaited if its advice were not followed:

> We are confident that, with the necessary and appropriate changes in the government of India's policies and practices and with a higher level of aid for at least the next five to ten years, India can within the next few years significantly accelerate the growth of its economy, can begin measurably to raise the level of living of its peoples, and can, at the same time, move on to a path which will eventually permit sustained growth on a self-supporting basis.
>
> We are equally confident that without the combination of important changes in the government of India's policy and practice with additional aid for at least the next five to ten years, there will be no acceleration of growth and no progress towards either improved living levels or eventual sustained and self-supporting growth. We would expect, in fact, retrogression in all these respects.[26]

The Bank's threats and promises were backed up by a report prepared by USAID in India. This report predicted that if additional foreign exchange of some $654 million were made available for maintenance imports, the increased output made possible by these imports would amount to $2·6 billion and would add 1 per cent to the growth rate of Indian industry. Substantial benefits in employment would also result, according to this estimate; additional employment resulting from liberalized imports would amount, the report said, to no less than two million jobs![27]

When the devaluation, and the associated import liberalization measures, were announced by the government in June 1966, however, these glowing promises were apparently not the motivation so much as the fact that the bottom of the barrel had been reached and India was desperate for funds just for the imports needed at that moment. This was clearly implied by the Finance Minister in a press conference when he was asked why the government had not waited another six months to see whether a good monsoon might make the devaluation unnecessary. He replied, 'If we had waited another six months, we would have had absence of imports in this country affecting the industries and there would have been fear of mass unemployment.' The implication was that aid was being made conditional on the devaluation, and that it had to be immediate. According to the Finance Minister, 'action could not be postponed because all further aid negotiations hinged on it'.[28]

The results of the devaluation package in no way lived up to the glowing promises of the Bell Mission and USAID reports. Although the devaluation was a severe one of 37·5 per cent, from 4·75 rupees to the dollar to 7·50, the expected boost to exports did not materialize; instead, they declined. The explanation for this paradoxical effect was simple: the previous structure of import tariffs and export subsidies, which was abolished with the devaluation, had amounted to a *de facto* devaluation by raising the prices of imports and lowering the price of exports which the government wanted to encourage.

It is arguable that the Indian devaluation is little more than an administrative device, a way to get rid of import restrictions and other controls, rather than a means of directly improving the balance of payments. No doubt the IBRD advisers urged the importance of the package deal as a means of loosening up the Indian economy.[29]

Post facto examinations of the reasons for the export decline confirmed the suspicion that exports had suffered more from the abolition of subsidies than they had gained from the effects

177

of the devaluation. The major traditional exports, jute and tea, were competitive without subsidies even before the devaluation and had to be taxed in order to absorb some of the windfall profits to exporters resulting from the devaluation. Most other export items – the new, non-traditional ones which the government wished to encourage – had a relatively high import content and thus suffered from the new higher import prices as well as the loss of their previous subsidies. The conclusion was that devaluation had not improved the overall position of the country's exports; some economists concluded that export subsidies should be re-introduced as the need for them still existed.[30]

Two days after the devaluation was announced, the World Bank called an urgent meeting of the Aid-India Club (whose original five members had been joined by five more European trading partners) in order to collect the $900 million in non-project aid which had been promised. The need was acute because India had again chosen not to seek an IMF stand-by credit and so could not expect immediate relief from that source. The United States announced the resumption of its own aid to India on 15 June. US aid to Pakistan was resumed at the same time, to demonstrate the supposed impartiality of American policy, but the timing of the announcement was clearly related to the Indian devaluation and the success of World Bank negotiations with India.[31]

It appeared, however, that the World Bank had considerably less leverage with the consortium members than it had with aid-hungry India. The promised $900 million was not immediately forthcoming, as the consortium members failed to pledge the necessary amounts. Japan in particular dragged its feet, reportedly because it had not been consulted on the matter.[32] Five months after devaluation, India had received only $465 million of the promised sum. The embarrassed Bank quickly replaced the official who had made the $900 million promise, and decided to abandon the search for firm pledges from the consortium in favour of a 'less formal' approach, in view of the difficulties it encountered in collecting firm pledges.

Indian bitterness at the shortfall in aid ran deep. 'You sold the country and have not even got the price', a legislator accused the government.[33] And nearly a year later, an Indian weekly editorialized:

... We seem to have been shortchanged on [stabilization aid for devaluation.] All we got was a promise of non-project assistance and we were left to do the bilateral negotiating with each aid-giver, with all the attendant consequences of delay and country-tying of commodity assistance.[34]

Import liberalization, which was the key to the entire package of measures, also did not have the predicted beneficial effects on industrial production. According to the government, fifty-nine priority industries, which accounted for fully 80 per cent of India's industrial production, were to be given permission to import whatever was needed – raw materials, spare parts and components – to enable them to work to their full capacity. However, the programme got off to a halting start because the promised non-project aid was slow in becoming available, and without it the country could not afford to liberalize imports. When imports were liberalized, the government issued licences that, according to critical comments, went 'beyond all justifiable needs'. It was predicted, all too accurately, that 'liberal import licensing, without specifications regarding use, is likely to lead to imports of many items which are produced in this country'.[35] The liberalization was not limited to its official purpose. Companies were granted 'replenishment' licences, without limitation to specific imports, in amounts which were far in excess of their import needs; and the favoured companies sold their licences to importers who could make big profits selling scarce goods on the protected market. The licences were even peddled via newspaper advertisements.[36]

It may be argued that these were abuses, perpetuated by a corrupt bureaucracy, of an essentially rational scheme; and that the World Bank cannot be blamed for its faulty administration. These 'abuses', however, were squarely in the spirit of liberalization, which was intended to give fuller scope to market forces as opposed to planning. The likely results of liberalization, however well administered, were those of giving a fillip to low priority industries, encouraging fresh investment and capacity creation in them, and diverting a much larger amount of foreign exchange than hitherto to uses which are of little relevance to the development of the economy – in sum, altering the patterns of industrial development ... The general relaxation of import control over a period of time cannot but shift priorities in favour of a pattern of development for which both aid and private capital can be shown to be more easily forthcoming.[37]

Five years later the import policy was still following the pattern set by the liberalization of 1966:

Nothing else could perhaps be expected at a time when the government appears so concerned about raising industrial output through better exploitation of established capacity. With the accent so much on production – *any* production – this is clearly the wrong time to be asking whether the government has any priorities in respect of the industrial sector.[38]

It is also quite likely that the liberalization is responsible for the sharp rise in the 'errors and omissions' item (which includes illegal capital flight) in India's balance of payments since the fiscal year of the devaluation, which means it has been a large contributor to the leakage of the country's foreign exchange.[39]

The devaluation decision was unpopular in India, for both good and bad reasons. It was widely recognized that the government had bowed to outside pressure in order to obtain aid. The unpopularity of the devaluation was believed to have contributed to the defeat of the Congress Party in the 1967 general elections; the party remained in power at the national level only because there was no nationwide opposition party which could concentrate the anti-government vote. The opposition to devaluation also seems to have influenced the Prime Minister. She subsequently fought and won a battle for control of the Congress Party with the 'bosses' who had put her into power, splitting the Party but bringing the large majority with her.[40] She has subsequently shown a desire to take a tougher line against US and World Bank pressure. 'Self-reliance', a slogan almost forgotten in the decade from 1956 to 1966, has become a favourite word once again.

India has, however, already given so much ground to the Western aid-givers, and is so deeply indebted to them, that it has virtually no room to manoeuvre. The Fourth Five-Year Plan, which was to have begun in 1966, had to be postponed for three years because the Plan was dependent on external aid and the amounts to be anticipated from it were too uncertain to allow the planning to proceed. The dependence was so great that the government had to take seriously the advice offered by a second Bell Mission from the World Bank in 1967, 'even if it cannot take seriously its promise of aid', as a journalist remarked.

Those who have read the successive Bell reports in full maintain that it is only from these reports that one can get an idea of the coherence in all the things that the government keeps announcing from time to time and in the things that it has promised to continue to do in return for aid.[41]

The type of planning which the World Bank advice favours is hardly that which the Indians embarked on in the early 1950s. The Bank's agricultural programme aims at the creation of a stratum of prosperous capitalist farmers and encourages the use of expensive commercial inputs such as fertilizers; it has exerted specific pressure (during the 1966 exchange crisis) for favourable conditions for foreign investment in India's fertilizer industry; it is a vigorous advocate of birth control; and it continues to press for further import liberalization and the relaxation or elimination of most domestic controls as well.

Foreign aid utilized in India for the fiscal year 1969–70 was vitally important to the economy: it amounted to 3 per cent of national income, 20 per cent of national investment, and over 50 per cent of imports.[42] 'Self-reliance', as embodied in the recently formulated Fifth Five-Year Plan (for 1974–9) is defined as a reduction of *net* aid to zero, and a surplus sufficient to cover interest charges on the foreign debt. It should be emphasized that although this is better than India has managed to do in the past in living within its means, and probably more optimistic than realistic, it still will require new borrowing in order to cover amortization of the existing foreign debt.

Unless India decides to repudiate its debts – a course which the government has thus far shown no signs of following – this will require continued obedience to the wishes of its creditors.

If it does repudiate the debts, its import-dependent economy will be vulnerable to the trade reprisals that are likely as a result. In 1962 an IMF official, himself an Indian, wrote that India would need the continued injection of external capital for 'another ten years or so', by which time India would presumably be over the 'balance-of-payments hump' and able to earn its own way with its exports.[43] That ten years has passed, and the situation is worse than ever. The proud anti-Western stance taken by India at the time of its most recent war with Pakistan, in support of the secession of Bangladesh, has already softed because India's dependence on consortium aid does not permit prolonged defiance of the interests of consortium members.

Despite its quantitatively large drawings on the IMF (corresponding to its large quota), India has, by conscious decision, never drawn into its third credit tranche which would have meant submission to a full scale stabilization programme. Since the World Bank has fulfilled the role of disciplinarian for the aid consortium, India's gain from this decision has been slight; but there may have been some marginal advantages. For example, the World Bank does not seem to have insisted on tight domestic credit as part of its exchange reform package; thus India may have escaped the severe recession which is the usual result of IMF stabilization programmes.

India's problems are so immense that it may seem beside the point to apportion blame for its present plight – yet such judgements are always relative. It might be recalled that in 1947 China was considered the hopeless case in Asia, and India seemed relatively well endowed for independent development, with the nucleus of a national industry, a highly educated élite, democratic government, and a leadership committed to development planning. It has been argued that the very existence of a capitalist class in India, and the commitment to a type of development which did not attack the class structure, has led inevitably to the type of dependent development – or stagnation – in which India is floundering.[44] The role of the international institutions has been to exploit the difficulties of national capitalist development in order to ensure the success of their own variety. But are there any alternatives to this type of development?

9

The Breakaways: Chile, Ghana, North Korea

Chile provides a timely illustration of the problems confronting a nation which tries to restructure its foreign economic ties. The foreign trade of Chile is dominated by copper, which provides about 80 per cent of its foreign exchange earnings. Until 1971 the copper mining industry was dominated by American corporations – Kennecott, Anaconda, and Cerro.

The resentment of Chileans against foreign domination of their vital copper production was of long duration and shared by broad sectors of the population. The government of President Eduardo Frei (1964–70) had tried to co-opt this resentment by 'Chileanizing' the mines. The government purchased 51 per cent of the stock, while allowing the American corporations to continue operating the mines and to take out substantial profits each year.

The high prices received for copper on the world market, and an influx of loans which reflected American confidence in Frei's government (and their hopes of giving him a boost in order to counter the appeal of Allende's more radical nationalism) gave a deceptive glow of health to the external payments position of Chile during Frei's term. Internally, however, the economy was a mess, due in part to the requirements imposed by the IMF as a condition for keeping Chile's credit rating in order. Domestic industry was stagnant, inflation was at a level of 35 per cent, and unemployment was high.

The 'Popular Unity' coalition led by Dr Salvador Allende won the elections of 1970 with promises to nationalize the copper mines, raise the standard of living of the poorer Chileans, and diversify the nation's economy. To this end Allende made another specific promise: to 'terminate agreements with the International Monetary Fund and put an end to the scandalous devaluations of the escudo'.[1]

Carrying out such a programme of economic restructuring and reorientation is a difficult and dangerous task, however; and there is reason to believe that Allende's government underestimated just how difficult it would be. For one thing, the increased income expected as a result of the nationalization of copper played a major part in his development programme – although copper had to be sold on the world market and earnings were therefore partially beyond Chile's control. In the event, Chile's copper receipts have suffered threefold: from a sharp drop in the world price of copper, from retaliatory attempts by the international corporations to boycott or confiscate Chilean copper exports, and from internal production difficulties arising from the government's policies.

One of the first acts of the Allende government was to raise the wages of the lower-paid sectors of the population by about 50 per cent. This gave their living standards an immediate boost and produced a modest boom in the economy but, as any economist could have predicted, in the absence of exchange controls and import restrictions it was bound to increase imports. This was a serious matter at a time when Chile could expect restricted access to credit on international markets and debt repayment threatened to take huge bites out of the available foreign exchange.

The Allende government nevertheless chose not to impose controls on imports or foreign exchange. Some valuable insight into the thinking of the government can be gleaned from the published proceedings of a conference held in Chile in March 1972, which brought Chilean officials together with scholars and officials from a number of other Western, socialist, and Third World countries.[2] The impression given by this conference report is that the outsiders were far more concerned about the approaching foreign exchange crunch than were the Chileans. Anxious questioning about how Chile was to get through its short-term balance of payments crisis was met with optimism, incomprehension, or reference to political necessity on the part of Chilean officials.

The Deputy Director of ODEPLAN, the government planning agency, 'concluded that there had been some misunderstanding concerning the trade model, arising from the statement that it was not an export model'.

It was really a question of emphasis and, in contrast with the previous government's efforts to increase copper exports to provide the imports for development, export and import policies were now to be a direct function of the government's principal objective of increasing the standard of living of the mass of the population, by organizing the population to produce the goods necessary for raising these living standards, and providing employment, etc. The import requirements necessary to fulfil this objective were calculated first and the level of exports necessary to facilitate these imports were derived from that figure. The government regarded this as a complete change from the previous model though it was recognized that it still required a tremendous export effort.[3]

So far so good; as a statement of general principle as to what a trade strategy should be this is not bad. Just how was the desired level of imports to be determined, though; and what would happen in the event that export earnings could not be expanded to cover the costs of the desired imports? The Minister of Planning gave an evasive answer when he reported that Chile was discovering 'enormous' new import-substitution possibilities:

The copper nitrate and coal-mining industries were important examples for which sound possibilities existed of producing, nationally, a large quantity of spare parts, machinery, and in the future, heavy transport vehicles ... Similarly, substantial import-substitution possibilities existed for agricultural implements and machinery ... The government regarded agrarian reform as one of the principal instruments for achieving import-substitution of foodstuffs ...[4]

The idea that consumption should be curbed either directly by rationing, or indirectly by import restrictions, was brushed aside.

... [T]he Chilean official view was that it was essential to maintain the level of popular consumption, and that import restrictions should only apply to the more luxurious goods and the inputs for industries producing non-essential products.[5]

Rationing and import restriction, as a solution to the short-term problem, was regarded as too economistic a way of looking at the matter and was rejected by government participants, who stressed that the starting-point for any realistic discussion of the matter was the recognition of the objective internal political situation. Sufficient details had been given about the political background for participants to see that the government had to take account of the fact that the Popular Unity was an alliance of groups whose interest was not completely identical. The government therefore had to steer a difficult course between internal and external pressures.[6]

This last statement deserves careful attention because there is no question that the government was in fact walking a political tightrope and therefore felt that they could not afford to ask sectors of the population whose support was, at best, conditional, to make sacrifices. The Popular Unity government had been supported by only a minority of the voters and most probably would have lost if their opponents had been able to unite against them. The coalition itself was composed of six different parties whose interests, as mentioned, did not always coincide.

The Chilean constitution is a complicated masterpiece of checks and balances, with elections for Congress and for the presidency held in different years. The system makes it very difficult for any party, let alone a minority coalition, to control all vital branches of the government. From his inauguration, President Allende had faced a Congress controlled by the non-socialist opposition, which nevertheless lacked the two-thirds majority which would be necessary to override a presidential veto. The March 1973 Congressional elections merely confirmed this stalemate for the remainder of Allende's six-year presidential term.

The composition of the ruling alliance created additional problems because a complicated quota system had to be observed in the distribution of official posts to be shared by the parties in the victorious alliances. This political necessity added another layer of checks and balances to frustrate the exercise of power, and supplied a large element of simple incompetence as well. The *New York Times* reported that a United Nations technical expert found himself frustrated by his inefficient Chilean assistant.

'The man was useless', the civil servant said. 'I knew it and the minister knew it, but the job belonged to the Socialist party and it took us a year to get him changed.' Each of the six parties in the governing coalition guards its quota of government jobs.[7]

Given the built-in frustrations of the Chilean constitution and political situation, a dictatorial solution (the suspension of elections, or of Congress) must have tempted Allende. It certainly appealed to the more radical leftists in his coalition. There was a good pragmatic reason for resisting the temptation, however: the Army. The Chilean Armed Forces were believed to be more devoted to constitutional rule than many of their Latin American counterparts. It was thought that so long as the Allende government observed the constitution they would refrain from intervention and even support him actively, but if he should depart from constitutional procedures, the neutrality of the Armed Forces could not be depended upon, and a counter-coup might throw him out of office.

These political difficulties were real and serious ones, as the event has shown. Having admitted this, however, it must still be questioned whether the Allende government was very wise in permitting the *laissez-faire* foreign trade policies inherited from previous administrations to continue when the government was attempting the momentous transition from an export- and import-dependent economy to a more autonomous one. The fact that imports would *have* to be restricted sooner or later could have been predicted from the first. It would have been wise in an economic sense to institute the restrictions *before* the nation's reserves ran out, so that their use could have been fitted into a careful plan rather than determined by development-indifferent market forces. It might well have been wiser politically to warn the electorate that sacrifices would be necessary when popular enthusiasm for the nationalization of the copper mines was high. However, the government itself seemed only dimly aware of the looming crisis until the foreign exchange treasury was empty; it is astonishing that so little was done from the beginning to plan and control foreign exchange expenditure. At the March 1972 conference, an economist from a socialist country warned:

State control of *all* external flows was ... an essential feature of any attempt to achieve a transition from capitalism to socialism. The experience of his country had shown how important it was to create a barrier, by controlling trade and capital movements, behind which the government could do what it deemed necessary to transform the structure of the economy.[8]

The failure to exercise this control made foreign exchange difficulties the Achilles heel of the Chilean revolution.

In the first year of the new government, no crisis was as yet apparent. The government awarded large wage increases to workers, with the result that the share of wage-earners in national income rose from 42 per cent to 50 per cent. Private consumption rose by 13 per cent. This stimulated national industry, and with its idle capacity brought back into operation, gross domestic product rose by 8·5 per cent in 1971, compared with 3·1 per cent the previous year, the last of the Frei administration. This represented a per capita rise of 6·2 per cent, compared with 0·7 per cent the previous year. Unemployment declined, and thanks to strict price controls on items of basic consumption, the official price index rose by only 20 per cent, a reasonable figure given Chile's inflationary history.[9]

The new prosperity was sweet, and national unity was high as the nationalization of the American-owned copper mines was celebrated as Chile's second independence day. Foreign banks in Chile were also nationalized, but the government was determined to keep lines of foreign credit available to Chile, so terms agreeable to the banks were negotiated for the nationalization and no question of 'inadequate' compensation arose in this case, as it did in the case of copper.

The government kept its promise not to limit imports for consumption. Under the previous administration Chile had never imported more than $170 million worth of foodstuffs in a year; in 1971 the bill was more than $250 million, and a figure of $400 million was predicted for 1972. Chile's agriculture, which has a potential productivity comparable to that of California, could not be turned around overnight to fulfil the expanding consumer demand created by the wage rises and controlled prices. The agrarian reform caused disruptions in

189

production which contributed to the food shortage; it was reported that livestock owners threatened with expropriation had driven huge herds across the border into Argentina. The government responded by sponsoring airlifts of beef imports from Argentina, a measure which is hard to justify as contributing to the consumption of the poorest Chileans.

The foreign exchange reserves inherited from the Frei administration ran down quickly. It is certainly a myth that these reserves had built up because Frei was a good administrator and were dissipated because Allende was a bad one: the international price of copper had fallen drastically, which was a severe blow to a nation so exclusively dependent on copper exports. Furthermore, Frei's reserves were accumulated thanks to public and private loans from the US, which had to be repaid by the Allende government.

Chilean officials denied that the inherited reserves had been squandered by their import policy. They asserted:

During 1971 no significant changes had taken place in the relative magnitudes of imports and exports, imports having increased only 5·6 per cent over the previous year. The fact was that a large part of these reserves had to be used to repay the inherited short-term debts which had partly been contracted to finance the copper industry's expansion plans.[10]

This much being allowed, it may still be asked whether the relative magnitudes of imports and exports should not have been changed before the point of crisis was reached – and US hostility to the Allende government virtually guaranteed a crisis.

In the summer of 1971 Allende, empowered by a unanimous vote of Congress, nationalized the copper mines. He did not reject the principle that just compensation should be paid, but countered that with a calculation of excess profits that the companies had taken out of the country in recent years.* When the excess profits were deducted from the compensation due

*They used the same formula that Peru's military government had applied to the nationalization of an American petroleum company subsidiary in 1968. Peru's action did not provoke such drastic sanctions as did Chile's.

for the nationalized property, the Chileans calculated that the American copper companies *owed them* several hundred million dollars.

The two largest companies, Anaconda and Kennecott, were infuriated by this unilateral action, and the US government supported their protests. The retaliatory measures which followed worsened Chile's balance of payments problems. In August, the US Export–Import Bank rejected a request from Chile to finance their purchase of three commercial aircraft. It was leaked to newspapers that this was the first application of a 'new tough policy' made on the 'White House level', under the pressure of private American companies, to refuse credit to any foreign country that nationalizes American private property without an immediate commitment on acceptable terms of compensation.[11]

Two months later the Chilean Foreign Minister conferred with Henry Kissinger in Washington. The press reported that both men agreed that the 'one-time' copper nationalization issue should not jeopardize long-term relations between the two countries, but apparently agreement on specifics could not be reached. Less than a week later the US Secretary of State William Rogers issued an unusually harsh press statement charging that Chile's action 'could jeopardize flows of private funds and erode the basis of support for foreign assistance with possible adverse effects on other developing countries'.[12] Chile angrily rejected this American effort to rally other poor countries against Chile. A few days later Rogers reportedly told representatives of six major United States corporations affected by expropriations in Chile that Washington would take steps to cut off aid to Chile unless prompt and fair compensation was forthcoming.[13]

The copper companies were meanwhile proceeding on their own behalf, taking legal action in the United States to attach the property of Chilean state enterprises and blocking the export to Chile of spare parts and machinery essential to keep the mines operating. They also sued in the European states which were the major consumers of Chile's copper to embargo the proceeds from its sale. Although most of the European lawsuits went against the companies, their actions were sufficient to frighten the international banking community out of extending their usual credit on copper contracts.

The World Bank and the Inter-American Development Bank ceased making loans to Chile under US pressure, and the line of short-term credit from North American banks dropped from a level of $220 million a month just before Allende's election to a trickle of about $20 million at the beginning of 1972. Meanwhile the international terms of trade had turned sharply against Chile. According to the Chilean Copper Corporation a ton of Chilean copper in 1969 would have bought 2·61 metric tons of frozen beef or 2·07 tons of butter. In 1972 the same amount of metal bought only 1·01 tons of beef or 0·82 tons of butter.

With all these pressures on the balance of payments, the question of debt service became acute. The Allende government had inherited over $2 billion worth of foreign obligations from the previous government. Upon nationalization of the copper mines the government assumed responsibility for another $642 million of debts owed by the copper companies to international organizations and banks for their recent expansion programme. The assumption of these debts meant that the Unidad Popular government agreed to pay for investments which had been made by foreign companies before it took over the government.

In November 1971 Allende announced that Chile was suspending payments due on its foreign debts and was requesting its creditors to re-negotiate payments falling due in the years 1971 to 1973. These payments would amount to $300 million in 1971, $400 million in 1972, and another $400 million in 1974 – altogether fully one-third of Chile's normal export earnings. In requesting the rescheduling, Allende said that repayment of the debts on schedule was incompatible with sustaining an adequate rate of development in the new socialist structure of investment in Chile.[14]

Why did the Chileans not repudiate the debts outright? Like other nations in a similar fix, they probably feared that the sanctions, in the form of withheld credit, would outweigh the advantages of shedding the repayment burden. The discussion at the March 1972 conference brought out some of the problems of such a choice:

A participant from a developing country, with a debt problem at least as acute as the Chilean one, pointed out that implicit in the debt repudiation strategy was the idea that the debtor country could turn to a highly autarchic solution, since reneging the debt would lead to retaliation and escalating trade disruption. The long-term costs and benefits of this solution should therefore be considered rather more carefully, especially when, as in the Chilean case, there was a democratic framework involving periodic elections.

The suggestion that debt repudiation was an answer to Chile's problems was rejected by another economist from a developing country. Refusal to repay would mean that all further transactions between Chile and the lender would stop. In his opinion, Chile could not possibly face such consequences since the foreign exchange components of even the unambitious 1972 investment programme were considerable and absolutely vital. It was not possible to think of bringing to a halt the copper expansion programme, or the plans for the iron ore complex, the Concepción oil refinery, etc.[15]

It is possible to quarrel with this reasoning. It is clear, however, that the Chilean authorities did not believe that their economy or political system could tolerate a sudden plunge into autarchy. Their foreign economic strategy revealed a consistent concern for keeping credit lines open as much as possible, a concern that was seriously contradicted only by the top priority nationalization of copper. It seems clear that the Chilean authorities showed more concern and skill in managing their credit contacts than they did in planning the imports to be financed with those credits.

An essential part of the Allende strategy was the attempt to cultivate and maintain good relations with the European powers, which are the major customers for Chile's copper, and thus leave the United States isolated in its pique over its nationalized copper companies. Since the US holds over half of Chile's foreign debt, the renegotiation sessions proved a good test of the Chilean strategy.

The first year's negotiations stretched over four rounds, from February to April 1972, and bargaining was hard on all sides.

The United States took a hard line against Chile on two points: it wanted a pledge of prompt and adequate compensation for the nationalized copper; and it wanted Chile to submit to the discipline of an IMF stand-by arrangement.* For three rounds of the negotiations the US succeeded in getting other creditor countries to insist on the IMF stand-by, but Chile stood firm against that condition. In a speech after the second round of negotiations Allende announced that Chile was ready to accept food rationing and give its creditors guarantees that it would hold back on public spending, but it rejected the terms of the proposed stand-by as demanding too much interference with internal investment, wage and price policies.[16]

In the third round of negotiations, Chile presented as a counter-proposal an offer to submit semi-annual balance of payments reports to 'an international financial organization such as the IMF'. This offer was at first rejected by the creditors, but in the fourth round of negotiations the European nations came over, at least part of the way, to the Chilean position. The demand for an IMF stand-by was dropped, and Chile's counter-proposal to submit periodic voluntary reports was accepted. On the issue of compensation for the nationalized copper, a compromise formula (which probably meant different things to the two sides), by which Chile undertook to give 'adequate compensation' was accepted. The terms of the rescheduling itself were not as favourable as those Chile had hoped for. A moratorium was granted on debt servicing only till the end of 1972, and the 1973 debts would require another set of negotiations. The creditors were giving Chile one year to show what it could do.

The general agreement had to be followed up by bilateral negotiations with each of the fourteen creditor nations involved. Most of these were easily concluded, but the US showed how reluctant was its acquiescence in the rescheduling compromise

* The IMF has in fact twice granted Chile a credit under its compensatory finance facility, as a result of the drop in the world price for copper. Because these credits were made under the special facility, and not as part of the regular tranches, Chile was not forced to agree to the conditions which would be required for a stand-by arrangement.

by dragging out its part of the discussions without coming to an agreement during the lifetime of the Allende government.

Some loans had been obtained from socialist countries, notably China and Romania, but they were insufficient to fill the gap. The Russians reportedly advised Allende to mend fences with the Americans and open the credit lines of the World Bank and the Inter-American Development Bank if he wanted to receive more Soviet aid. They were not eager to repeat their costly experience of subsidizing Cuban independence from the US[20] (Castro also reportedly warned Allende against becoming dependent on the Russians for financial support).

Aside from suspending, and then re-negotiating, payments on the foreign debt, the measures taken by the Chilean government to deal with the exchange crisis of Allende's second year seemed curiously capitalist, and alarmingly inadequate to cope with the crisis. Despite Allende's campaign promise to end devaluations, the escudo was devalued in December 1971 and again in August 1972. The December 1971 devaluation saw also the re-introduction of a system of multiple exchange rates, as the government attempted to make an exchange tax on luxury imports pay for a continued subsidy on items of basic consumption, especially foodstuffs. While the adoption of multiple rates represented a step backward in terms of the IMF's preferences, it underlined the fact that Chile's foreign trade economy was still thoroughly capitalist since imports were to be controlled through the exchange rate, rather than directly. The fact that whisky, caviare, and cigars could still be imported, even at a particularly high rate of exchange, indicated how far Chile remained from its goal of a socialist society.

The second year of Allende's government saw the emergence of the crisis which had been threatening ever since his election. The crisis was both economic and political. Economically, the lack of foreign exchange and credit led inevitably to severe shortages of food and other consumer items, and thus to inflation. The rate of inflation rose to 160 per cent in 1972, the highest in the world. Although the government continued to favour the poorer sectors of the population by granting wage rises to keep pace with the cost of living, without an increase in production the rises could only fuel the inflation.

The economic difficulties emboldened the political opposition. The opposition-controlled Congress slapped statutory limitations on the President's power to nationalize industries by fiat. 1972 saw the 'March of the Empty Saucepans' by middle-class women and, more seriously, the 'Bosses' Strike' which crippled the country for nearly a month. The strike ended only when the military authorities showed their support for Allende by consenting to be included in his cabinet.

It was not until mid-1972 that the Chilean leadership began to admit its economic difficulties, and warn the population that the confrontation with imperialism would require sacrifices. In June the Minister of Economics told a group of workers from the public sector that they must strive to 'avoid all possible imports'. He said:

Our enemies, both domestic and foreign, consider the foreign exchange shortage to be the Achilles heel of this government's entire economic policy. This is where they centre their attacks to bring us under. This shortage is the principal limitation preventing us from advancing in our economic expansion plans as outlined for 1972.[17]

President Allende called in July for an austerity policy of 'work, sacrifice, and savings', but promised that this austerity would hit the rich harder than the poor: 'If workers have to take in one notch of the belt, the rich will have to take in four.'[18] The government sponsored the formation of neighbourhood 'supply and price committees' to monitor the sales of essential consumer goods.

In September the Minister of Economics announced that the government was suspending indefinitely all imports of beef and butter, saying, 'We cannot afford to spend foreign exchange on imports of this kind.' He denied, however, that the next step would be food rationing. It is remarkable that the government displayed such a consistent allergy to the idea of rationing. In times of severe shortage rationing is the only fair and equitable alternative to allowing those with money to buy up all the scarce commodities. In rich countries, it is accepted as necessary in times of crisis, notably wartime; but in poor countries in a chronically desperate condition it has come to be regarded as an admission of failure, and thus politically unacceptable. In Chile, some sections of Allende's own coalition had been urging the government to adopt it; yet the government, worried for its popularity in the crucial March 1973 Congressional elections, shied away from the word even while announcing some measures which could be construed as rationing.

In January 1973 Allende admitted that his government had made some serious mistakes in both economic and political management since taking office. The first mistake, he said, had been in failing to take an inventory of the country when taking office.

Next, he said:

... we should have informed the people that we found the country with an immense foreign debt ... We should have started to re-negotiate the foreign debt right then in November 1970, and not have waited a year to begin talks.

We should have said that the only way to solve the meat problem was to establish a livestock policy whose results would be seen in eight or ten years ...

... But above all, we should have warned that our posture of confrontation with imperialism was going to bring us acute problems.

He admitted to another error of political calculation. Each president in Chile has the right to dissolve parliament and call a plebiscite in the hope of winning a favourable majority for his own party and policies. Since this is allowed only once during a president's six-year term, Allende had decided to hold this weapon in reserve, but now admitted that the early months would have been the most favourable time, in terms of his government's popularity, to have called the election.[19]

Despite these calls to austerity, before the March 1973 congressional elections it was reported that the government was attempting to defuse the shortage issue by unloading its stockpile of foodstuffs and by massively stepping up imports. The election results showed that both the support for and opposition to Allende's government had remained remarkably stable despite the ups and downs of his first two and a half years in office. The results seemed to promise that the constitutional stalemate would continue for the remainder of Allende's term, with the opposition controlling a majority in congress, but not the two-thirds majority necessary to make the President powerless.

By July 1973 (winter in the southern hemisphere), however, the nation was in a boiling crisis. Key sectors of the bourgeoisie such as the independent lorry owners were ready to sabotage the government by strikes or any other means, and the failure to ration foreign exchange and consumption only ensured that the inevitable shortages would be out of the government's control.

The military coup against Allende in September followed the inexorable pattern of the events we have surveyed in Indonesia, Cambodia, and Brazil. The military junta taking power as the new rulers of Chile immediately reversed the major economic policies of the Unidad Popular government because they knew that this was the precondition for a resumption of credit flows.

The IMF sent a mission to Chile in December, and announced on 30 January 1974 that a new stand-by arrangement had been concluded. As usual, this stand-by is less important for the amount of money directly involved than for the much larger amounts it will unlock in the form of bilateral and World Bank credits.

The murder and imprisonment of political opponents is a predictable part of this pattern, but Chile has changed with horrifying rapidity from one of the least repressive societies in Latin America to one experiencing institutionalized violence on a scale previously unknown on that continent, even in Brazil.

The Chilean revolution accomplished many good things in its short lifetime. Infant mortality declined because health services were improved and each child guaranteed half a litre of milk every day. The nation's industrial and farm workers were encouraged to become involved in the process of management and to make production decisions for the benefit of society rather than a capitalist ownership. Many of the changes were so fundamental, and so popular, that reversion to the old society seems impossible. This is probably the reason for the vicious severity of the repression.

And yet, those gains could not be defended. The Allende government made a fatal mistake in failing to husband its foreign exchange resources more carefully, and in putting more emphasis on obtaining new credit than on conserving what little it had. When a bourgeois government squanders scarce foreign exchange it is criminal; when a government supposedly committed to socialism does the same it is tragic, for it will doom the entire enterprise.

*

When new government aid fails to even equal the amount required of a particular country for current debt repayment, repudiation may become an attractive proposition. Consider this table, reproduced from the Pearson report:

Debt service as percentage of gross lending, 1965–7 and 1977

	Africa	Europe	East Asia	South Asia & Middle East	Latin America
1965–7	73	92	52	40	87
1977					
Variant A: Assumption that the gross flow of new lending remains unchanged:	121	109	134	97	130
Variant B: Assumption that new lending increases by 8% per annum:	77	71	88	60	89

From: *Partners in Development* ['Pearson Report'], Report of the World Bank Commission on International Development. September 1969, Praeger. Table 3–4, p. 74.

199

But gross lending has in fact been *declining* since 1968. This, and the corollary that as the debts mount aid is losing its efficacy as a bribe, is the real 'crisis in aid' that is upsetting the World Bank! There is a genuine contradiction here, since the creditor governments have to reconcile the demands of their exporters for easy export credit guarantees with the unwillingness of legislatures to provide unlimited funds to salvage the bad debts. Generous export credits and private lending can also frustrate, at least temporarily, the efforts of the IMF and the World Bank to discipline an errant government:

The governments of DAC member countries have repeatedly expressed their concern about the harmful effects of export credits, but they have failed to evolve a coherent policy which could reconcile their trade interests with the objectives of their development assistance.[21]

In order to prevent the system from breaking down, and the debtor countries unilaterally throwing off their debt burdens, the World Bank commission recommends more lenient terms be offered for both new aid and debt rescheduling. They also recommend

a strong 'early warning system' based on the external debt reporting which is being evolved by the OECD and the World Bank. The World Bank should be charged with the responsibility of issuing definitive recommendations against further encouragement of export credits to countries which are in the danger zone from the standpoint of debt liabilities and interest burden. It should fix ceilings which should not be exceeded. *Export credits beyond these ceilings should, in the event of any debt rearrangement, enjoy significantly less favourable treatment than other claims.*[22]

The alarm of the World Bank (and other components of the international development establishment) about excessive debts is real. But they are concerned not to destroy or dismantle the system, but to rationalize it so it can continue to function. Excessive use of export suppliers' credits is the monkey wrench in the system.*

*The case of India, however, where they are a very small proportion of the total, shows that curbs on suppliers' credits would not change the basic nature of the problem.

Recent events in Ghana illustrate this dilemma.

The Ghanaian army treated us in January 1972 to the novel spectacle of an *anti*-IMF military coup. Colonel I. K. Acheampong, leader of the coup which ousted the elected President Kofi Busia, took the very unusual step of actually reversing a devaluation which had been effected on IMF advice two weeks before the coup. The Colonel then announced a unilateral but selective repudiation of some of Ghana's external debts, and the unilateral rescheduling of much of the rest.

The size of the external debt which Kwame Nkrumah left to successor governments of Ghana is well known.[23] Less publicized is the fact that the rescheduling of those debts negotiated between Nkrumah's ouster in 1966 and the coup of 1972 has in itself added considerably to the burden.* Two years, and two rescheduling agreements, after Nkrumah's downfall, the additional interest which Ghana had been forced to agree to pay in return for the postponement of repayment obligations amounted to 40 per cent of the original debt. At the third rescheduling in 1970, Ghana's Finance Minister J. H. Mensah protested to the creditors that because repayment conditions were so harsh, per capita income in Ghana had fallen from $261 in 1965, under Nkrumah, to $239 in 1969, and that unemployment was as high as 30–35 per cent. The following year he complained bitterly, while signing one more loan agreement dictated by the intransigent creditors;

[T]he agreement we are signing not only threatens to sanctify, with the concurrence of our government, the principle of *relieving* debts by *increasing* them, but also embodies a particularly harsh application of that principle.

He added darkly:

... It is impossible to convince any Ghanaian that public money

* 'We were very unfortunate in Ghana, because we had a debt meeting right after the Indonesian one. Like the good bankers they are, they decided that, when you have been kind to one man, you must be very hard to the next man. Otherwise all your debtors will get into bad habits.' J. H. Mensah, [ex-Finance Minister of Ghana 1969–72], 'Some Unpleasant Truths about Debt and Development', *Development Dialogue* (Uppsala) 1973, no. 1, p. 16.

should be spent on paying such debts rather than on developing the country.[24]

On still another occasion he recalled to a Ghanaian audience the post-war era when Britain blocked payment on the sterling balances owed to its colonies:

... It is pertinent to record that Britain unilaterally adjusted the rate at which she satisfied the claims of her creditors after the war in accordance with the capacity of the British economy to pay.[25]

The military government which threw out President Busia (and Finance Minister Mensah) acted on this implied threat. Colonel Acheampong, as mentioned, reversed the devaluation decision which the Busia government had taken as the price for IMF support in the fourth debt re-negotiations, which had been scheduled for March 1972. Acheampong then announced a unilateral repudiation of a small proportion of the debts which were notorious because of the large kickbacks which the suppliers had paid to members of Nkrumah's government to obtain the original contracts.

The military government carefully and cannily distinguished between the different categories of their foreign debt. Long term debts owed mainly to the United States and the World Bank (which totalled $264 million) were fully accepted. Short-term trade debts ($286 million), which had been massively incurred as a result of the Busia government's disastrous decision to liberalize imports, were accepted as legitimate but would be paid back behind schedule, only as money became available for them. Medium-term credits incurred after Nkrumah, which totalled only $18·6 million, were also to be honoured. For the medium-term suppliers' credits negotiated by Nkrumah's government, however, Acheampong proposed that repayment be on the model of the very low-interest long-term loans made by the World Bank's soft loan affiliate, the International Development Association. This meant the effective repudiation of a large chunk of the debts, most of which ($218 million) was owed to World Bank members. The hated 'moratorium interest' burdening Ghana as a result of its three debt reschedulings was also repudiated.

Ghana, like Chile, was making a clever attempt to divide its creditors; but Ghana was appealing to the US and the World Bank, which it hoped would be sources of new aid, against Great Britain, to whom the bulk of the old Nkrumah debts were owed. The military government was not at all hostile to foreign investment and continued its efforts to attract more of it.

When Britain and the EEC countries cut off export credit insurance to Ghana, Acheampong's government showed it meant business by mobilizing internally to make good the shortage of imports. It launched an 'Operation Feed Yourself' movement to lessen its extraordinarily high dependence on food imports and imposed the strictest import rationing in history. Factories which were dependent on imported agricultural raw materials were advised to go into farming to produce their own raw materials. Eight months after taking power, Acheampong announced that the budget for 1972–3 would be financed entirely from domestic sources.

Although the debt repudiation was popular with Ghanaians, the resulting consumer shortages and price inflation were not. So, when the World Bank, negotiating on behalf of Ghana's creditors, offered a debt resettlement which came half-way towards meeting Ghana's conditions, Acheampong's government said it would be willing to talk and even hinted that the repudiated debts might eventually be paid after all.

No settlement had been reached as this book went to press. High export prices have enabled Acheampong to hold out for more than two years, although the balance is still precarious and could tip in the other direction again in the future. Many other debt-ridden countries must have noted that the Ghanaians have extorted an offer which is much more generous than anything that was offered to the more compliant governments between 1966 and 1972. Ghana's example must be giving the debt managers of the capitalist world some sleepless nights.

*

We find the most extreme opposition to the IMF formula for development in the centrally planned socialist states, for in those countries the direct control of foreign trade by the state is a principle as essential to socialism as the public ownership of the means of production. (In this respect, as Chapter 6 shows, Yugoslavia is the exception that proves the rule.) Here we will ignore the better-known cases of China and Cuba in order to survey briefly the pattern of development in North Korea. This country is more relevant as a model because it is much smaller than China, and more successful in building an industrial economy with its own efforts than Cuba.

When two journalists from the *New York Times* were allowed to visit North Korea in the summer of 1972, they discovered with some astonishment that that country 'about the size of the state of Mississippi' with a population of only fourteen million, had developed 'a well organized and highly industralized socialist economy, largely self-sufficient, with a disciplined and productive work force' and an overall industrial plant which 'compared favourably to anything in Asia outside Japan', including China. The Koreans export machine tools, sixty-ton freight cars, and synthetic fabrics.[26] Although only about 20 per cent of the territory is suitable for cultivation (the southern part of Korea had been the nation's 'breadbasket' before the country was divided at the 38th parallel in 1945), North Korea achieved agricultural self-sufficiency by 1961 and 'now has higher mechanization of this sector than any other developing country in Asia, with the possible exception of Taiwan'.[27] Yet it was only about twenty years ago, as the Korean War ended, that the country was scarcely more than a pile of rubble, bombed to bits by the United States armed forces.

As in China, steep differences in income and standard of living among classes and individuals are a thing of the past. Most workers enjoy a wide range of non-cash benefits: free rice for all family members, free work clothes, medical care, education, and holiday and recreation facilities. The cost of house rent, electricity, heating, and common consumer goods are low, although the country is not yet rich in consumer goods in comparison with the West.[28] North Korea is one of the few countries of the world to have a problem of labour shortage, rather than high unemployment; despite this, working hours are reasonable: eight hours a day normally, but six for heavy or dangerous work. Workers receive paid holidays of fifteen days a year (a month for those doing heavy or dangerous work).[29]

Most interesting for our purpose is the fact that almost all of these achievements were accomplished through the efforts of Koreans and with Korean raw materials. The Koreans themselves use the word *juche*, usually translated as self-reliance, as the motto of their development strategy.

It is true that substantial aid was received from the Soviet Union and China during the seven years following the Korean War. According to their own figures, foreign aid contributed 33·4 per cent of total state revenue in 1954, the year after the armistice. It had dwindled to less than 5 per cent in 1958, and by 1961 it was zero.[30] This aid was significant, but it cannot explain the actual achievements of the North Korean economy. It is likely that the Koreans embraced the *juche* strategy out of necessity, because the aid was not sufficient to match their ambitions. Kim Il Sung, in an extended discussion of *juche* given in answer to a foreign journalist's question,* said simply that 'Korea had not enough money' to invite foreign technicians and procure equipment from abroad for the construction of blast furnaces; similarly, 'we could not afford to buy from foreign countries lots of electric locomotives needed in our country'. The solution to both problems, according to Kim, was to give Korean technicians, including students not yet graduated from technical colleges, the task of designing and building blast furnaces and electric locomotives. The furnaces and locomotives were built; and the Koreans discovered that they got them faster by designing and building themselves than they could have by importing.

There is a vivid description of the manner in which North Korea began to produce its own lorries.

At an early stage in the revolution Marshal Kim Il Sung instructed one factory to start manufacturing them. Since no blueprint was available the workers pulled an imported one apart, noting the design of the parts and where they fitted together. Having reproduced the parts they then produced a duplicate lorry. The first lorry to

* See appendix IV.

205

be manufactured was able to go only backwards but the matter was soon rectified and lorries began to be produced in great amounts.[31]

Korea began manufacturing tractors in 1958 in the same manner. Employees of a farm tool works took a tractor apart and made a blueprint by copying the parts, and after thirty-five days of intensive work (and 32 failures) they produced Korea's first tractor. By 1971 that factory was manufacturing 10,000 tractors a year.[32]

The Koreans have scored an original technical success with the development of vinalon, an artificial fibre made from limestone (cotton cannot be grown in the country). By this means they are able to produce clothing with domestic raw materials. The psychological effects of devising new products through their own efforts, rather than by importing technicians and equipment, must be incalculable.

If the Koreans were forced out of necessity to adopt the strategy of self-reliance, they are firmly convinced by now that it is a real virtue to do as much as possible by their own efforts. In Kim's own words:

If too much stress is laid on foreign assistance or an attempt is made to rely entirely on others, it will cause people to lose faith in their own strength and neglect their endeavours to tap the inner resources of their own country, blindly pinning hopes on others and imitating them only. Then, it will be impossible to succeed in building a sovereign, independent state in the end.[33]

10

Conclusion: Dependence or Autonomy?

Prose works are subject to demands of form which are as strict in their way as those of the sonata or haiku. It is a time-honoured convention that in a critical work such as this book the final chapter must be a call to action pointing the way to a solution – the non-fiction version of a happy ending.

This conviction is understandable (some wit has remarked that anyone who writes a book must be an optimist) but in practice it may be unfortunate. A physician who does not know how to cure a cancer may nevertheless accurately diagnose it and record its progress. The only optimism in this process would lie in the hope that another specialist may know the cure, or that with the passage of time and the accumulation of many observations and experiments some other scientist may discover a cure.

The burden of my final chapter must be that there are no glib formulas for an easy solution. There may be happy endings, but they will not be achieved without determination, sacrifice, and a clear-sighted view of the available alternatives. Reform of the IMF will not be considered at all; I have set down my views on that subject in appendix III. The problem which must be tackled is the larger and more difficult one of how national governments can learn to manage their economies without recourse to the IMF and submission to its pernicious demands on behalf of its sponsors.

In an ideal world, production would be organized for the benefit of people rather than for the extraction of profits. In such a world, there would be no national boundaries and no balance of payments problems; goods could move freely where they were most needed and best utilized. If all kinds of useful labour were (as it should be) equally valued, then each man and woman could be recompensed equally for a day's work, and the amount of time which each were forced to spend on necessary drudgery could be steadily diminished in favour of activities indulged in for pleasure and for the development of human talents and capabilities. The division of labour among individuals, regions, and continents could be examined rationally, so that it could be promoted where it contributed to this human objective and rejected where it threatened to frustrate it.

But, although this Utopia is important as a vision of what should be possible, it is obviously no guide to what can be done in the present. Even more sobering is the thought that what is possible now is not only very difficult to attain, but may not even lead logically to that Utopia. There is no world government* which can be overthrown at a stroke, or even after protracted war, by socialist revolution. There are only nation states, some much more powerful than others, that may experience revolutions at different times. And even socialist governments, forced to survive in a hostile environment where balance of payments problems and prices determined by profits are the rule, may develop vested interests in protecting their own people which run counter to the interest of international revolution.

It is possible that the present upheaval in international monetary relations among the rich nations will disrupt the trading system so severely that it creates the opportunity for revolution in many countries simultaneously. The rich nations will certainly not let this happen if they can foresee and prevent it, and their mutual infighting must become very severe indeed before they become so preoccupied as to drop the leash they are holding. Much more probable, given their irreducible dependence on raw materials from the Third World, is that the rich nations will split into rival blocs, each binding their client states much more tightly to *one* outlet for their products and *one* source for their imports.

The current international monetary scene contains several new features which may undermine the system described in previous chapters. Between 1971 and 1973 the United States, and with it the other major capitalist powers, abandoned the Bretton Woods 'par value' system of exchange rates and now all

* Not even the IMF is powerful enough to fill this role!

currencies are floating. But while the 'strong' currencies float against each other, the poorer nations keep their exchange rates pegged to the strong currency of their most important trading partner, more concerned to preserve the existing trade structure than to revolutionize it.

In recent months the price of primary commodities, which form the bulk of the Third World's exports, have soared to new record heights. This has enabled some nations, such as the Philippines and Ghana, to evade for the time being the direst consequences of the debt trap. But the price of petroleum has seen the steepest rise of all, and most of the countries used as examples in this book are importers of petroleum. The rise in the price of foodgrains, wheat and rice, will benefit the rich exporting countries but penalize the Third World, which is a heavy net importer of grain. India will suffer particularly from heavy rises in the cost of imports, but Brazil is also being affected by the high price of imported oil and grain. Additionally, the very nature of Brazil's current export success will make that country particularly vulnerable to a contraction in world trade which is a likely outcome of the present international mess. And even a country like Indonesia with oil to sell will not benefit much from the price rise, since Japan is seeking to bind Indonesia's resources ever more tightly to itself as petroleum gets scarcer and more expensive.

Another new development is the rapid rise in 'Eurodollar' lending to Third World countries. From a modest sum of about $455 million borrowed in 1970, Eurodollar loans to Third World countries have mushroomed to something like $10,000 million in 1973. These loans carry extremely high interest rates, and thus represent a new burden to the balance of payments in the long run while relieving it in the short run. They also involve less political and economic supervision than does foreign aid offered by bilateral donors or multilateral agencies, and are attractive to borrowers for that reason. These loans, like high export prices, are temporarily easing the debt repayment situation at present, but they are obviously not the solution but rather a new aspect of the problem.

A government which is determined to regain its autonomy

and benefit its people should be able to utilize *either* the collapse of the old trading system *or* an unexpected windfall of export earnings and new loans as an opportunity to restructure its economy and its foreign trade. A corrupt client government (and these predominate, thanks to the aid system) will squander any windfall earnings as similar bonanzas were squandered after the Second World War and the Korean War, without lasting benefit to the economy or people. Such a government will respond to a collapse of the present trading system with panic and repression, as well it might, for such a collapse would enhance the possibility, by underlining the necessity, of revolutionary change.

The rich nations hope to restore the Bretton Woods system with only minimal repairs, which may not be sufficient to prevent future breakdowns. If they do not succeed in patching up their monetary relations, then crisis after worsening crisis will occur, and all predictions are up for grabs. If the rich nations do succeed in restoring some sort of order, then the regressive system of trade and finance will continue in effect with minor changes which will make it marginally more or less tolerable for the various poor nations. If we make the second assumption, then it is possible to draw a few positive lessons, from the mostly negative examples surveyed in this book, for the poor country which wishes to gain some autonomy over its own economic policy.

The IMF is perfectly correct when it tells governments that financial discipline, and occasional painful adjustments in the structure of production, are necessary for the health of the balance of payments. My quarrel with the Fund stems from the fact that by conniving in the rich countries' use of foreign aid as a bribe, the IMF is deliberately frustrating the very type of financial discipline and production adjustments which are most badly needed. The nation which wishes to break out of imperialism's grip must not only say nay to the IMF's demands, but must also have the courage to discipline its own consumption and channel it along the most constructive lines.

Historically speaking (and ignoring the original distorting effects of colonialism which have set the present patterns) nations have failed to develop not because they had too little international money, but because they had too much. All nations will find that some imports are genuinely essential, and many more are useful if properly utilized, when they develop new industries and a new productive capacity. But imports are somewhat analogous to medicines administered to an ailing body. The same medicine which, in small doses, aids and stimulates the body's own powers of recovery may, in massive amounts, enervate and addict the patient beyond hope of recovery.

The analogy to an addictive drug can be carried to some length. Just as a 'pusher' finds it good business to provide free samples on which potential users can get 'hooked', so the grant aid of the 1950s served to make poor nations dependent on Western brand names and accustomed to the idea of development via imports, rather than by their own efforts, thus paving the way to the debt slavery of the 1960s and 1970s. And, just as the absence of heroin means nothing to the non-addict but is shattering for the addict, so the nation which has once accepted the pusher's wares will find the denial of aid much more difficult and dangerous than the one which has never succumbed to, or been offered the chance of, temptation. The nation which is trying to break out of the system is bound to suffer withdrawal pains, the severity of which will be proportional to the previous degree of aid dependence. And (as the story of Cambodia demonstrates) the political dangers of the memory of aid dependency may linger long after the economic difficulties have been surmounted.

If this analysis is correct, then large-scale aid would be a pernicious influence on development *even if no conditions whatsoever were imposed as a quid pro quo.* Further, the conclusion applies *pari passu* to any reformist scheme which proposes to allocate more foreign exchange to poor governments. This would include commodity agreements intended to secure better prices for raw material exports and the IMF scheme of compensatory finance for fluctuations in export earnings (both, like aid, bribes to *prevent* change in the traditional system of production), or the proposed allocation of newly created SDRs

– the 'international money' issued by the IMF – to poor countries as a backdoor sort of untied foreign aid.

In an ideal world, it would probably be deemed morally desirable to sacrifice some efficiency in total production for the sake of the equitable development of human capabilities, above and beyond the equitable distribution of the fruits of production. In the real world, which is hostile to attempts at revolutionary change, a high degree of self-sufficiency is imperative for the sake of survival alone.

A socialist IMF might or might not be a desirable institution, depending on the motives of the nations that funded and controlled it. Experience has shown that aid from older socialist countries to struggling new ones can be at best a marginal supplement to sincere indigenous efforts to turn the economy around, and at worst can create a pernicious dependency just as capitalist aid does.

There is no doubt that economic self-sufficiency, if only at a low level of technology, is possible for any nation possessing arable land potentially capable of feeding its population. (The fact that a particular nation is currently importing food indicates very little about its potential, since resources now devoted to export crops or inefficiently utilized might be diverted to the production of food.) The difficulty lies in the aspirations of most poor countries towards the development of industries with a high level of sophistication.

It is now fatuously asserted that China was able to develop without reliance on Western aid only because it was a large continental nation with a huge population, and thus a 'large market'. But so is India. And if China *hadn't* done it, very few people would now recognize that the potential was there.

There is no doubt that, given the way national boundaries of the ex-colonies have been drawn, resources are distributed very inequitably among nations. The smallest, which do not resemble real nations in any respect except in the possession of a flag and a UN seat, may never be able to aspire to autonomous and diversified industrial development. But if North Korea, which is not exceptionally endowed with either population or natural resources, can do it, then most of the nations described in previous chapters can do it. Some, like Brazil and Indonesia, have a truly outstanding potential.

The question which aspiring revolutionary leaders have to decide is what kind of development they are aiming for. One type is built on servicing the needs of the rich countries, or more precisely, of the corporations in the rich countries. Development of this type will bring in the latest technological gadgets, but only for the purposes which suit the corporations, such as extracting mineral ores. The other type of development starts by ensuring that everybody has enough food to eat and works up from there to provide more amenities as it becomes possible to produce them. No very high level of technology is needed for the first stages of this type of development, although the states which take this route often prove to be the most efficient in the application of the fruits of technology when given a chance.* The two types of development are so different that it is unfortunate that the same word should be used for both.

There is no great economic problem preventing the adoption of a strategy of self-sufficiency. There are, however, grave political problems, since, as we have seen, powerful classes in poor countries benefit from aid, suffer from its termination, and provide an active fifth column for the external enemies of autonomy. This is the most difficult dilemma, and repression of these classes may be the only solution of it.

The fact that economic self-sufficiency is possible for most countries does not mean that there are no economic problems involved in getting there. As we have remarked already, the refusal of heroin to an addict causes severe problems although it is imperative for the sake of health. The problems of transition are always the most difficult and the most interesting.

But those who predict catastrophe for the poor countries if aid declines, or their exports are shut out of protected markets, or their reserves depreciate with the dollar, are shutting their eyes to the costs of the present system. At the moment of writing people are starving to death in large areas of India and

---

*For example: Cuba and North Vietnam are the most efficient 'adopters' of the 'Green Revolution' improved seeds, which in the capitalist Third World can only be afforded by the richer farmers.

West Africa, for reasons which have less to do with the failure of the monsoon than with the corruption and indifference of governments who have failed in the past to invest modest amounts in water conservation facilities, and are now failing to distribute relief supplies where they are needed. The injuries suffered in a period of transition would surely be less than the suffering caused by the present system, and more significantly, the injuries of transition would be borne largely by the classes which are now consuming the fruits of both aid and exploitation and which share the responsibility for present sufferings.

A prescription for administering an economic revolution is beyond the scope of this book, and will in any case have to be worked out separately for each nation on the basis of its real and potential resources. The moral of this work is both simple and old-fashioned: that nations, like individuals, cannot spend more than they earn without falling into debt, and a heavy debt burden bars the way to autonomous action. This is particularly true when one's creditors are also one's customers, suppliers, and employers.

Self-reliance has become such a fashionable phrase that there is a danger we will forget the stern reality it stands for. It is not just a groovy thing to do, like baking your own bread; it is a deadly earnest matter of survival and one can't always run to the store if the bread-making fails. Some hunger pangs – particularly for those who are likely to be reading this book – are probably inevitable if mass starvation is to be prevented. But in the long run it is more realistic to withdraw from an exploitative system and suffer the dislocations of readjustment than it is to petition the exploiters for a degree of relief.

Appendix I: The Fund and the World Bank

There is understandable confusion about the relationship between the IMF and the World Bank (International Bank for Reconstruction and Development, or IBRD). The two institutions were both founded at the 1944 Bretton Woods conference, and membership in the IMF is a prerequisite to membership in the World Bank and eligibility for its loans. The headquarters of the two institutions sit side by side in Washington, joined Siamese-twin style by corridors at several levels. Executive Board meetings of the two are held on alternate days of the week to allow the same persons to serve on both Boards when convenient. Their annual meetings are always held jointly, and they jointly publish a magazine, *Finance and Development*, which attempts to popularize their projects and philosophy. Since both institutions depend on the support of the major capitalist governments, and the World Bank in addition must keep the confidence of Western capital markets in order to continue lending, they share a pro-capitalist ideology.

In theory, there is a clear division of labour between the two. The Fund makes short-term loans for balance-of-payments support, and the Bank serves as a loan broker and guarantor for specific projects which supposedly contribute to development. In practice, as both institutions have gradually usurped new functions not foreseen at their founding, their roles have overlapped to some extent. The Bank has recently decided that it too can legitimately provide balance of payments support and enforce liberalization and financial discipline on borrowing countries, as chapter 8 has shown in the case of India. Similarly, although it is usually the Bank which organizes aid consortia, the IMF is invariably a key member of them and occasionally takes the role of organizer.

In 1966 the Fund and the Bank agreed on the definition and delimitation of their respective spheres of responsibility and on the terms of their liaison:

It was agreed that the Fund has primary responsibility for exchange rates and restrictive systems, for adjustment of temporary balance of payments disequilibria, and for evaluating and assisting members to work out stabilization programmes as a sound basis for economic advance. On the matters thus identified, the staff of the Bank would inform themselves of the established views and position of the Fund and adopt these as a working basis for their own activities. On the other hand, the Bank was recognized as having primary responsibility for the composition and appropriateness of development programmes and project evaluation, including development priorities. On these matters, the Fund staff would adopt the views of the Bank. In spheres which were not the primary responsibility of either institution, such as the structure and functioning of financial institutions, the staff of the Fund would acquaint itself, before visiting a member country, with the views of the Bank; and vice versa.[1]

Appendix II: The US and the Fund

From its inception the Fund has been dominated by the wishes of its largest member, the United States of America. Until 1956, this dominance was so absolute that decisions were made effectively by the US Secretary of the Treasury, to the point that the Fund's staff had no authority to negotiate conditions for drawings.[1]

As the European states and Japan have become more economically powerful in the 1960s, the American dominance has declined relatively, but it is still safe to assume that no major decisions are taken against the strong wish of the United States. The resignation in 1973 of Pierre-Paul Schweitzer as Managing Director, after the US indicated that it did not have confidence in him, is an illustration.

The Managing Director is by agreement and tradition always a European, as the President of the World Bank is always an American. The Fund's Deputy Managing Director has been an American ever since the post was created in 1949.

The Fund, like the World Bank, is nominally a part of the United Nations system. It has, however, its own constitution and is in no way subject to the one-nation one-vote principle of the UN General Assembly. The Fund is controlled by its member states in proportion to the size of their quotas. It is thus ruled firmly by the rich countries. When the Fund was inaugurated, the US quota was by far the largest and amounted to about 36 per cent of the total. As periodic readjustments of quotas have been made since then, the percentage held by the US has declined to 23 per cent. However, as certain important questions – including that of quota adjustment – have to be decided by an 80 per cent majority, the US has formal veto power over such decisions. The EEC countries have recently been given a collective veto by a new requirement of an 85 per cent voting majority for certain types of decisions; the quotas

217

of the original six amount collectively to about 16 per cent of the total.

The five members with the largest quotas (currently the US, UK, France, Germany, and India – but not Japan) each appoint an executive director. The two countries whose currency has been most drawn from the Fund in the previous year also have the right to appoint a director, if they are not already in the 'big five'. The rest of the twenty-member Board are elected by combinations of countries and their votes are weighted according to the total of the countries electing them. Formal votes are usually avoided in the Executive Board, but everyone concerned has a good idea of each director's voting power, and how a vote, if taken, would turn out!

Formal voting strength is a less important factor, however, than the well-recognized economic power which the US wields in the international monetary system by virtue of the key role of the dollar and the sheer size of the country as importer and exporter. The international monetary crisis of recent years has shown that the IMF has no power to impose discipline on the US, and in this crisis the Fund has been reduced to a mere forum for negotiations.

The US Executive Director cannot cast his vote at his own discretion, but is bound by law to accept the instructions of the Secretary of the Treasury.[2] The Fund's sensitivity to US wishes is underlined by the location of its headquarters in Washington, DC, just a phone call away from top American officials.

An ugly incident from the McCarthy era illustrates how subservient the Fund was to US wishes in its early years. A US citizen, Frank Coe, was serving as Secretary of the Fund when he was summoned to appear before a US Grand Jury. Before the Grand Jury he refused to answer questions, claiming the privilege of the Fifth Amendment against self-incrimination. He also refused to testify before a subcommittee of the US Senate. The Fund's Managing Director, after consulting the Executive Directors, requested Mr Coe's resignation.[3]

The United States is now the major debtor country of the world. Although it has benefited massively from the Fund's resources, both through stand-by arrangements and by other means, it has never been subjected to the type of dictation which is imposed on smaller countries (including the United Kingdom) as a matter of course. As Susan Strange has explained,

Without it ever being stated in so many words, the Fund's operational decisions made its resources available neither to those in the greatest need nor yet to those with the best record of good behaviour in keeping to the rules, but paradoxically to those members whose financial difficulties were most likely to jeopardize the stability of the International Monetary System.[4]

As the US changed from a creditor to a debtor country in the 1950s and 1960s its position in the Fund reflected this transformation. The IMF was a major source of finance for the US deficit, as its creditor position in the Fund was run down and then a debtor position was built up.[5] The IMF financed fully 10 per cent of the US deficit from 1960 to 1967.[6]

In 1964 the Fund deliberately bent its rules which specify which currencies could be used in repurchasing drawings, in order to provide additional finance to the US deficit. An official Fund publication explains:

Owing to an excess of repurchases in US dollars over drawings of dollars, Fund holdings of dollars had been rising towards a point (75 per cent of quota) beyond which, in accordance with Article V, Section 7(c), repurchases in dollars could no longer be accepted. *The rise in the Fund's holdings of dollars was of assistance to the United States in helping to finance its balance of payments deficits. In order to permit this assistance to the US balance of payments to continue* ... it was understood that the United States would, under its stand-by arrangement, draw currencies from the Fund which it would sell for dollars to other members who in turn would use them to repay the Fund.[7]

There is yet another way in which the Fund is consciously assisting the US balance of payments deficit. It has invested its own sizeable funds in US government securities, thus loaning the American government money quite outside the Fund system of purchases and repurchases of currency. The double standard of power ensures that debtors on a grand scale receive much more cooperation than small debtors.

Appendix III: Reform of the IMF?

The question of the motives of IMF officials has not been touched on, except obliquely, in the body of the text. The question of motive or intent is not relevant to a description of the system in operation, but it becomes important when the possibilities of change are considered. The Fund staff are frequently criticized by other economists as being too narrowly orthodox in their theory, the implication being that they are behind the times in economic fashions and out of touch with the real world.

It is true that the Fund staff is small and intellectually inbred. Its policy of promoting from within, and the movement of personnel between the Executive Board and the staff guarantees a high degree of conformity: in 1968, eight of the twelve 'decision-making' senior staff had either been on the staff since 1950 or had served previously as Executive Directors.[1] The Fund neither hires nor generates mavericks. It cannot, however, be argued that the Fund staff are out of touch with the modern world; rather, they are deeply and intimately involved with the economies of all their member countries, and they possess confidential information not made available to others. Further, the articles published in the *IMF Staff Papers* show that they are perfectly aware of outside criticism, since many of the articles are, at least implicitly, refutations of such criticism. Their policies cannot be ascribed to ignorance.

'In policy, as in law, men must be held to intend the natural consequences of their acts', according to J. S. Furnivall's famous phrase. The Executive Directors and staff of the IMF have had by now nearly thirty years' experience in which to observe the consequences of their policies, so we must conclude that if they do not significantly change those policies, they intend and approve the consequences.*

*To be sure, there is a catch here: the consequences of an IMF pro-

It is scarcely credible that the US would entrust the Fund with the key task of certifying a borrowing country's credit rating if that institution were mistaken in its recommendations and out of touch with new economic theories. It is much more logical to assume that the Fund's economic philosophy suits the material interests of the creditor governments which control it.

As I have attempted to show in chapter 2, criticism of the Fund which accepts its pretension to promote a healthy balance of payments situation for each individual member must miss its mark. The Fund is bound by its Articles of Agreement to promote the smooth running of the capitalist international system, and to oppose restraints on international payments and trade. When a poor country deems it necessary for balance of payments reasons to control imports and profit remittances, the Fund *must* oppose it. Since the international monetary system is controlled by the rich nations, it is Utopian to expect the guardian of the system to be the champion of the have-nots as well. For all these reasons I have offered no suggestions for changes in the operations of the Fund itself, for it would have to tear up its constitution and become a different animal altogether before it could conceivably play a positive role in the development of the Third World.

---

gramme are so dire that few nations find it possible to follow one faithfully. Therefore, where critics blame economic difficulties on the IMF programme, the Fund may blame difficulties on the failure to follow the programme faithfully.

Appendix IV: The North Korean Formula for Self-Reliance

(Excerpt from an interview given by Kim Il Sung to Abdel Hamid Ahmed Hamrouche, General Manager of *Dar-el-Tahrir* for Printing and Publishing, of the United Arab Republic, 1 July 1969. Reprinted in Kim Il Sung, *Answers to the Questions Raised by Foreign Journalists*, Pyongyang, Korea, 1970.)

The entire people of our country, in active response to the Party's call, rose as one and waged a courageous struggle devoting all their physical strength, wisdom and technical skill. Our working people manufactured machines for themselves and rebuilt factories, turning out what they had not and searching out more what was not enough. Furthermore, they made new scientific inventions, technical innovations and creative suggestions, thereby solving bottlenecks and knotty problems facing our country with their own efforts. Especially the patriotic intellectuals of our country made a great contribution.

Let me cite a few examples.

Under Japanese imperialist rule there was hardly any textile industry in the northern half of our country. There were no more than a few thousand spindles and the per capita output of fabrics was barely 14 centimetres. Even after liberation it was not so easy to resolve the problem of clothing for the people. Our country has a poor harvest of cotton because we have much rain in summer, so the question of fibres still remained a headache.

Our scientists displayed the spirit of self-reliance, and solved this difficult question satisfactorily. Some scientists devised the method of making vinalon from limestone which abounds in our country, while others invented the method of turning out fibres from reed which grows in plenty in our country. Thus we came to solve completely the problem of clothing for the people with the efforts of our own scientists and domestic raw materials.

Previously our country had many bottlenecks in the iron industry, too. Coking coal is not produced in our country, and we had to import it from abroad to turn out iron. But our scientists succeeded in producing iron with anthracite which is inexhaustible in our country, with the result that we opened up an avenue to the production of iron with our domestic raw materials. This was another great contribution to consolidating the foundations of the country's independent economy.

Now some countries produce fertilizers by means of electrolyzing water. But this method requires too much electricity, so it does not suit us. Our scientists, therefore, devised the method of producing fertilizers by gasifying the coal of our country.

Besides, various kinds of minerals have been found, which used to be taken for being absent in our country and they have helped to develop industry rapidly, and a great deal has been done also in the irrigation of agriculture by devising ways and methods which other countries do not know. The constructive work, too, could be pushed ahead rapidly because it was done with our domestic raw materials and building materials ...

... When we were rebuilding and constructing blast furnaces soon after the armistice, we had no technicians and were short of equipment and materials. To make things easy, we would have had to invite foreign technicians and procure equipment from abroad. But we had not enough money to do so at that time. So, we took bold measures. We provisionally graduated the third-year students of the technical college in advance and asked them to design and build furnaces. There were about 200 of them, and they worked hard day and night and succeeded in building excellent furnaces in a little more than a year.

Had we built the furnaces with foreign help, it would have cost us much time as well as much money. It would have taken a year to design, another year to manufacture the equipment plus a considerably longer period of time to bring them in; it would have taken four to five years at least to complete the construction of a furnace after all.

If you rely on foreign countries in building a furnace, it requires such a large amount of fund and much time at that, but if you rely on your own efforts, you can build a good furnace in the short period of a year. How nice it is to rely on your own efforts!

It also needs much money to import such things as electric locomotives from abroad, too. We could not afford to buy from foreign countries lots of electric locomotives needed in our country. Therefore, we assigned our college students and technicians the task of designing and building locomotives with their own efforts. Our technicians are now in a position to turn out fine electric locomotives by their own techniques and efforts and are electrifying nearly all the railway lines in the country with electric locomotives of their own make.

Whenever we got a good machine, we, modelling after it, unfolded machine multiplying movements everywhere and thus developed the nation's machine-building industry. Today we manufacture automobiles, tractors, and various kinds of weapons on our own efforts ...

... In our country today up-to-date machines made by ourselves are working at the construction sites and tractors made by ourselves are ploughing the fields; strings of Charyokkaeng-saeng (Self-reliance) lorries are running along the roads of our country. Our brave People's Army men are safeguarding the defence-line of the country impregnably with the weapons made by our working class. It is true that our people's livelihood is not so plentiful as that in advanced countries. However, we all eat our fill with the rice we produce in our country without purchasing it from foreign countries, and lead a decent life, living in the houses built by ourselves, dressed in clothing made of the fabrics produced in our own country and using the daily necessaries of our own make.

As a result of the establishment of *Juche* and the self-reliant efforts we have turned our country, once a backward colonial agrarian nation, into such an advanced socialist industrial-agricultural country in a very short span of time. Today our people have become a dignified nation whom no one would dare to flout.

Some say that a small country need not have a comprehensively developed industry and others say that it is better to produce for itself only some of the things which are needed in the country and to buy the rest from foreign countries. Certainly, at a given stage of development of the productive forces you may buy from abroad those things which are not produced or are in slight demand in your country. But the main thing is to set it as a principle to build an independent national industry with your own efforts and the resources of your own country all along. Particularly, you must produce yourselves things which are in great demand at home and also important raw materials and other materials. Only by so doing can you ensure the independence of the national economy ...

... By establishing *Juche* and relying on our own efforts we never mean that we reject international solidarity, mutual co-operation and assistance among fraternal countries and solve everything by ourselves. We invariably insist that international solidarity should be further strengthened among the fraternal countries and deem it necessary to cooperate and assist each other.

We were given active support and encouragement of the socialist countries and the peace-loving peoples of the world in the difficult days of post-war rehabilitation and construction. We also received no small assistance from the fraternal socialist countries. The successes made in the post-war rehabilitation and construction of our country are associated also with the helping hands of the peoples of the fraternal countries. We are grateful for this and remember this.

We learn advanced things from foreign countries and draw on their good experiences. We also get foreign help when undertaking something we do not know or tackling something new to us and purchase from foreign countries things we do not have in our country. We have built a thermal power station with the help of Soviet technicians. We are building an oil refinery also with the help of Soviet technicians because oil is not yet produced in our country. Certainly, next time we will build thermal power stations and oil refineries on the strength of our own technicians.

We consider it necessary to work together and assist each other among the fraternal countries and get help from foreign countries, but we do not consider it to be the main thing. Even in the days of post-war rehabilitation and construction we invariably set it forth as the basis to rely on our own efforts and did not attach importance to foreign assistance. It is all the more so today. Foreign assistance has limitations, however sincere it may be, and can only play an auxiliary role in building the national economy. It is impossible to meet our own demands in time and satisfactorily with the assistance of foreign countries.

If too much stress is laid on foreign assistance or attempt is made to rely entirely on others, it will cause people to lose faith in their own strength and neglect their endeavours to tap the inner resources of their own country, blindly pinning hopes on others and imitating them only. Then, it will be impossible to succeed in building a sovereign, independent state in the end. You are a writer, and in writing too, you cannot write a good article or improve your writing if you just imitate or copy others' articles. You can write a good article and raise your ability of writing only when you use your own brains in writing.

Our experience shows that it is possible to build an independent national economy with success and bring prosperity and progress to the country only when *Juche* is thoroughly established and self-reliance maintained as the basis.

Notes

Introduction

1. Harry Magdoff, *The Age of Imperialism* (New York: Monthly Review Press, 1969) pp. 144–9 and passim.; Teresa Hayter, *Aid as Imperialism* (Penguin, 1971) pp. 33–46 and passim.; Andre Gunder Frank, *Capitalism and Underdevelopment in Latin America* (Penguin, 1971) p. 339.

Chapter 1

1. International Monetary Fund, *Balance of Payments: Concepts and Definitions*, Pamphlet series no. 10 (Washington, DC, International Monetary Fund, Second Edition, 1969) p. 14.
2. See Branislav Gosovic, *UNCTAD: Compromise and Conflict: The Third World's Quest for an Equitable World Order through the United Nations* (Leiden: A. W. Sijthoff, 1972) chapter VI.
3. Angus Maddison, *The Balance of Payments of Developing Countries* (Paris: Organization for Economic Cooperation and Development, Development Centre Reprint No. 1, 1966) table 5 and p. 12.
4. This paragraph and several other points in this chapter have been drawn from B. J. Cohen, *Balance of Payments Policy* (Penguin, 1969) chapter 1.
5. Poul Høst-Madsen, *Balance of Payments: Its Meaning and Uses*, Pamphlet series no. 9 (Washington, DC, International Monetary Fund, 1967) pp. 16–17.
6. J. Marcus Fleming, *The International Monetary Fund, Its Form and Function* (Washington, DC, International Monetary Fund, 1964) p. 33.

Chapter 2

1. J. Marcus Fleming, *The International Monetary Fund, Its Form and Function* (Washington, DC, International Monetary Fund, 1964), p. 13.
2. For example, see E. M. Bernstein and I. G. Patel, 'Inflation in

Relation to Economic Development', *International Monetary Fund Staff Papers*, vol. 2, no. 3, 1952.

3. See the interview given by Pierre-Paul Schweitzer, Managing Director of the Fund, to *The Banker* (London), August 1967, p. 669; Robert Mundell, 'The International Monetary Fund', in *The Journal of World Trade Law*, vol. 3, no. 5, 1969, pp. 496–7; and Edward M. Bernstein, 'The International Monetary Fund', in *The Global Partnership: International Agencies and Economic Development,* Richard N. Gardner and Max F. Millikan, eds., Frederick A. Praeger, 1968, p. 131.

4. For a study of post-war aid to Europe which shows many parallels to the subject of this book, see Joyce and Gabriel Kolko, *The Limits of Power: The World and United States Foreign Policy, 1945–1954,* Harper & Row, New York, 1972, passim.

5. Seymour J. Rubin, *The Conscience of the Rich Nations: The Development Assistance Committee and the Common Aid Effort,* Harper & Row, 1966, pp. 34–5.

6. John White, *Pledged to Development*, Overseas Development Institute, 1967, p. 103.

7. *Financial Times* (London), 1 August 1958.

8. *Manchester Guardian*, 30 June 1958.

9. Fleming, op. cit., pp. 8–9. My emphasis.

10. *The International Monetary Fund 1945–1965: Twenty Years of International Monetary Cooperation,* vol. I, Chronicle, by J. Keith Horsefield, International Monetary Fund, Washington, DC, 1969, p. 469.

11. Fleming, op. cit., p. 9.

12. Eprime Eshag and Rosemary Thorp, 'Economic and Social Consequences of Orthodox Economic Policies in Argentina in the Post-war Years', *Bulletin* of the Oxford University Institute of Economics and Statistics, vol. 27, no. 1, 1965, pp. 41–3.

13. Graeme Dorrance, 'Rapid Inflation and International Payments', *Finance and Development*, vol. 2, no. 2, 1965, p. 67.

14. ibid., p. 69.

15. N. M. Perera [Minister of Finance], *Budget Speech 1970–71,* Department of Government Printing, Ceylon, 25 October 1970, p. 7.

16. Poul Høst-Madsen, 'What Does It Mean: A Deficit in the Balance of Payments', *Finance and Development,* vol. 3, no. 3, 1966, p. 174.

17. For an example, see the *Financial Times* (London) supplement on Ghana, 10 January 1973, p. 24. On the practice of transfer

pricing see Michael Z. Brooke and H. Lee Remmer, *The Strategy of the Multinational Enterprise*, Longmans, 1971, pp. 16–18.

18. D. L. Cohen and M. A. Tribe, 'Suppliers' Credits: Ghana and Uganda', *Journal of Modern African Studies*, vol. 10, no. 4, 1972, pp. 535–6.

19. Joseph Gold, ' "To Contribute Thereby to ... Development ..." Aspects of the Relations of the International Monetary Fund with its Developing Members', *Columbia Journal of Transnational Law*, vol. 10, 1971, p. 295.

20. Laurence Whitehead, 'Aid to Latin America: Problems and Prospects', *Journal of International Affairs*, vol. 24, no. 2, 1970, final section.

Chapter 3

1. Miguel Cuaderno, Sr., *Guideposts to Economic Stability and Progress*, Manila, 1955, pp. 146–7.

2. Shirley Jenkins, *American Economic Policy Toward the Philippines*, Institute of Pacific Relations, New York, 1954, p. 63.

3. Salvador Araneta, quoted in Jenkins, op. cit., p. 159.

4. Jenkins, op. cit., p. 57.

5. ibid., p. 118.

6. Cuaderno, op. cit., pp. 146–7.

7. Frank H. Golay, 'The Philippines', in Frank Golay et al, *Underdevelopment and Economic Nationalism in Asia*, Cornell University Press, Ithaca, New York, 1969.

8. Fernando S. David, 'The Philippine Economy: A Brief Postwar Perspective 1945–1968', First National City Bank, Manila, January 1970, p. 4.

9. Golay, op. cit., p. 36.

10. Filemon Rodriguez, *Our Struggle for Power*, Manila, 1967, p. 312.

11. Golay, op. cit., pp. 87–8.

12. ibid., pp. 33, 82.

13. Senator Jose W. Diokno, essay in *The Role of Nationalism in Economic Development and Social Justice,* Araneta University Institute of Economic Studies and Social Action, Report No. 20, Manila, 1968.

14. Miguel Cuaderno, Sr., *Problems of Economic Development (The Philippines – A Case Study)*, Manila, 1960, p. 32. The date of the incident is not given but from the context it must have occurred in 1950.

15. Golay, op. cit., p. 107.
16. ibid., pp. 92–3.
17. Cuaderno, *Problems of Economic Development* (*The Philippines – A Case Study*), p. 44.
18. ibid., p. 45.
19. ibid., pp. 70, 72.
20. ibid., p. 71.
21. ibid., pp. 75, 77.
22. John Power and Gerardo Sicat, *The Philippines: Industrialization and Trade Policies*, Oxford University Press, 1971, p. 38.
23. Rodriguez, *op. cit.*, p. 239.
24. Cuaderno, *Problems of Economic Development* (*The Philippines – A Case Study*), pp. 179–80.
25. Amado A. Castro, 'Philippine Export Development 1950–1965', in *Economic Interdependence in Asia,* Theodore Morgan and Myle Spoelstra, eds., University of Wisconsin Press, Madison, 1969, p. 194.
26. Emmanuel Q. Yap in the *Manila Bulletin*, 12 October 1963.
27. Cuaderno, *Problems of Economic Development* (*The Philippines – A Case Study*), Manila, 1960, pp. 80–81.
28. ibid., p. 83.
29. ibid., p. 83.
30. Alejandro Lichauco, speech, 30 November 1969. My emphasis.
31. ibid. Emphasis in original.
32. For an excellent summary of the policy package and prediction of its effects, see Benito Legarda y Fernandez [Benito Legardá Jr.], 'Foreign Exchange Decontrol and the Redirection of Income Flows', *Philippine Economic Journal*, vol. 1, no. 1, First Semester 1962, pp. 18–27.
33. ibid., p. 23.
34. Power and Sicat, op. cit., pp. 46–7.
35. M. Treadgold and R. Hooley, 'Decontrol and the Direction of Income Flows: A Second Look', *The Philippine Economic Journal*, Second Semester 1967, pp. 117–20.
36. Power and Sicat, op. cit., pp. 46, 47.
37. Interview with Ramon del Rosario in David Zenoff, *Private Enterprise in the Developing Countries,* Prentice-Hall, Inc., Englewood Cliffs, New Jersey, 1969, pp. 106–7.
38. Richard Butwell, 'The Philippines: Changing of the Guard', *Asian Survey,* vol. 6, no. 1, 1966, pp. 46.
39. *Southeast Asia's Economy in the 1970s*, Longman's for the Asian Development Bank, 1971, p. 652.

Chapter 4

1. Bank of Indonesia, *Report for the Financial Years 1960–1965*, p. 93.
2. J. A. C. Mackie, *Problems of the Indonesian Inflation* (Ithaca, New York, Cornell University Modern Indonesia Project, 1967) p. 35.
3. This dispute was settled quickly, to the satisfaction of the oil companies, with the assistance of a personal envoy from President Kennedy. See Roger Hilsman, *To Move a Nation* (Garden City, New York, Doubleday, 1967) p. 390.
4. Usha Mahajani, *Soviet and American Aid to Indonesia 1949–68* (Athens, Ohio: Ohio University Center for International Studies, Southeast Asia Program, 1970) p. 22.
5. USA National Advisory Council on International Monetary and Financial Policies, *Special Report to the President and Congress on the Indonesian Debt Rescheduling* (March 1971), p. 1; and Economist Intelligence Unit, *Threemonthly Economic Report: Indonesia*, no. 46 (October 1963).
6. Mahajani, loc. cit.
7. Quoted in Guy J. Pauker, 'Indonesia in 1964: Towards a "Peoples' Democracy"?' *Asian Survey*, vol. 5, no. 2 (February 1965), p. 95.
8. *Bulletin of Indonesian Economic Studies* (Melbourne) [vol. 1], no. 2 (September 1965) p. 1.
9. Mahajani, op. cit., p. 34; and *Bulletin of Indonesian Economic Studies* (Melbourne) [vol. 2], no. 4 (June 1966) p. 6.
10. *Bulletin of Indonesian Economic Studies* (Melbourne) [vol. 3], no. 6 (February 1967) p. 11.
11. Robert Shaplen, *Time Out of Hand* (Harper and Row, 1969) p. 167. Also G. A. Posthumus, *The Inter-Governmental Group on Indonesia (IGGI)* Rotterdam University Press (1971), pp. 29–30.
12. *Bulletin of Indonesian Economic Studies* (Melbourne) vol. 8, no. 1 (March 1972) p. 6.
13. Alex Hunter, 'The Indonesian Oil Industry' in Bruce Glassburner, ed., *The Economy of Indonesia* (Cornell University Press, Ithaca, New York, 1971); *Bulletin of Indonesian Economic Studies* (Melbourne) vol. 5, no. 3 (November 1969) pp. 21–22; and ibid. vol. 8, no. 1 (March 1972) p. 12.
14. *Bulletin of Indonesian Economic Studies* (Melbourne) vol. 8, no. 1 (March 1972) p. 19.

15. Ingrid Palmer and Lance Castles, 'The Textile Industry' in Glassburner, ed., op. cit., pp. 333–4.
16. Gunnar Tómasson, 'Indonesia: Economic Stablization 1966–69', *Finance and Development* vol. 7, no. 4 (1970) p. 48.
17. *Bulletin of Indonesian Economic Studies* (Melbourne) [vol. 4], no. 11 (October 1968) p. 23.
18. Sumitro Djojohadikusumo, *Trade and Aid in Southeast Asia*, vol. 1: Malaysia and Singapore (Melbourne: F. W. Cheshire, 1967) p. 110.
19. *Bulletin of Indonesian Economic Studies* (Melbourne) vol. 8, no. 1 (March 1972) pp. 5, 29.
20. ibid. vol. 7, no. 1 (March 1971) pp. 25–6; David Cole, 'New Directions in the Banking System', *Bulletin of Indonesian Economic Studies* (Melbourne) vol. 5, no. 2 (July 1969) p. 69.
21. Figures taken from *Bulletin of Indonesian Economic Studies* (Melbourne) vol. 6, no. 2 (July 1970) p. 17; and table prepared by the Arbeitskollecktiv Köln-Bonn in *Sudostasien Korrespondenz* no. 2 (July 1971) p. 16.
22. Posthumus, op. cit., p. 44.

Chapter 5

1. *US Economic Assistance for Laos – Stabilization Programs*. A report of the Committee on Government Operations, US House of Representatives (Washington: Government Printing Office, 1971) p. 2.
2. Roger Hilsman, *To Move a Nation*, (Garden City, New York, Doubleday, 1967) p. 112.
3. ibid., pp. 113–14.
4. *Far Eastern Economic Review*, 24 December 1964.
5. Hilsman, loc. cit.
6. Those interested in learning more about the recent political history of Laos are referred to Nina S. Adams and Alfred W. McCoy, eds., *Laos: War and Revolution*, Harper and Row, 1970; and Hilsman, op. cit.
7. Clark Joel, 'The Foreign Exchange Operation Fund for Laos: An Interesting Experiment in Monetary Stabilization', *Asian Survey* vol. 6, no. 3 (March 1966) p. 136.
8. Quoted in Hilsman, op. cit., p. 153.
9. Joel, op. cit., p. 139.
10. ibid., pp. 134–5.

11. *Economy and Efficiency of US Aid Programs in Laos and Cambodia*, Hearings before a Subcommittee of the Committee on Government Operations, House of Representatives, Ninety-Second Congress, First Session, 12 July 1971, pp. 75–6.

12. *Economy and Efficiency of US Aid Programs in the Khmer Republic (Cambodia)*, Hearings before a Subcommittee of the Committee on Government Operations, House of Representatives, Ninety-Second Congress, Second Session, 17 and 24 February 1972, p. 28.

13. *Economy and Efficiency of US Aid Programs in Laos and Cambodia*, Hearings before a Subcommittee of the Committee on Government Operations, House of Representatives, Ninety-Second Congress, First Session, 12 July 1971, p. 30.

14. Joel, op. cit., p. 140.

15. Joel, loc. cit.

16. Frances Starner in *Far Eastern Economic Review*, 20 May 1972.

17. *US Economic Assistance for Laos – Stabilization Programs*. A report of the Committee on Government Operations, US House of Representatives (Washington: Government Printing Office, 1971) p. 1.

18. *Economy and Efficiency of US Aid Programs in Laos and Cambodia*, Hearings before a Subcommittee of the Committee on Government Operations, House of Representatives, Ninety-Second Congress, First Session, 12 July 1971, p. 13; and T. D. Allman in the *Guardian*, 8 November 1971.

19. *US Economic Assistance for Laos – Stabilization Programs*. A report of the Committee on Government Operations, US House of Representatives (Washington: Government Printing Office, 1971) p. 23.

20. For the role of Laos in the heroin network see David Feingold, 'Opium and Politics in Laos' in Adams and McCoy, op. cit., pp. 322–39.

21. Frances Starner in *Far Eastern Economic Review*, 20 May 1972.

22. T. D. Allman in *New York Times*, 25 February 1972.

23. Norodom Sihanouk and Wilfred Burchett, *My War with the CIA: Cambodia's Fight for Survival* (Penguin, 1973) p. 135.

24. Roger M. Smith, *Cambodia's Foreign Policy* (Cornell University Press, Ithaca, New York, 1965) pp. 125–6.

25. ibid., p. 127.

26. Report of Sihanouk's press conference in *Realités Cambodgiennes*, 15 November 1963.

27. Sihanouk's speech on 10 November 1963, reprinted in *Réalités Cambodgiennes*, 15 November 1963.
28. Press communiqué of the Cambodian Embassy in the United Kingdom, 22 November 1963.
29. Quoted in the *New York Times*, 13 November 1963.
30. *Réalités Cambodgiennes*, 23 November 1963.
31. ibid.
32. *Far Eastern Economic Review*, 16 April 1964.
33. ibid., 13 May 1965.
34. Sihanouk and Burchett, op. cit., p. 92.
35. ibid., p. 94.
36. ibid., p. 95.
37. *Economy and Efficiency of US Aid Programs in Laos and Cambodia*, Hearings before a Subcommittee of the Committee on Government Operations, House of Representatives, Ninety-Second Congress, First Session, 12 July 1971, p, 77.
38. *Far Eastern Economic Review*, 16 July 1970.
39. Donald Kirk, 'Cambodia's Economic Crisis', *Asian Survey*, April 1971, p. 144.
40. ibid., p. 250.
41. International Monetary Fund report on Cambodia, reprinted in *Economy and Efficiency of US Aid Programs in Laos and Cambodia*, Hearings before a Subcommittee of the Committee on Government Operations, House of Representatives, Ninety-Second Congress, First Session, 12 July 1971, p. 100.
42. Kirk, op. cit., p. 243.
43. Kirk, loc. cit., and *Far Eastern Economic Review*, 16 July 1970.
44. *New York Times*, 18 September 1971.
45. Kirk, op. cit., p. 247; *Neue Zürcher Zeitung*, 26 February 1971.
46. *Neue Zürcher Zeitung*, 15 July 1971.
47. ibid.
48. The report and recommendations have been published (although probably not in complete and confidential form) in *Economy and Efficiency of US Aid Programs in Laos and Cambodia*, Hearings before a Subcommittee of the Committee on Government Operations, House of Representatives, Ninety-Second Congress, First Session, 12 July 1971, pp. 81–120.
49. Henry Kamm in *New York Times*, 29 October 1971; *United Press International*, 20 October 1971.
50. Kamm, loc. cit.
51. IMF report in *Economy and Efficiency of US Aid Programs in Laos and Cambodia*, Hearings before a Subcommittee of the

Committee on Government Operations, House of Representatives, Ninety-Second Congress, First Session, 12 July 1971, p. 97.

52. *Economy and Efficiency of US Aid Programs in the Khmer Republic (Cambodia)*, Hearings before a Subcommittee of the Committee on Government Operations, House of Representatives, Ninety-Second Congress, Second Session, 17 and 24 February 1972, p. 22.

53. ibid., p. 13.

54. *New York Times*, 12 January 1972.

55. The pledging figures are from the *Japan Times*, 15 January 1972, except for the figure for Britain, which was supplied by Larry Wright.

56. *Economy and Efficiency of US Aid Programs in the Khmer Republic (Cambodia)*, Hearings before a Subcommittee of the Committee on Government Operations, House of Representatives, Ninety-Second Congress, Second Session, 17 and 24 February 1972, pp. 66 and 101.

57. ibid., pp. 28, 29, and 66.

58. ibid., p. 5.

59. ibid., p. 124.

60. Testimony by Roderic O'Connor, AID Coordinator for Supporting Assistance, in *Economy and Efficiency of US Aid Programs in the Khmer Republic (Cambodia)*, Hearings before a Subcommittee of the Committee on Government Operations, House of Representatives, Ninety-Second Congress, Second Session, 17 and 24 February 1972, p. 100.

61. *Economy and Efficiency of US Aid Programs in the Khmer Republic (Cambodia)*, Hearings before a Subcommittee of the Committee on Government Operations, House of Representatives, Ninety-Second Congress, Second Session, 17 and 24 February 1972, p. 114.

62. Nicholas Turner, *Observer Foreign News Service*, 25 January 1972.

63. *Japan Times*, 27 February 1972.

64. Kirk, op. cit., p. 255.

65. *Far Eastern Economic Review*, 25 May 1967.

66. Nguyen Trong Hy and Le Quang Trong, 'Sud-Vietnam 70: Déséquilibre et Dépendance Economique', *Tiers-Monde*, vol. 11, nos. 42–3, 1970, p. 377.

67. *Far Eastern Economic Review*, loc. cit.

68. *An Investigation of the US Economic and Military Assistance*

Programs in Vietnam, Committee on Government Operations, US House of Representatives, Government Printing Office, Washington, DC, 1966, pp. 12–13.

69. ibid., p. 8.
70. *Far Eastern Economic Review,* 17 July 1969, 13 November 1969, and 26 May 1970.
71. *Economy and Efficiency of US Aid Programs in Laos and Cambodia,* Hearings before a Subcommittee of the Committee on Government Operations, House of Representatives, Ninety-Second Congress, First Session, 12 July 1971, p. 52.

Chapter 6

1. Fred Singleton in the *Financial Times,* 29 March 1972 (special supplement on Yugoslavia).
2. George W. Hoffman and Fred Warner Neal, *Yugoslavia and the New Communism,* Twentieth Century Fund, New York, 1962, p. 144.
3. C. L. Sulzberger in the *New York Times,* 2 March 1950.
4. *Financial Times,* 23 February 1950, and *New York Times,* 21 April 1950.
5. *New York Herald Tribune,* 23 July 1950.
6. *New York Times,* 20 February 1950.
7. *Neue Zürcher Zeitung,* 23 November 1950.
8. J. V. Mladek, E. Sturc, and M. R. Wyczalkoski, 'The Change in the Yugoslav Economic System', *International Monetary Fund Staff Papers,* vol. 2, no. 3 (1952) pp. 407–38.
9. *New York Herald Tribune,* 29 December 1951.
10. John Michael Montias, 'Economic Reform and Retreat in Jugoslavia', *Foreign Affairs,* vol. 37, no. 2 (1959) p. 297.
11. *New York Times,* 22 October 1951 and *Christian Science Monitor,* same date.
12. Montias, op. cit., p. 298.
13. *New York Times,* 12 November 1951.
14. *Christian Science Monitor,* 8 October 1951.
15. *New York Times,* 2 March 1952.
16. *Christian Science Monitor,* 9 January 1952.
17. *New York Times,* 14 October 1952.
18. *Neue Zürcher Zeitung,* 26 November 1952.
19. Hoffman and Neal, op. cit., pp. 258–9.
20. Montias, op. cit., pp. 301–2.

21. *Neue Zürcher Zeitung,* 2 May 1956.

22. Vladimir Pertot, 'Long-term Tendencies in Development of the Yugoslav Balance of Payments', *International Problems* (Belgrade), 1971, pp. 46–9.

23. *New York Times,* 28 December 1960.

24. *New York Times,* 10 July 1960.

25. *New York Times,* 29 August 1960.

26. *New York Times,* 4 December 1960.

27. *Financial Times,* 8 December 1960; *Frankfurter Allgemeine Zeitung,* 8 December 1960; *The Times,* 28 December 1960.

28. *Neue Zürcher Zeitung,* 2 June 1961.

29. John C. Campbell, 'Jugoslavia: Crisis and Choice', *Foreign Affairs,* vol. 41, no. 2 (1963) p. 386.

30. *New York Times,* 3 January 1961, and *The Times,* 28 February 1961.

31. *Neue Zürcher Zeitung,* 1 April 1965, and *Le Monde,* 24 July 1965.

32. Pertot, op. cit., pp. 48–9.

33. *The Times,* 26 July 1965.

34. *The Times,* 27 July 1965.

35. *Neue Zürcher Zeitung,* 17 July 1965, and *The Times,* 26 July 1965.

36. *New York Times,* 20 October 1965.

37. Nenad D. Popovic, *Yugoslavia: The New Class in Crisis,* Syracuse University Press, Syracuse, New York, 1968, p. 177; and *Financial Times,* 24 August 1967.

38. *Japan Times,* 29 November 1967.

39. Ernest Bauer, 'Auslandskapital in jugoslawischen Betrieben', *Der Donauraum,* vol. 13, no. 3 (1968) pp. 182–3.

40. Popovic, op. cit., pp. 177–8.

41. *Financial Times,* 19 July 1967.

42. *Financial Times,* 25 January, 12 February, and 15 February 1972; *Neue Zürcher Zeitung,* 22 February 1971; *Guardian,* 11 August 1971.

43. Michael Simmons in the *Financial Times,* 29 March 1972.

44. Mladek, Sturc, and Wyczalkoski, op. cit., p. 425.

45. *Financial Times,* 3 June 1971, and 15 February 1972.

46. *Financial Times,* 3 June 1971.

47. Aleksander Lebl in the *Financial Times,* 29 March 1971.

48. *Le Monde,* 29 December 1971.

49. Deborah Milenkovitch, *Plan and Market in Yugoslav Economic Thought,* Yale University Press, 1971, pp. 299–300.

50. 'Peaceful Transition from Socialism to Capitalism', *Monthly Review*, vol. 15 (March 1964) p. 588.
51. Mladek, Sturc, and Wyczalkoski, op. cit., p. 423.

Chapter 7

1. *Economist*, special survey on Brazil, 2 September 1972, p. 15; *New York Times*, 14 March 1965, 21 August 1965, and 9 August 1972.
2. This paragraph and much of what follows is drawn from the work of Thomas E. Skidmore and Albert Fishlow. Professor Skidmore's study, *Politics in Brazil 1930–1964: An Experiment in Democracy* (Oxford University Press, 1967) is recommended for those who want to learn more about the failure of democracy in Brazil than can be given in this brief compass. I am indebted to Professor Fishlow for the opportunity to read his studies of pre- and post-coup economic policies before they were available in published form, as well as for detailed comment on an earlier draft of this chapter.
3. Donald Huddle, 'Furtado on Exchange Control and Economic Development: An Evaluation and Reinterpretation of the Brazilian Case', *Economic Development and Cultural Change*, vol. 15, no. 3 (1967) p. 279.
4. Werner Baer, *Industrialization and Economic Development in Brazil* (Richard D. Irwin, Inc., Homewood, Illinois, 1965) p. 193.
5. Huddle, op. cit., p. 280.
6. Lincoln Gordon and Engelbert L. Grommers, *United States Manufacturing Investment in Brazil: The Impact of Brazilian Government Policies*, Harvard Graduate School of Business Administration, Boston, 1962, pp. 147–8.
7. Skidmore, op. cit., p. 164.
8. ibid., pp. 158–61.
9. ibid., pp. 174–82 and note 40, p. 386.
10. *Financial Times*, 16 March 1961.
11. *New York Times*, 17 March 1961.
12. *New York Times*, 27 August 1961.
13. *Sunday Telegraph*, 30 July 1961.
14. *New York Times*, 26 August 1961.
15. Skidmore, op. cit., p. 241.
16. The fortunes of one multinational company before and after the military coup are described in *The Brascan File*, Project Brazil, Toronto, 1973.

17. *United States Policies and Programs in Brazil,* Hearings before the Subcommittee on Western Hemisphere Affairs of the Committee on Foreign Relations, United States Senate, Ninety-Second Congress, First Session, on 4, 5, and 11 May 1971, Government Printing Office, Washington, DC, 1971. Testimony of William. A Ellis, Director of USAID, Brazil, p. 150.

Testimony of Thomas C. Mann, Assistant Secretary of State for Inter-American Affairs in May 1964, shortly after the overthrow of Goulart, is quoted in Carlos Diaz-Alejandro, 'Some Aspects of The Brazilian Experience with Foreign Aid', in *Trade, Balance of Payments and Growth: Papers in international economics in honor of Charles P. Kindleberger,* ed. Jagdish Bhagwati et al., North-Holland Publishing Company, 1971, pp. 443–72.

18. *New York Times,* 5 April 1964. There is a careful account of the US role in the coup in Skidmore, op. cit., pp. 322–30.

19. *New Directions for the 1970s: Toward a Strategy of Inter-American Development,* Hearings before the Subcommittee on Inter-American Affairs of the Committee on Foreign Affairs, House of Representatives, Ninety-First Congress, First Session, Government Printing Office, Washington, DC, 1969, Testimony of James R. Fowler, Deputy US coordinator for the Alliance for Progress, AID, p. 576.

20. *New York Times,* 10 May 1964.

21. *New Directions for the 1970s: Toward a Strategy of Inter-American Development,* Hearings before the Subcommittee on Inter-American Affairs of the Committee on Foreign Affairs, House of Representatives, Ninety-First Congress, First Session, Government Printing Office, Washington, DC, 1969. Testimony of William A. Ellis, AID Mission Director in Brazil, p. 572.

22. John Wills Tuthill, 'Economic and Political Aspects of Development in Brazil – and US Aid', *Journal of Inter-American Studies,* vol. 9, no. 2 (1969) pp. 205–6. See also letter from Robert J. Alexander in the *New York Times,* 15 February 1966.

23. *New York Times,* 14 March 1966 and 8 January 1967.

24. Tuthill, op. cit., p. 199.

25. Skidmore, op. cit., p. 320.

26. *New York Times,* 3 October 1964; and Jerome Levinson and Juan de Onis, *The Alliance That Lost Its Way,* Quadrangle Books, Chicago, 1970, p. 197, note 7.

27. Carlos Diaz-Alejandro, 'Some Aspects of the Brazilian Experience with Foreign Aid', in *Trade, Balance of Payments and*

Growth: Papers in international economics in honor of Charles P. Kindleberger, ed. Jagdish Bhagwati et al., North-Holland Publishing Company, 1971, p. 452; and *New Directions for the 1970's: Toward a Strategy of Inter-American Development,* Hearings before the Subcommittee of Inter-American Affairs of the Committee on Foreign Affairs, House of Representatives, Ninety-First Congress, First Session, Government Printing Office, Washington, DC, 1969. Testimony of James R. Fowler, Deputy US coordinator for the Alliance for Progress, AID, p. 577.

28. Levinson and de Onis, op. cit., p. 209.
29. *New Directions for the 1970's: Toward a Strategy of Inter-American Development,* Hearings before the Subcommittee on Inter-American Affairs of the Committee on Foreign Affairs, House of Representatives, Ninety-First Congress, First Session, Government Printing Office, Washington, DC, 1969. Testimony of William A. Ellis, AID Mission Director in Brazil, p. 580.
30. Albert Fishlow, 'Brazilian Income Size Distribution – Another Look' (unpublished) p. 23, Table 8.
31. Carlos Widmann in *Suddeutsche Zeitung,* 19 July 1972.
32. ibid. His assumption that there was rationing in Chile was not accurate, however. (See the discussion of Chile in chapter 9 of this book.)
33. *Financial Times,* 7 July 1972.
34. *Le Monde,* 16 May 1972.
35. *New York Times,* 1 April 1972.
36. *Frankfurter Allgemeine Zeitung,* 2 October 1972.
37. *The Times,* 29 August 1972.
38. Bart S. Fisher, *The International Coffee Agreement,* Praeger 1972, pp. 133–46.
39. *Neue Zürcher Zeitung,* 17 November 1972.
40. John Donnelly, 'External Debt and Longterm Servicing Capacity', in *Contemporary Brazil: Issues in Economic and Political Development,* ed. H. Jon Rosenbaum and William G. Tyler. (Praeger, 1972) p. 112–14.

Chapter 8

1. Edward M. Bernstein, 'The International Monetary Fund', in *The Global Partnership: International Agencies and Economic Development,* ed. Richard N. Gardner and Max Millikan, Praeger, 1968, Table, p. 138.

2. Ravi I. Gulhwati, 'India's External Debt', *India Quarterly,* vol. 28, no. 1 (1972) p. 3.
3. M. Narasimham, 'India's Third Five-Year Plan', *International Monetary Fund Staff Papers,* vol. 9, no. 3 (1962) p. 381.
4. Thomas E. Weisskopf, 'Dependence and Imperialism in India', in *Remaking Asia: Essays on the American Uses of Power,* ed. Mark Selden (Pantheon, New York 1974) p. 205.
5. ibid., p. 206.
6. Columbia University School of Law, *Public International Developing Financing in India,* Public International Development Financing Report no. 9, Columbia University, New York, 1964, p. 367.
7. Asok K. Chanda, Auditor-General of India, in *Hindu,* 31 August 1958.
8. A. H. Hanson, *The Process of Planning: A Study of India's Five-Year Plans 1950–1964,* Oxford University Press, 1966, p. 150.
9. ibid., p. 153.
10. *New York Times,* 6 September 1957.
11. *New York Herald Tribune,* 16 September 1957.
12. Hanson, op. cit., p. 158.
13. Quoted in *Hindu,* 6 February 1958.
14. Michael Kidron, *Foreign Investments in India,* Oxford University Press, 1966, p. 150.
15. Columbia University School of Law, *Public International Development Financing in India,* Public International Development Financing Report no. 9, Columbia University, New York, 1964, pp. 48–9.
16. *Hindu,* 31 August 1958.
17. *New York Times,* 29 August 1958.
18. *Hindu,* 16 February 1958.
19. Ranjit San, 'The "New Economics" ', *Economic and Political Weekly* (Bombay), Special Number, August 1972, p. 1573.
20. Weisskopf, op. cit., Table 4, p. 241.
21. *Hindu,* 21 February 1965.
22. Michael Kidron, *Foreign Investments in India,* Oxford University Press, 1966, passim.
23. Weisskopf, op cit., p. 212.
24. *Financial Times,* 10 March 1966.
25. *New York Times,* 13 April 1966.
26. Bell Mission report, quoted in *Hindu,* 20 June 1966.
27. *Hindu,* 23 April 1966.

28. K. Sundaram, 'Political Response to the 1966 Devaluation – II', *Economic and Political Weekly*, 9 September 1972, pp. 1887–8.
29. Sidney Wells, 'Foreign Trade: A Commodity Study', in *The Crisis Of Indian Planning*, ed. Michael Lipton and Paul Streeten, Oxford University Press, 1968, p. 307. See also the article by Deepak Lal in *Far Eastern Economic Review*, 23 June 1966.
30. I. S. Gulwati, 'Export Promotion after the Devaluation', *Economic and Political Weekly*, Special Number, August 1967, p. 1597. See also *Economic and Political Weekly* for 24 December 1966, pp. 795–7, and 24 June 1967, pp. 1131–4.
31. *Hindu*, 8 June 1966; *New York Times*, 16 June 1966.
32. *Hindu*, 10 July 1966.
33. *The Times*, 23 July 1966.
34. *Economic and Political Weekly*, 6 May 1967, p. 826.
35. *Economic and Political Weekly*, 29 October 1966, p. 466.
36. *Economic and Political Weekly*, 8 April 1972, p. 735.
37. *Economic and Political Weekly*, 8 April 1967, p. 659.
38. *Economic and Political Weekly*, 8 April 1972, p. 734.
39. *Economic and Political Weekly*, 13 May 1972, p. 954.
40. Jagdish Bhagwati, K. Sundaram, and T. N. Srinivasan, 'Political Response to the 1966 Devaluation – I', *Economic and Political Weekly*, 2 September 1972, p. 1836.
41. *Economic and Political Weekly*, 8 July 1967, p. 1196.
42. *Economic and Political Weekly*, Special Number, August 1972, p. 1459.
43. Narasimham, op. cit., p. 425.
44. Weisskopf, op. cit., pp. 222–8.

Chapter 9

1. *New York Times*, 11 December 1971.
2. J. Ann Zammit, ed., *The Chilean Road to Socialism*, Institute of Development Studies, Brighton, 1973.
3. ibid., pp. 164–6.
4. ibid., p. 162.
5. ibid., p. 169.
6. ibid., p. 170.
7. Joseph Novitski in the *New York Times*, 28 January 1973.
8. Zammit, op. cit., p. 176.
9. *Neue Zürcher Zeitung*, 30 January 1972.
10. Zammit, op. cit., pp. 170–71.
11. *The Times*, 16 August 1971.

12. William P. Rogers press statement. US Department of State, 13 October 1971.

13. Benjamin Welles in the *New York Times*, 23 October 1971.

14. Juan de Onis in the *New York Times*, 10 November 1971.

15. Zammit, ed., op. cit., p. 172.

16. *Financial Times*, 1 March 1972.

17. *Financial Times*, 14 June 1972.

18. *New York Times*, 23 July 1972.

19. *Financial Times*, 22 January 1973.

20. *Financial Times*, 27 March 1973.

21. *Partners in Development* ('Pearson report'). Report of the World Bank Commission on International Development, Praeger, 1969, p. 156.

22. ibid. Second emphasis mine.

23. For an excellent account of the Nkrumah years and after, including the role of the IMF, see Ruth First, *The Barrel of a Gun: Political Power in Africa and the Coup d'État* (Penguin, 1972) pp. 169–201 and 376–407.

24. *The Guardian*, 19 July 1971.

25. *Observer Foreign News Service* (Cameron Duodu) 5 May 1970.

26. John M. Lee in the *New York Times*, 4 June 1972.

27. Harald Munthe-Kaas in the *Far Eastern Economic Review*, 1 July 1972, p. 38.

28. ibid.

29. Joan Robinson, 'Korean Miracle', *Monthly Review*, vol. 16, no. 9 (January 1965) p. 545.

30. Byung Chul Koh, *The Foreign Policy of North Korea* (Praeger, 1969) p. 38, note 61.

31. *Far Eastern Economic Review*, 1 January 1972, p. 40.

32. 'The Korean People March Ahead', *China Reconstructs*, December 1971, p. 14.

33. Interview given by Kim Il Sung to Abdel Hamid Ahman Hamrouche of the United Arab Republic, 1 July 1969. Published in Kim Il Sung, *Answers to the Questions Raised by Foreign Journalists*, Pyongyang, 1970.

Appendix I: The Fund and the World Bank

1. *The International Monetary Fund 1945–1965: Twenty Years of International Monetary Cooperation*, vol. I, Chronicle, by J. Keith Horsefield, International Monetary Fund, Washington, DC, 1969, pp. 603–4.

Appendix II: The United States and the Fund

1. Brian Tew, 'The International Monetary Fund', mimeographed, 1969, p. 86.
2. Susan Strange, 'IMF: Monetary Managers', in Robert W. Cox and Harold K. Jacobson et al, *The Anatomy of Influence: Decision-Making in International Organizations*, Yale University Press, New Haven, Connecticut, 1973, p. 284.
3. *The International Monetary Fund 1945–1965: Twenty Years of International Monetary Cooperation*, vol. I, Chronicle, by J. Keith Horsefield, International Monetary Fund, Washington, DC, 1969, p. 339.
4. Strange, op. cit., p. 272.
5. Robert Mundell, 'The International Monetary Fund', *The Journal of World Trade Law*, vol. 3, no. 5 (September–October 1969) p. 492.
6. Fred Hirsch, *Money International* (Penguin 1969) pp. 364–5.
7. J. Marcus Fleming, *The International Monetary Fund: Its Form and Functions*, International Monetary Fund, Washington, DC, 1964, p. 64. Emphasis mine.

Appendix III: Reform of the IMF?

1. Brian Tew, 'The International Monetary Fund', mimeographed, 1969, p. 71.

Index

MONTHLY REVIEW

an independent socialist magazine
edited by Paul M. Sweezy and Harry Magdoff

Business Week: ". . . a brand of socialism that is thorough-going and tough-minded, drastic enough to provide the sharp break with the past that many left-wingers in the underdeveloped countries see as essential. At the same time they maintain a sturdy independence of both Moscow and Peking that appeals to neutralists. And their skill in manipulating the abstruse concepts of modern economics impresses would-be intellectuals. . . . Their analysis of the troubles of capitalism is just plausible enough to be disturbing."

Bertrand Russell: "Your journal has been of the greatest interest to me over a period of time. I am not a Marxist by any means as I have sought to show in critiques published in several books, but I recognize the power of much of your own analysis and where I disagree I find your journal valuable and of stimulating importance. I want to thank you for your work and to tell you of my appreciation of it."

The Wellesley Department of Economics: " . . . the leading Marxist intellectual (not Communist) economic journal published anywhere in the world, and is on our subscription list at the College library for good reasons."

Albert Einstein: "Clarity about the aims and problems of socialism is of greatest significance in our age of transition. . . . I consider the founding of this magazine to be an important public service." (In his article, "Why Socialism" in Vol. I, No. 1.)

DOMESTIC: $13 for one year, $25 for two years, $10 for one-year student subscription.

FOREIGN: $16 for one year, $29 for two years, $12 for one-year student subscription. (Subscription rates subject to change.)

62 West 14th Street, New York, New York 10011

Selected Modern Reader Paperbacks